Corporate Dividend Policy

Studies of Government Finance

TITLES PUBLISHED

Federal Fiscal Policy in the Postwar Recessions, by Wilfred Lewis, Jr.

Federal Tax Treatment of State and Local Securities, by David J. Ott and Allan H. Meltzer.

Federal Tax Treatment of Income from Oil and Gas, by Stephen L. McDonald.

Federal Tax Treatment of the Family, by Harold M. Groves.

The Role of Direct and Indirect Taxes in the Federal Revenue System, John F. Due, Editor. A Report of the National Bureau of Economic Research and the Brookings Institution (Princeton University Press).

The Individual Income Tax, by Richard Goode.

Federal Tax Treatment of Foreign Income, by Lawrence B. Krause and Kenneth W. Dam.

Measuring Benefits of Government Investments, Robert Dorfman, Editor.

Federal Budget Policy, by David J. Ott and Attiat F. Ott.

Financing State and Local Governments, by James A. Maxwell.

Essays in Fiscal Federalism, Richard A. Musgrave, Editor.

Economics of the Property Tax, by Dick Netzer.

A Capital Budget Statement for the U.S. Government, by Maynard S. Comiez.

Foreign Tax Policies and Economic Growth, E. Gordon Keith, Editor. A Report of the National Bureau of Economic Research and the Brookings Institution (Columbia University Press).

Defense Purchases and Regional Growth, Roger E. Bolton.

Federal Budget Projections, Gerhard Colm and Peter Wagner. A Report of the National Planning Association and the Brooking Institution.

Corporate Dividend Policy, by John A. Brittain.

Corporate Dividend Policy

JOHN A. BRITTAIN

Studies of Government Finance

THE BROOKINGS INSTITUTION

WASHINGTON, D. C.

THE BROOKINGS INSTITUTION is an independent organization devoted to nonpartisan research, education, and publication in economics, government, foreign policy, and the social sciences generally. Its principal purposes are to aid in the development of sound public policies and to promote public understanding of issues of national importance.

The Institution was founded December 8, 1927, to merge the activities of the Institute for Government Research, founded in 1916, the Institute of Economics, founded in 1922, and the Robert Brookings Graduate School of Economics and Government, founded in 1924.

The general administration of the Institution is the responsibility of a self-perpetuating Board of Trustees. The trustees are likewise charged with maintaining the independence of the staff and fostering the most favorable conditions for creative research and education. The immediate direction of the policies, program, and staff of the Institution is vested in the President, assisted by the division directors and an advisory council, chosen from the professional staff of the Institution.

In publishing a study, the Institution presents it as a competent treatment of a subject worthy of public consideration. The interpretations and conclusions in such publications are those of the author or authors and do not purport to represent the views of the other staff members, officers, or trustees of the Brookings Institution.

Foreword

CORPORATE DIVIDENDS increased at an annual rate of about 6 percent per year for fifteen years following World War II. During this period, after-tax net profits of corporations rose only 2 percent per year. These divergent trends have had significant impacts on corporate saving, income distribution, and investment. In this volume, John A. Brittain of the Brookings Institution economics staff attempts to explain the trends in corporate dividends on the basis of an econometric model of developments since World War I.

The author is grateful for the valuable criticisms and suggestions of a number of professional specialists. The Reading Committee consisted of George F. Break, Richard Goode, Myron J. Gordon, Daniel M. Holland, and Merton H. Miller. Many helpful comments were also received from William C. Brainard, Eugene F. Brigham, Samuel B. Chase, Jr., Sergei Dobrovolsky, Gary Fromm, Joseph A. Pechman, Dan Throop Smith, George Terborgh, Norman B. Ture, J. Fred Weston, and others. The study was initiated when the author was the recipient of a Ford Foundation Faculty Fellowship.

The author also wishes to acknowledge the capable research assistance he received from Sheau-eng Lau, Marcia Douglass and, for briefer periods, from Ilse Higgins and Alex Kim. Margaret Markley provided efficient secretarial services throughout the project, and typed the drafts of the manuscript in its several stages. The manuscript was edited by Charlene Semer. Florence Robinson prepared the index.

This study is part of a special program of research and education on taxation and public expenditures, supervised by the National Committee on Government Finance and financed by a special grant from the Ford Foundation.

The views expressed in the study are those of the author and do not purport to represent the views of the National Committee on Government Finance or the Advisory Committee, or the staff members, officers, or trustees of the Brookings Institution, or the Ford Foundation.

Robert D. Calkins
President

January 1966
The Brookings Institution

Studies of Government Finance

Studies of Government Finance is a special program of research and education in taxation and government expenditures at the federal, state, and local levels. These studies are under the supervision of the National Committee on Government Finance appointed by the trustees of the Brookings Institution, and are supported by a special grant from the Ford Foundation.

MEMBERS OF THE ADVISORY COMMITTEE

Contents

Text Tables

Charts

Appendix Tables

CHAPTER I

Introduction

THE RELATIONSHIP BETWEEN dividend payments and corporate earnings has varied widely since the 1920's. These changes in the payout ratio have had a significant effect not only on the current income of stockholders, but also on the value of corporate securities, total investment, and the nation's economic growth and stability. The goal of this study is to isolate the major determinants of corporate dividend policy and, by implication, the complementary corporate saving policy.

The analysis is based on a statistical model designed to explain changes in corporate dividend payments in the United States since World War I. Primary attention is given to the determinants that are subject to public policy control—particularly individual tax rates and tax provisions concerning depreciation. The effect of the corporation tax is estimated through its depressing effect on after-tax earnings. Major emphasis is placed on the changes over time in the payout ratios for all corporations and manufacturing corporations, rather than on interfirm differences, but the model is also applied to the dividend behavior of industries and individual firms.

Trends in Aggregate Corporate Dividends

Commerce Department estimates of dividends and profits after taxes reveal three pronounced trends in the aggregate payout ratio since the first World War.[1] The first was an upward trend in the payout ratio through the twenties. The ratio then fell from about 70 percent to about 35 percent during the period from 1929 to 1947 as dividends rose far less rapidly than the profit base.[2] This downward trend is most clearly visible in the seven-year interval between 1939-40 and 1947. In 1939-40, the ratio was near the 1927-29 level; it was then rapidly cut in half by 1947. Finally, since the war, the payout ratio has recovered steadily to the levels of the late twenties.

These trends during the period studied—1920-1960—are illustrated by data for selected years in Table 1. The halving of the aggregate payout ratio between 1929 and 1947 is a striking development in light of the generally assumed rigidity of the desired payout ratio of corporations. So is the subsequent rise in the ratio, which ultimately doubled by 1961-62. The 1929-47 decline in the manufacturing payout ratio was somewhat less pronounced than that for the nonmanufacturing sector which fell from 81 percent to 38 percent.

Although profits after taxes averaged 90 percent greater in 1946-47 than they were in 1929, aggregate dividends were up only 3 percent. Since profits[3] are less reliably measured than dividends,

[1] The "aggregate payout ratio" is the ratio of net corporate dividends to net profits after taxes and capital consumption allowances. Net dividends and net profits estimates are from the Department of Commerce, Office of Business Economics. Both series exclude the "rest of the world" component; the dividends series also excludes dividends paid out of capital gains by investment trusts.

It should be noted that variations in the payout ratio reflect changes in profits as well as direct adjustments of dividends, and thus are not necessarily indicative of short-run variations in the level of dividends.

The series used throughout the study are those available before some substantial revisions in the aggregate data were presented in the *Survey of Current Business*, August, 1965. The main significance of these revisions for the problem of dividend policy is that they raised the estimates of corporate profits and thereby reduced payout ratios for each year. However, the relative changes in these series remained basically the same as before. Nevertheless, as a precaution, some of the key empirical work of the study was redone with the new data (available for the corporate aggregate only), and the results are reported in Appendix G. There it may be seen that the general upward revision of the payout base did not disturb the conclusions of the study. The estimated coefficients changed considerably, but not in sign or significance.

[2] This description of a decline in payout after the twenties bypasses the Great Depression years (1930-38) when the undistributed profits tax (effective 1936-37) and negative or near-zero profits produced erratic and wide swings in the ratio and undermined its usefulness as a measure of the propensity to pay dividends.

[3] Here and elsewhere "profits" refers to profits after taxes and depreciation.

TABLE 1. Dividends and Profits After Taxes, and Payout Percentages, Selected Years[a]

(Dollar amounts in billions)

Year	All Corporations			Manufacturing Corporations		
	Dividends	Net Profits	Payout Percentage	Dividends	Net Profits	Payout Percentage
1920	$2.98	$4.65	64.1	$1.46	$2.65	55.1
1929	5.72	8.03	71.2	2.65	4.23	62.6
1947	6.24	17.55	35.6	3.41	10.06	33.9
1960	13.05	21.11	61.8	6.67	11.46	58.2

[a] The three latest years are Office of Business Economics estimates, after removing estimated capital gains of investment trusts and the "rest of the world" component. For earlier sources and data processing procedures, see Appendix A.

the behavior of the latter alone is also worth noting. During the 1946-62 interval, aggregate dividends rose steadily at roughly a 6 percent annual rate,[4] which almost tripled dividends by 1962. This postwar rate of growth of aggregate dividends was not far off the 8 percent pace of the 1919-29 period when dividends more than doubled in a single decade. The recent liberality of dividend payments is an especially tempting subject for investigation, because it occurred in the seemingly hostile environment of a "profit squeeze" which limited the postwar trend in after-tax net profits to a 2 percent annual gain.

Trends in aggregate dividends were roughly parallel to those in individual industries and firms. Although there are some disparities in individual behavior, dividends for industries and firms tend to show the same trends with a high degree of consistency.

If it is assumed that the ability to pay, as measured by corporate income, should have a heavy influence on dividend payments, the data pose several questions: (1) Why did dividends rise faster than profits in the twenties? (2) Why were payout ratios cut in half between the start and finish of World War II? (3) Why did dividends rise at a 6 percent per year postwar rate when profits were barely moving at 2 percent per year?

[4] Here and elsewhere "annual rate" of increase refers to the growth rate derived from a least squares trend line fitted to the logarithms of the observations. Such trend estimates avoid the excessive influence of particular starting and finishing years.

Significance of the Swings in Payout Policy

These trends in dividend payments produced—or were associated with—a number of other developments of significance for public policy. It may be worthwhile to summarize two of them here.

Effects on Corporate Saving

Corporate saving, an important source of corporate liquidity and investment potential, is inversely related to changes in dividend policy.[5] Large changes in the payout ratio are associated with relatively larger swings in corporate saving. In Table 2, the actual level

TABLE 2. Actual and Hypothetical Levels of Retained Earnings, All Corporations, Selected Years[a]

(In billions of dollars)

Year	Actual Corporate Saving	Hypothetical Corporation Saving Under:	
		1929 Payout Ratio	1947 Payout Ratio
1920	1.67	1.34	2.99
1929	2.31	2.31	5.17
1947	11.31	5.07	11.31
1960	8.06	6.10	13.59

[a] Derived from Table 1.

of retained earnings (after taxes and depreciation allowances) is contrasted to levels that would have been attained with alternative payout policies. It can be seen that if the payout ratio had not been halved between 1929 and 1947, corporate saving would have been $5.1 billion, rather than $11.3 billion, in 1947. The actual corporate saving that year accounted for practically all net private saving[6] according to Office of Business Economics (OBE) estimates, so the halving of the corporate payout ratio accounted for—*ceteris*

[5] There is no intention at this point to portray changes in either savings or dividends as caused by the other. Corporate policy may be made with respect to one, with the other emerging as a residual. It will be suggested later that dividends appear to be most directly subject to policy, with saving primarily a residual. Here the discussion is focused simply on magnitudes.

[6] Net of depreciation allowances and after inventory valuation adjustment.

paribus—about one-half of the saving of the entire economy.

On the other hand, if the low payout ratios of the early postwar period had been maintained, corporate saving would have been $13.6 billion instead of $8.1 billion in 1960. This gap between actual corporate saving and the hypothetical level at the 1947 rate became even greater as the payout ratio continued to climb after 1960.

Effects on Measured Individual Income Distribution

A second important consequence of the trends in dividend payments is their effect on changes in the measured degree of inequality of individual incomes. Since most studies of individual income distribution do not impute corporate saving to individual stockholders, the fall in the dividend payout ratio was reflected in these studies as a leveling effect on the distribution of income. A rough indication of the effect of lower payout on the shape of the income distribution curve is obtainable from Kuznets' figures on the "basic" income variant and his estimate of the contribution of dividends to the income of the top one percent in 1947.[7] A dividend payout ratio equal to that of the late twenties would have given this group an income 22 percent greater than actually recorded. Its share in the total would have been 10.0 percent rather than the 8.5 percent indicated by Kuznets' series. Lower payouts account for about one-quarter of the 1929-47 decline of the income share of that group.[8] In order to allow for the effect of corporate taxation also, a 1947 payout ratio equal to the 1929 ratio to *pre-tax* income was analyzed similarly. The total income of the top one percent would have been 40 percent greater than recorded, making its share 11.2 percent. The lower payout thus accounts for 44 percent of the drop in that share between 1929 and 1947.

This indication that restriction of dividends by corporations in the early postwar period played a significant role in the apparent equalization of individual incomes clouds the meaning of the income

[7] Simon Kuznets, *Shares of Upper Income Groups in Income and Savings* (New York: National Bureau of Economic Research, 1950).

[8] This estimate is based on a hypothetical doubling of 1947 dividends to conform with the 1929 payout ratio, Kuznets' estimates of dividends as a source of income of the top one percent (*ibid.*, p. 668), relative shares of this group in 1929 and 1947 (*ibid.*, p. 582), and Internal Revenue Service estimates of dividends as a percentage of total individual income in 1947.

distribution statistics. Increased retention cuts the share of the wealthy in total personal income, but this may be misleading because any resulting capital gains are generally excluded from data on personal incomes. Stockholders as a whole are likely to prefer high retention for tax-saving purposes. Even those who do not prefer high retention remain the legal owners of the resulting increments to wealth, although they may be inconvenienced by lack of control over its disposition.

Whether or not the imputation of undistributed income to individual stockholders is a defensible exercise, it would be interesting to know the extent to which the leveling of measured individual incomes was the result of tax factors. Studies of the declining inequality of individual incomes have often given the impression that it was a leveling in the "market place"—a "natural" phenomenon which proceeded independently of fiscal policy through some undirected tendency of the economic system.[9] However, the indications are that the change in "after-tax" income distributions toward equality was partly the indirect effect of taxes on the dividend payout ratio and on its net profits base. In this respect, a more or less "natural" economic leveling of income is in doubt. It is evident that even "pre-tax" individual income data already reflect the pressures of taxation. The corporate tax rose from the 12 percent level of 1929 to take a bigger bite from profits, thus presumably reducing dividends to individuals.[10] In addition, it seems likely that the rise in individual tax rates also heightened the incentive to retain corporate income in order to avoid taxes. Any leveling of individual incomes arising from such pressures on dividends can hardly be regarded as independent of fiscal policy.

[9] For example, speaking of England, R. G. D. Allen noted "a massive redistribution of income even before the incidence of taxation and social services is considered." (Royal Commission on the Taxation of Profits and Income, Minutes of Evidence, Eighth Day, Friday, 30th May, 1952, p. 185.)

[10] This assumes less than 100 percent shifting of the tax. Some estimates of short-run shifting of more than 100 percent were obtained by M. Krzyzaniak and R. A. Musgrave in *The Shifting of the Corporation Income Tax* (Baltimore: Johns Hopkins Press, 1963). Their findings would suggest that corporations basing their dividends on profits would tend to pay more dividends the higher the corporate tax rates, since the higher taxes are more than completely recouped through higher prices or other adjustments. If this discovery of a favorable effect of corporate taxation on after-tax profits were accepted as valid, it would suggest that businessmen, in order to maximize profits, might be well advised to go to Washington and lobby for higher corporate tax rates.

Other Effects of Payout Policy

There are other important consequences of changing dividend policy besides the two discussed here. For example, a restriction of dividends in an inflationary period may cause difficulties for some individuals dependent on the income from equities. Greater profit retention may not immediately produce capital gains; in fact, stock prices may even be depressed. Even if gains are realized, stockholders may not consider them equivalent to dividends. Dividend policy may also affect the outcome of collective bargaining insofar as unions tend to compare the wage share with dividends, rather than with net profits. Finally, the dividend decision may have a stabilizing impact on the economy to the extent that it is primary and corporate saving is residual. That is, insofar as dividends are relatively stable, corporate saving varies with corporate profits, and partially offsets the impact of profit swings on aggregate demand.

Alternative Measures of Corporate Income

In this study it was taken for granted at the outset that after-tax income is the primary determinant of dividend payments. This was in accord with the earlier work of others to be outlined in the next chapter. However, within this framework, the initial problem was the appropriate measurement of the income base.

Net earnings is a misleading measure of income when capital consumption allowances vary because of changes in accounting practice or for legal or procedural, rather than economic, reasons.[11] It was suspected that the much-discussed postwar "profit squeeze" was, at least in part, such an accounting phenomenon. Insofar as postwar depreciation charges were "liberalized" over time, it suggests that the trend in measured net profits carries a downward bias.[12] For this reason, net earnings—after taxes and capital consumption allowances as measured in the national income accounts

[11] For an excellent treatment of this problem from the accounting point of view, see Allan R. Drebin, " 'Cash-Flowitis': Malady or Syndrome?," *Journal of Accounting Research,* Vol. 2, No. 1 (Spring 1964), pp. 25-34.

[12] This does not imply that any particular position is being taken on the issue of whether or not actual allowances were or are now "adequate," or whether profits are overstated or understated in any given time.

—may not be a reliable indicator of the ability to pay dividends or of the source of funds from which they are paid. Although some corporations have reported tying dividends to net earnings,[13] it seems in order to seek a measure of income that is free from the distortion produced by differing accounting practices.

The Problem of Varying Depreciation Allowances

The first significant and explicit interference by the Treasury in corporate depreciation accounting for tax purposes occurred with its issuance in 1934 of Bulletin F, *Tables of Useful Lives Of Depreciable Property*.[14] Although these guidelines probably constrained depreciation charges somewhat, the vagaries of capital consumption allowances first produced a major distortion of the profit data during World War II. Five-year amortization and later liberalizing regulations and practices have clouded the meaning of the tax return profit data. This liberalization process also distorts the regular profit series appearing in the national income accounts, since these rely upon tax return depreciation allowances.

The overall effect of liberalized allowances is to give a downward bias to the reported growth of corporate incomes since liberalization began. Many corporations try to avoid this downward bias by charging less depreciation against profits reported to stockholders than they do for tax purposes. They may report the tax saving to stockholders as a liability for deferred income tax, or allow it to "flow through" to increase reported earnings. Those who report depreciation differently to stockholders and tax authorities apparently agree with the advice of the Committee on Accounting Procedure of the American Institute of Certified Public Accountants which stated that "sound financial accounting procedures do not necessarily coincide with the rules as to what shall be included in 'gross income' or allowed as a deduction therefrom, in arriving at taxable net income."[15] However, it appears that most corporate accountants tend to follow the gyrations of tax laws and definitions in making

[13] See John Lintner, "Distribution of Incomes of Corporations Among Dividends, Retained Earnings and Taxes," *American Economic Review*, Vol. 46, No. 2 (May 1956), pp. 97-113.

[14] The corporate tax itself affected depreciation accounting, but this was an indirect result.

[15] *Accounting Research Bulletin*, No. 43 (1953), p. 76.

their reports.[16] The bulk of corporate profits are reported in about the same way in stockholder reports as in tax returns.

As an illustration of the effect of acceleration of depreciation charges on measured profits consider the case of the United States Steel Corporation, which reported a decline in net profits from $190.2 million to $163.7 million between 1961 and 1962—a decline of 14 percent.[17] The chairman of the company's finance committee noted that "the 1962 profit margin was smaller than that of any nonwar year since the depression year of 1938."[18] A different picture is obtained if one allows for the fact that U. S. Steel took higher depreciation by adopting the shorter "guideline" lives (issued by the Treasury Department in 1962) in its depreciation accounting. An adjustment for this is made in the following table:

Reported net income of U. S. Steel	$163.7 million
Add: Additional depreciation charged by adoption of "guideline" lives	44.0 million
Less: Taxes saved by this additional depreciation	−22.9 million
Adjusted net earnings	$184.8 million

After this adjustment, net earnings fell only three percent. What happened was that in 1962 U. S. Steel took the extra depreciation in order to save almost $23 million in taxes, but in so doing reduced its reported net earnings by $21 million.[19]

Corporation accountants are undoubtedly aware of such distortions and presumably regret that in order to achieve the tax saving they create an artificially low profit estimate. Apparently, most of them are reluctant to report different and economically more realis-

[16] Accountants are not alone in this. It is surprising to find so few doubts expressed by economists using the official net profit figures. For data on depreciation reporting, see George H. Sorter and others, "Corporate Personality as Reflected in Accounting Decisions," *Journal of Accounting Research,* Vol. 2, No. 2 (Autumn 1964), pp. 183-96.

[17] The information for this example is taken from Allan R. Drebin, *op. cit.,* pp. 27-30.

[18] United States Steel Corporation, *1962 Annual Report,* p. 23.

[19] Net earnings are reduced by only about half the added depreciation because of the compensating effect of the tax saving.

tic figures to their stockholders.[20] Instead there is often resort to informal qualification of the reported profits by reference to the "quality" of earnings. For example, in reference to the steel industry, *Business Week* reported (August 8, 1964):

It hurts to set sales and tonnage records and yet not come within hailing distance of old profit marks (even though today's profits may be of "higher quality" due to cash-flow benefits of higher depreciation).

Measuring Income by Cash Flow

The initial hypothesis of this study, that net earnings is a poor measure of the ability to pay dividends, is accompanied by the corollary that "cash flow" (net earnings plus depreciation allowances) would be a better basis for the explanation of dividends.[21] The assumption was that firms take these liberalized allowances into account and base dividend payments either on their total cash flow, or on some conception they might have of their "true" earnings. Casual empiricism based on postwar data offers ready support for this conjecture. Because the dividend-net earning ratio doubled after the early postwar low, it is obviously difficult to explain dividend payments on the basis of a linear relationship with net earnings alone. On the other hand, the ratio of dividends to cash flow has held remarkably stable near 30 percent since 1941. This contrast in itself suggests that cash flow offers a better basis for explaining dividends. It may often fail, as in the case of the 1962 dividend cut by U. S. Steel when dividends were reduced in the face of a rise in cash flow achieved through the saving in taxes. However, it appeared likely that cash flow would usually explain aggregate dividends better than net earnings.

[20] The disappointment of those stockholders who fail to understand this process may be at least partially offset by advantages that may be gained in the context of collective bargaining. However, the unions themselves are not unaware of the downward bias caused by liberalized depreciation. See, for example, a report on a statement issued by the AFL-CIO, June 2, 1962 in William A. Paton, "The Cash-Flow Illusion," *The Accounting Review*, Vol. XXXVIII, No. 2 (April 1963), p. 243.

[21] It would have been desirable to include in the cash flow measure all capital consumption allowances rather than depreciation allowances alone. It was necessary to omit accidental damage to fixed capital and capital outlays charged to current expense because data were not available on an industry basis. However, these allowances are small, and there is no evidence that they were liberalized over time.

This line of reasoning has already appeared in the accounting and financial literature. While rejecting cash flow as a substitute for an accounting improvement of the net income measure, Perry Mason stated:[22]

The *concept* of "cash flow" can be used effectively as one of the major factors in judging ability to meet debt retirement requirements, to maintain regular dividends, to finance replacement and expansion costs, . . .

A similar comment was made by another writer under the heading of "Depreciation—Not a Cash Outlay":[23]

. . . The more rapid the rate of depreciation the larger the amount of such cash flow and the lower the demands for after tax retained earnings and external financing. . . . The analyst must realize that dividend payments will generally be based on *cash flow* remaining after capital expenditures deemed necessary by corporate directors.

Other financial writers have, for similar reasons, explicitly dismissed the "profit squeeze." For example:[24]

And lastly—and possibly most important—is the fact that much of the profit margin squeeze is artificial, because one of the most rapidly increasing cost items is depreciation charged off against the newly created facilities.

The significance of this cannot be overstated. What has happened is that industry's binge of capital spending, combined with the newer methods of accelerating depreciation charges, has created an enormous expense item on corporate income statements that reduces reported profits but nevertheless allows enormous cash earnings to flow into the company coffers. In effect, corporate profits today are being understated as never before—and this process will continue until the capital spending boom drops to much lower levels.

Obviously cash flow is not an ideal indicator of the ability to pay dividends, and the last statement above may be criticized for failing to recognize that accurately measured depreciation is as le-

[22] American Institute of Certified Public Accountants, *"Cash Flow" Analysis and the Funds Statement,* Accounting Research Study No. 2 (1961), p. xv.

[23] Douglas H. Bellemore, *Security Analysis* (Simmons-Boardman, 1959), pp. 140-41.

[24] Ward Gates, "A Sound Approach to 1960 Third Quarter Reports," *The Magazine of Wall Street and Business Analyst* (Nov. 19, 1960), p. 224.

gitimate a deduction as any other cost. However, financial analysts can hardly be blamed for falling back on this crude measure when they are given nothing more reliable than tax return profits. They obviously prefer to be consistent—and possibly wrong—than to be consistently wrong.

In this study, the first hypothesis tested was that cash flow would do a better job of explaining dividends than net earnings. However, in recognition of the crudity of the cash flow measure, two related alternatives were tested. One was to test income measures other than either of these for a better explanation of dividends. The other was to include depreciation allowances or measures of depreciation liberality explicitly, along with net profits, in the explanatory models.[25]

Variations in the Propensity to Distribute

In addition to the initial rejection of net earnings as an income measure, it was also hypothesized from the start that the target (desired long-run) ratio of dividends to any income measure would vary substantially over time. It would be surprising if any simple fixed relationship between dividends and income could survive the great changes since the thirties, especially in the tax structure.

In contrast, Lintner had concluded that there is no evidence "that the normal or target or equilibrium ratio of dividends to profits for corporations as a whole is any different during the postwar years than during the preceding quarter century."[26] This statement appears to be confirmed by the stability of the ratio of dividends to cash flow since 1941. However, although the ratio was stable at around 30 percent since 1941, it is well below the nearly 50 percent levels of the late twenties.

The Effect of Individual Tax Rates

The primary hypothesis about the payout ratio was that it would tend to vary inversely with the differential between the higher tax rates on ordinary income and the rates on capital gains. To the extent that stockholders do not rely on any particular after-

[25] The problem of depreciation allowances is discussed in detail in Chapter III.
[26] Lintner, *op. cit.*, p. 112.

tax dividend level, this association would seem likely in light of the tax saving (or shelter effect) afforded by corporate retention. The behavioral rationale underlying this hypothesis is that the payout ratio adopted by boards of directors is influenced by the desire of stockholders for a tax shelter. This influence could be transmitted in a number of ways, so that payout may lag as income tax rates rise if directors themselves are interested in a tax shelter, or are forced to take the interests of stockholders into account.

Even if it is presumed that this hypothesis is correct and that corporate boards of directors adjust their dividend policy in order to save taxes for the owners, it is not surprising that explicit references to this by company officers or reports are rare. Perhaps it is considered distasteful to take pride even in perfectly legal tax avoidance. In addition, there is always the risk that admission of the tax-avoidance objective may lead to imposition of the "accumulated earnings tax" on retentions "beyond the reasonable needs of the business." However, some direct statements on this have been made. For example, Carl Gilbert, head of the Gillette Safety Razor Corporation, remarked:[27]

We can't distribute any more in dividends. But there will come a time when having cash in the bank will mean being able to buy something at an advantageous price. Anyway the stockholders are better off with artificial courage in the bank than in being paid higher dividends out of which Mr. Dillon gets his share. It's better off in our hands than his.

Corporations not so inclined to consider the tax position of their high-income, appreciation-minded stockholders may be moved to do so by the demands of stockholders as expressed by their concentration in low-payout growth stocks. One investor, with an income of about $100,000, for example, has been quoted on his own quest for such stocks as follows:[28]

We, that is, my wife and I, prefer common stocks as an investment, but not for all our funds. We choose corporations which pay out a minimum

---

[27] Walter Guzzardi, Jr., "Gillette Faces the Stainless-Steel Dragon," *Fortune,* Vol. LXVIII, No. 1 (July 1963), pp. 159-60.

[28] J. K. Butters, L. E. Thompson, and L. L. Bollinger, *Effects of Taxation: Investment by Individuals* (Boston: Division of Research, Graduate School of Business Administration, Harvard University, 1953), p. 200.

of earnings in order to have our holdings grow in intrinsic value. We like to save by having corporations plow back a substantial portion of their earnings tax-free to us. If the corporations pay us dividends, we have to pay taxes on the income.

Butters, Thompson, and Bollinger, who reported the above comment, indicate that a large number of other investors questioned made similar remarks.[29]

Corporations may not necessarily respond directly to such preferences on the part of one segment of their stockholders, especially those corporations whose officials may have different interests and objectives from those of the owners. However, managers and boards of directors would undoubtedly be disturbed by any weakness in stock price caused by a desertion of stockholders seeking appreciation in place of dividends. Finally, if the decisionmakers of a corporation hold a substantial amount of its stock themselves, their own interest may call for increasing retention in the face of higher tax rates.

Other Factors Affecting the Payout Ratio

The structure of individual tax rates is not the only factor prompting variations in the payout ratio. Higher interest rates may encourage a higher rate of retention to avoid the high costs of external finance or rationing or restrictions imposed by lenders at given interest rates. High investment demand may encourage retention to avoid the need for external finance. A rise in liquidity may stimulate dividends if the funds are not needed internally. A high rate of growth of profits may lead to a reduction of the fraction paid out if corporate officials believe such growth rate may not be maintained. Finally, the degree of liberality of depreciation allowances is likely to affect the ratio of dividends to officially measured net profits, especially because of recognition of the downward bias in the postwar trend of the profit series. In other words, in addition

[29] A recent study appears to have found less evidence of openly expressed "tax consciousness." However, without being asked explicitly about taxes, 17 percent of a high-income group volunteered that they preferred growth stocks to income stocks because of tax considerations. See James N. Morgan, Robin Barlow, and Harvey E. Brazer, "A Survey of Investment Management and Working Behavior among High-Income Individuals," *American Economic Review*, Vol. 55, No. 2 (May 1965), pp. 257-58.

to seeking a better income measure than net earnings, it seemed appropriate to introduce the depreciation variable explicitly to explain that part of variations in payout ratios that arises from inadequacies of net earnings as a measure of income.

The Analytical Approach and Some Findings

This study of factors affecting corporate dividends relies primarily on statistical models of dividend behavior. Regression models have been fitted to annual data for the years 1920-60 in an effort to isolate the impact of various factors. The models were developed primarily to bring out long-run relationships rather than the nature of short-run adjustments.

The investigation was carried out in three phases, representing three different types of analysis. The first was a highly aggregative time series analysis of the relationship between changes in dividends and movements in presumably related variables. The relationships were studied separately for the corporate aggregate and for all manufacturing corporations which comprise, on most criteria, about one-half of the aggregate.

The results of the aggregative analysis are in brief as follows: (1) Because of the exaggeration of the squeeze on net earnings by liberalization of depreciation allowances, the measurement of income by "cash flow" gives a better explanation of dividends since the beginning of World War II (Chapter III); (2) allowing for long-run variations in the ratio of dividends to net profits in response to individual tax rates and depreciation liberality gives a satisfactory explanation of dividends in the entire 1920-60 interval (Chapter IV); (3) these two tax factors appear sufficient to account for the sharp drop in the payout ratio between the late 1920's and the early postwar period, and its subsequent recovery (Chapter IV); (4) the rate of corporate taxation was found to influence aggregate dividends, but not the payout ratio (Chapter V); (5) three other factors, rising interest rates, rapid sales increases, and diminishing corporate liquidity, were all found to depress the fraction of income paid out in dividends, although their influence was far less significant (Chapter V).

The second phase of the study was a similar, though less detailed, time series analysis of the dividend policy of industries and firms. The study of industries strongly supported the depreciation and tax rate hypotheses, and interest rates appeared influential in a majority of cases (Chapter VI). The same models fitted to a sample of forty large firms suggested that depreciation and individual tax rates were each influential in the case of about one-third of the firms (Chapter VII).

The third phase of the investigation introduced an entirely different approach. The data for the forty large firms studied in Chapter VII were again utilized. This time cross-section and time series information was pooled, and the variations among firms and over time were analyzed simultaneously. This more efficient analysis of the dividend behavior of these firms reaffirmed strongly the influence of depreciation and individual tax rates even though the time series models for firms had shown only infrequent influence by the tax variables. It also reestablished interest rates as a significant factor. Liquidity was found to stimulate dividends, and, for the first time, high investment demand was found discouraging to dividends (Chapter VIII).

After an outline of the general methodology adopted (Chapter II), the findings of this study are reported in the same sequence as the tests were conceived and the results obtained. Theil has remarked that an evaluation of an empirical result cannot be made independently of the manner in which it is obtained; that is, it makes a difference whether the final hypothesis is the first one, or the result of much experimentation along the way. "Since every econometric analysis is an essay in persuasion—just as is true of any other branch of science—the line of thought leading to the finally accepted result must be expounded."[30] This study began with the hypothesis that liberalized depreciation beginning with World War II led to higher dividends than could be explained by artificially squeezed profits (Chapter III). The next hypothesis was that higher individual tax rates since the interwar period produced a structural change in the relation between dividends and income and could explain changes in dividend policy since World War I (Chapter IV). Next, rival hypotheses that might augment or undermine the preliminary success of the depreciation and tax hypotheses

[30] H. Theil, *Economic Forecasts and Policy* (Amsterdam: North-Holland Publishing Co., 1958), p. 207.

were considered (Chapter V). The next step was to ask whether the successful aggregative time series models could explain the dividend policy of industries and firms (Chapters VI and VII). Finally, more conclusive confirmation of the hypotheses was sought by simultaneous use of time series and cross-section information (Chapter VIII). Some of the implications of the findings are considered briefly in the conclusion.

CHAPTER II

Antecedents and Methodology

THE IMPACT OF DEPRECIATION liberalization, individual tax rates, and corporate taxes on the dividend decision was tested primarily by means of regression models. Although this statistical analysis was preceded by *a priori* reasoning and supplemented by description of corporate behavior, the main reliance is on the statistical results.

The Basic Model

The main approach was the generalization of models of dividend behavior previously proposed by others by introducing depreciation allowances, tax rates and other plausible explanatory variables. The objective was to isolate the separate influences of these tax factors. An underlying theoretical device relied upon repeatedly is a model proposed by John Lintner.[1] Although the model was proposed as descriptive of individual firm behavior, it was also used to relate aggregate corporate dividends to lagged dividends and net

---

[1] See "The Determinants of Corporate Saving" in *Savings in the Modern Economy*, edited by Walter W. Heller (Minneapolis: University of Minnesota Press, 1953), pp. 230-55, and "Distribution of Incomes of Corporations Among Dividends, Retained Earnings and Taxes," *American Economic Review*, Vol. 46, No. 2 (May 1956), pp. 97-113.

profits (after depreciation and taxes). Writing current dividends as D, profits as P, lagged dividends as D_{-1} and the unexplained error term as u, the relation estimated by Lintner was

$$(2\text{-}1) \qquad D = a + b_1 P + b_2 D_{-1} + u$$

The simplest rationale for this model is that dividends depend directly on current net income but are also influenced by past dividends because of reluctance to cut dividends or to raise them to levels which may not be maintained.

A more detailed theoretical rationale for (2-1) is the speed-of-adjustment model suggested by Lintner and backed by behavioral claims made by interviewed firms. Lintner was led to relation (2-1) by the following more explicit model of corporate dividend policy:

$$(2\text{-}2) \qquad D - D_{-1} = a + c(rP - D_{-1}) + u$$

Corporations were pictured as pursuing a "target" payout ratio r which they applied to current earnings P. If dividends were fully adjusted each year to achieve the target level rP, they would be changed by $(rP - D_{-1})$ between times $t - 1$ and t. However, a conservative bias against large revisions leads them to move only a fraction of the way, given by a speed-of-adjustment coefficient c. The constant term a—expected to be positive—was added to allow for a presumed greater reluctance to cut dividends than to raise them. If a is positive, the model says that dividends will tend to drift up even if the rest of the model calls for no change. Thus, the target level of D must be enough below D_{-1} to offset the constant term in order for a cut in dividends to be indicated.

This expectation of a positive constant term pertains to the macroeconomic level, rather than to the microeconomic context in which the rest of the model was conceived. It allows for the mixture of profitable and unprofitable firms, with the latter tending to maintain dividends in the face of disappointing profits.

There are other behavioral rationales that also lead to the estimating equation (2-1). Dividends may be assumed to depend on profits in all previous years according to a "distributed lag" formulation. Under simplifying assumptions, this reduces to relation (2-1). Alternatively, the distributed lag model may first be rationalized by an "adaptive expectations" framework in which dividends are assumed to depend on the *expected value* of profits on assets currently held, rather than on current profits. This rationale also leads, via the distributed lag model, to the same estimating equation (2-1). These alternative behavior rationales are discussed in detail in the first technical note following this chapter and compared there to the speed-of-adjustment framework proposed by Lintner.

One way of interpreting the Lintner theoretical framework is that dividends are determined by (1) capacity to distribute (approximated by P) and (2) a long-run propensity to distribute (r), modified by short-run inertia or resistance. The resulting equation has proved to be a useful vehicle for generalization in the present analysis. It performed well according to goodness-of-fit and the behavior of residuals. In addition, the treatment of short-run and long-run behavior in this model is convenient for the present problem. Since the primary objective is to account for the difference between prewar and postwar dividend policies, and for the rapid postwar rise in dividends, a relatively long-run analysis is necessary. It would be difficult, for example, to estimate the total influence of a cut in individual tax rates using a short-run model, because such a change might have only minor immediate effects.

Lintner's model provided an impressive explanation of interwar dividends and performed well when applied to the postwar period. However, some critics of the original formulation have stressed its aggregative character and its failure to explain the target ratio itself.[2] In his discussion of the model, Tarshis also commented that the ability of this "relatively simple formulation to 'explain' dividends over a very long time span," during which "everything else in the economy changed" was a ground for suspicion of the results rather than satisfaction.[3] His criticism of Lintner's results as "a bit too good" can be countered by an elaboration of the model, however. Using Lintner's model as the foundation, his results can be significantly improved by adding a propensity-to-distribute function

[2] See, for example, Jacob Michaelsen, "Determinants of Corporate Dividend Policy" (unpublished doctoral thesis, University of Chicago, 1961). Some other criticisms by Michaelsen are less convincing. His own concern with interfirm differences leads him to dismiss time series models, such as Lintner's, as unimportant and uninteresting, mere "historical description." However, he does admit that his emphasis ignores their possible usefulness in explaining macroeconomic behavior.

[3] "Economic Growth: Income Distribution—Discussion," *American Economic Review*, Vol. 46, No. 2 (May 1956), p. 118.

and by taking account of some of the changes mentioned by Tarshis, including important shifts in the tax structure.

The basic model was elaborated in two major respects. First, the net profits variable P was rejected as a measure of the ability to pay dividends; it was found necessary either to replace it by more adequate income measures or supplement it by explicit depreciation variables. Secondly, the fixed long-run target payout ratio r was replaced by a target function r_t which varied over time with tax and other factors.

Dividend Models with Alternative Variables

Lintner also tested various elaborations of his basic model. Adding gross and net investment variables proved useless, as did inclusion of current change in profits and the highest previous dividend outlay (when in excess of last year's dividend). Lintner also compared the predictive ability of his basic interwar model with those of more complicated models proposed earlier by others. He found the postwar forecasts by the simple speed-of-adjustment model (based only on profits and lagged dividends) better than the other forecasts.

Some additional factors in dividend policy which were explored in these earlier studies should be mentioned. Tinbergen and Modigliani used lagged profits and corporate surplus as explanatory variables with some success.[4] In his more detailed study,[5] Dobrovolsky found a significant positive association between dividends and surplus, but his results did not validate the lagged profits hypothesis.

[4] Jan Tinbergen, *Statistical Testing of Business Cycle Theories*, Vol. 2 (Geneva: League of Nations, Economic Intelligence Service, 1939), p. 115; Franco Modigliani, "Fluctuations in the Savings Income Ratio: A Problem in Economic Forecasting," *Studies of Income and Wealth*, Pt. V, Vol. II (New York: National Bureau of Economic Research, 1949), p. 414.

[5] S. P. Dobrovolsky, *Corporate Income Retention, 1915-43* (New York: National Bureau of Economic Research, 1951), especially pp. 39-40. His study also compared large, small, and medium-sized companies and was extended to cross-section analyses. These are less relevant to the present concern with tax factors than are the time series models. For more recent cross-section studies, which will not be taken up here, see J. Michaelsen, *op. cit.*, S. J. Prais, "Dividend Policy and Income Appropriation" in *Studies in Company Finance*, B. Tew and R. F. Henderson, eds. (Cambridge: Cambridge University Press, 1959), and Phoebus J. Dhrymes and Mordecai Kurz, "On the Dividend Policy of Electric Utilities," *The Review of Economics and Statistics*, Vol. 46, No. 1 (February 1964), pp. 76-81.

He also found dividends to be negatively and significantly associated with "expansion requirements," measured by actual growth of operating assets. Dobrovolsky's emphasis is directly on the corporate saving decision as influenced by the rate of return on investment. This is in contrast with Lintner's direct concern with the dividend decision, and the implication that saving is a passive or residual outcome of this decision.

The lagged profits hypothesis has been more recently proposed by Darling. He assumes that after a change in earnings, "the firm moves toward the new target (rP) by letting current dividends reflect the target *ratio, r,* applied to *recent past* levels of earnings (rP$_{-1}$) plus a smaller fraction, c, of the *current* change in earnings, that is plus c(P — P$_{-1}$)." This rationale leads to substitution of P$_{-1}$ for D$_{-1}$ in relation (2-1).[6]

The more important departure by Darling is that he adds successfully to this model the amortization of noncurrent assets and the change in sales over the previous two years. The former allows for the fact that rising and predictable depreciation charges diminish uncertainty with respect to the ability to maintain dividends out of a given level of profits. The sales change variable is a proxy for anticipated working capital needs. Dividends were found to be positively associated with amortization and negatively with the change in sales. Darling also treats an unmeasurable expectation (or confidence) variable—the expected departure of future cash positions from desired levels. By inspection, he concludes that this factor explains well the residuals from the fitted model.[7]

More directly addressed to the possible impact of corporate capital requirements on dividends is the work of David Smith.[8] Al-

[6] Paul G. Darling, "The Influence of Expectations and Liquidity on Dividend Policy," *Journal of Political Economy,* Vol. 65, No. 3 (June 1957), pp. 209-24. In his analysis of all corporations, Darling's lagged profit model showed strong evidence of autocorrelated residuals, and a residual variance more than double that of the model containing lagged dividends instead of lagged profits. However, Darling preferred the lagged profit model on other grounds (see p. 217).

[7] For example, low dividends in the early thirties (relative to measurable determinants) were interpreted as the consequence of low confidence, a variable not included in the model. For interpretations of other periods see Darling, *op. cit.,* pp. 220-21.

[8] David C. Smith, "Corporate Saving Behavior," *Canadian Journal of Economics and Political Science,* Vol. 29, No. 3 (August 1963), pp. 297-310.

though Modigliani-Miller and others have stressed the theoretical independence of the corporate investment and saving decisions,[9] Smith suggests that the cost of financial transactions will link the two decisions in practice. The cost imputed to internal funds should only be as great as the cost of external funds if there were no transaction costs connected with the latter. However, flotation costs, the risk of a poor showing by a new issue, and higher taxes on distributions all make for higher external costs.

Smith measured investment demand by averaging current investment less capital consumption allowances and a survey of investment intentions for the next year less current capital consumption allowances. He added this variable to the Lintner model and to another with lagged profits substituted for lagged dividends. Time series regressions based on postwar Canadian data showed a positive influence of investment demand on corporate saving, but the variable was of marginal significance.

The latest intensive analysis of corporate dividend policy was by Edwin Kuh.[10] He assumes a widespread preference for internal finance on the part of manufacturing firms. Consequently, the availability of internal finance must be taken into account in a theory of investment. This implies some kind of relation between investment demand and dividend policy. The link is found in the behavior of the speed-of-adjustment coefficient and the target payout ratio. Kuh's hypothesis is that firms that adjust dividends according to the Lintner model and capital stock according to the Chenery model[11] can select coefficients that are compatible with financing net investment from retained earnings on a continuing basis. However, his empirical work tended to refute this hypothetical link between the dividend and investment decisions by producing much larger speed-of-adjustment coefficients for the dividend models than for the capital stock models.[12]

---

[9] See, for example, F. Modigliani and M. H. Miller, "The Cost of Capital, Corporation Finance, and the Theory of Investment," *American Economic Review,* Vol. 48, No. 3 (June 1958), pp. 261-97; and F. Lutz and V. Lutz, *The Theory of the Investment of the Firm* (Princeton: Princeton University Press, 1951), p. 185.

[10] *Capital Stock Growth: A Microeconometric Approach* (Amsterdam: North-Holland Publishing Company, 1963), especially pp. 16-26 and Chap. 10.

[11] *Ibid.,* pp. 8-9.

[12] *Ibid.,* pp. 316-17.

Other Estimation Problems

In addition to the selection of explanatory variables, several decisions were necessary with respect to the structure of the dividend models.

Time Series

While the basic vehicle for this analysis was the speed-of-adjustment approach, a constant term (expected to be positive) was also included throughout. This was in keeping with Lintner's assumption that a given drop in profits would produce a smaller decline in dividends than the gain that would result from a profit increase of the same amount. The expected positive sign was found throughout the aggregative analysis, and the inclusion of the constant significantly improved the explanation of dividends in the case of most industries also. However, in the models for single firms, the constant terms were negative about as often as positive, and they were rarely statistically significant.

This inconsistent behavior of the constant terms for many firms lends some support to Kuh's conclusion that the dividend model is improved by excluding the constant.[13] His empirical argument for this is that actual average payout and target payout were much more closely correlated when the targets were estimated by models without the constant term. However, such a conclusion is not necessarily a sign of better performance by the model. It is to be expected that slow-growing or declining firms would tend chronically to pay more than called for by their target ratios—a phenomenon that can be allowed for by a positive constant term. The reverse might well be true of fast-growing firms, leading to the appearance of negative constant terms in many fitted models. The high frequency of these in the equations for firms may be the result of the known prevalence of fast-growing firms in the sample studied here. In any case, the constant term was retained in all models reported because of its success at the aggregate and industry levels. However, additional tests were carried out without the constant term, and these cast no

[13] *Ibid.*, Chap. 10.

doubt on the signs or significance of the coefficients in the models to be presented.[14]

Another methodological problem was the possibility that the magnitude of the residuals in the regression estimates of dividend change would tend to grow along with the explanatory variables as the latter drifted up over time. To guard against this "heteroscedasticity," the model was first put in relative change form—essentially by division of equation (2-2) by D_{-1}. Models of this form and more general versions were tested extensively and finally abandoned for two reasons. In the first place, there was strong evidence of serial correlation in the residuals (low Durbin-Watson statistics). Secondly, the transformation was probably unnecessary since the variance of the residuals in the models explaining $D - D_{-1}$ did not appear to increase with the explanatory variables.[15] This is evident from the fact that the standard error of estimate of models fitted separately to the first and second halves of the period of study were of about the same magnitude.

The generalization of the basic model involved another methodological decision. Either or both of its basic parameters (the speed-of-adjustment coefficient c and the target payout ratio r) could be allowed to vary over time with the tax variables and others. There were *a priori* reasons to expect r to vary, but it proved difficult to develop plausible hypotheses about variations in c. Nevertheless, this coefficient was allowed to vary with sales change and other variables in a number of tests aimed at improvement of the explanation of dividends. Treating c as a function of these other variables introduced greater multicollinearity among the explanatory variables, and no satisfactory results were obtained. It thus proved necessary to adopt the simplifying, and not altogether satisfactory, assumption that all long-run influences on dividend policy were reflected in changes in the target ratio. After preliminary tests,

---

[14] Lintner has noted that the constant term "a" is not the only way of handling the premium on growth in dividends and reluctance to cut them. This can (by complicating the rest of the function) be better handled directly in a homogeneous form. (J. Lintner, "Discussion," *American Economic Review*, Vol. 54, No. 3 [May 1964], p. 303n.)

[15] Therefore, it was the relative change model that exhibited the undesirable property of squared residuals which tended to decrease as the explanatory variables increased.

the speed-of-adjustment coefficient was treated as a parameter, as in the original Lintner model.

Pooled Time Series and Cross-Section Data

A stronger estimation technique was adopted to supplement the generalized speed-of-adjustment time series models discussed above. A combined cross-section and time series analysis was carried out for a sample of forty firms in the same thirty-eight-year period used for the time series models. Long-run marginal payout propensities were estimated each year for the sample aggregate by a cross-section regression of dividends on profits. Each year's coefficient for profits was taken as an estimate of this long-run propensity and then explained by time series regressions on tax factors and other variables as reported in Chapter VIII.

This technique proved especially valuable because it avoided some of the statistical difficulties discussed in the technical note on estimation problems following this chapter.

Estimation Procedures

The models were all fitted by means of the classical least-squares procedure. This technique is suspect for one main reason. The presence of the lagged exogenous variable D_{-1} as an explanatory variable in all models except those of Chapter VIII introduces a possible bias in the regression coefficients and their standard errors. An evaluation of the statistical results to be reported should take account of these statistical difficulties in the time series analysis.

These issues are discussed in detail in the second technical note following this chapter. However, it is shown there that the problem is probably not serious. Especially reassuring is the fact that the pooled time series and cross-section analysis of Chapter VIII, which avoids this problem, generally confirms the earlier time series findings.

Summary of the Methods Used

There were two basic approaches. Relation (2-2) was generalized by introduction of alternative after-tax income variables and by allowing the target payout ratio r to vary with time series variables. After multiplication of the income variable by the target function, the regression equations were fitted to the years 1920-60 (excluding 1936-38). The target functions implied by each such regression were taken as an estimate of the long-run relationship between dividends and the income variable of the model.

The second approach pooled the annual information for forty firms. Long-run relationships were estimated for each year by cross-section analysis and then explained by time series.

After some preliminary tests, it was assumed in all cases that the effect of corporate taxes on dividends could be allowed for by adoption of after-tax income as the explanatory variable. These equations show directly the long-run effect of depreciation liberalization, individual tax rates and other factors on dividends. On any given assumption about the incidence of the corporate tax, they also show the effect of that tax on dividends through its impact on after-tax income.

TECHNICAL NOTES

Alternative Rationales for the Basic Equation

The simple theoretical model given as relation (2-1) has been applied not only by Lintner, but also by Dobrovolsky, Prais and later by others.[16] While each writer had a different rationale, the same linear regression equation emerges in all three cases and in a fourth case to be discussed later.[17] Dobrovolsky added lagged dividends to the explana-

[16] Dobrovolsky, *Corporate Income Retention, 1915-43* (National Bureau of Economic Research, 1951); S. J. Prais, "Dividend Policy and Income Appropriation," in *Studies in Company Finance*, B. Tew and R. F. Henderson, eds. (Cambridge: Cambridge University Press, 1959); S. J. Prais, "Some Problems in the Econometric Analysis of Company Accounts" (unpublished paper presented at the 18th European meeting of the Econometric Society, aix-en-Provence, August 1956).

[17] In other words, the coefficients and predictions are the same regardless of the underlying rationale. However, the issue is relevant to the discussion of estimation problems in the second technical note to this chapter.

tory income variable to allow for relatively stable "dividend requirements." He reasoned that, "since corporations are, as a rule, reluctant to change their dividend policy abruptly, the preceding period's dividend payments may be taken as a rough measure of the requirements of the current period."[18]

In Prais' treatment of dividend policy, he sought to allow for uncertainty and variations in the firm's interpretation of current profit levels:

> Since the future is uncertain and obscure (to companies as well as to Man), the major short-term question that faces a company is the interpretation of any recent change in its profits. Is it due to some fundamental improvement in circumstances which may be expected to persist? Or is it nothing more than a temporary fluctuation? The effect on dividends will depend on how confidently the board of directors expects the change to persist.[19]

Prais approached this problem by assuming that dividends depend on a longer-term estimate of profits, approximated by a weighted average of past profits in which the weights for earlier years decline exponentially. Thus he also arrived at relation (2-1), but via the distributed lag rationale discussed by Koyck.[20] In the simplest version of this model, dividends are assumed to depend on profits in the current year and all previous years according to a two-parameter relation (and with an error term v added to Prais' formulation):

$$(2\text{-}3) \quad D = b_1(P + b_2 P_{-1} + b_2^2 P_{-2} + b_2^3 P_{-3} + \cdots) + v, \quad (0 < b_2 < 1)$$

Here b_1 is the "short-run propensity to distribute" since a unit increase in P increases current D by b_1. However, in the long run, the effect of a unit increase in profits is greater than this if the new level of profits is maintained. Dividends in the next year D_{+1} will be higher by $b_1 b_2$, and in the following year by $b_1 b_2^2$ as a result of the original unit increase. The aggregate (long-run) response of dividends to a unit increase in profits is:

$$(2\text{-}4) \qquad b_1(1 + b_2 + b_2^2 + b_2^3 \cdots) = b_1/(1 - b_2)$$

---

[18] Dobrovolsky, op. cit., p. 40. His model also includes an "asset requirements" factor, but the lagged dividend variable is stressed here for comparison with the basic Lintner model.

[19] Prais, "Dividend Policy and Income Appropriation," op. cit., p. 37.

[20] L. M. Koyck, Distributed Lags and Investment Analysis (Amsterdam: North-Holland Publishing Company, 1954).

Prais labels this the "long-run propensity to distribute." A standard manipulation of (2-3) plus addition of a constant term a leads to

(2-5) $$D = a + b_1 P + b_2 D_{-1} + (v - b_2 v_{-1})$$

With this, Prais has arrived at relation (2-1), except for the appearance here of a "composite error term."

The link between Prais' concept of a longer-term estimate of profits and the specified distributed lag equation (2-3) may be spelled out in more detail. "Even though [a directly specified distributed lag model such as (2-3)] may be too rigid and mechanistic, more general and perhaps more realistic assumptions still give rise to distributed lags."[21] These assumptions can be embodied in an "adaptive expectations" model of the type discussed by Nerlove and others.[22] This type of model is contrasted with the speed-of-adjustment interpretation by referring to the latter as a "rigidity" model. The expectation model may be regarded as implicit in Prais' work and in the discussion by Miller and Modigliani of the "informational content of dividends."[23] Miller and Modigliani stress that the profit variable in their share valuation equation is not *current* profits, which contains random disturbances and temporary distortions. Their preferred explanatory variable (to be labeled P*) is the *expected value* of the (uncertain) profits on the assets currently held. Dividends are presumed to contain considerable information about P*, and this implies that firms base their dividends on this unobservable "noise-free" profit potential. A simple dividend policy of the firm which embodies the Miller-Modigliani interpretation can thus be described in two equations.

First,

(2-6) $$D = kP^* + w,$$

where k is the normal payout ratio and w the disturbance term. Suppose further that changes in P* are generated by

(2-7) $$P^* - P^*_{-1} = s(P - P^*_{-1})$$

[21] J. Johnston, *Econometric Methods* (McGraw-Hill, 1963), p. 219.

[22] For a detailed survey of models of this type see Marc Nerlove, "Distributed Lags and Demand Analysis for Agricultural and Other Commodities," U. S. Department of Agriculture, *Agricultural Handbook 141* (1958).

[23] Franco Modigliani and M. H. Miller, "The Cost of Capital, Corporation Finance, and the Theory of Investment: Reply," *American Economic Review,*

This postulates an adjustment in expectation proportional to the discrepancy between the current value and the previous expectation. Adapting Nerlove's terminology, the coefficient s might be called the "profit expectation coefficient"; it is a smoothing coefficient that downgrades the importance of current profits (assuming $s < 1$). Paraphrasing Nerlove, equation (2-7) exactly expresses the distinction between the permanent and transitory components of a change in current profits. If the change in current profits is expressed as a deviation from the previous expected normal profits, the coefficient of expectation s is just the proportion of the change that is regarded as the *permanent* component of the change; 1-s is the proportion regarded as the transitory component.[24]

By algebraic manipulation it can be shown that (2-7) is equivalent to

$$(2\text{-}8) \qquad P^* = s[P + (1 - s)P_{-1} + (1 - s)^2 P_{-2} + \cdots]$$

Substitution of (2-8) in (2-6) and further manipulation leads to the same relation as that obtained by Prais, and reproduced in (2-5), with an error term added:

$$(2\text{-}9) \qquad D - D_{-1} = skP - sD_{-1} + w - (1 - s)w_{-1}$$

The only difference is that (2-9) was derived from the more specific behavioral rationale given in (2-6) and (2-7).

In summary, three different theoretical foundations for the basic estimating equation (2-2) have been suggested by Lintner, Dobrovolsky and Prais, and a fourth is obtained by supplementing Prais' formulation by the adaptive expectations argument. The first and last of these appear to offer the most complete behavioral descriptions. The Lintner speed-of-adjustment model and the expectations version of the distributed lag include explicit target or normal payout ratios that are essentially the same. The only differences of consequence are in the nature of the adjustment process and in the interpretation of the coefficients c and s. The Lintner model implicitly recognizes the transitory nature of current profits by assuming fractional adjustment c of dividends to target levels based on *current* profits. The expectations description bases dividends on *expected* profits but assumes only frac-

---

Vol. 59, No. 4 (September 1959), especially pp. 666-68; and Merton H. Miller and Franco Modigliani, "Dividend Policy Growth and the Valuation of Shares," *The Journal of Business,* Vol. 34, No. 4 (October 1961), especially p. 430.

[24] Nerlove, *op. cit.,* p. 23.

tional adjustment s of expected profits in response to current profit changes.

Lintner has reported that most of the firms interviewed by him actually rationalized their behavior as he described,[25] and his speed-of-adjustment phraseology will be used in reporting the statistical analysis that follows. However, no attempt has been made here to test the relative merits of the speed-of-adjustment and the expectations interpretations. They yield the same estimating equation embodying a long-run payout ratio; since variation of this payout ratio is the primary subject of this study, there is no need to choose between the two rationales. If the true behavioral process could be determined, however, a more accurate evaluation of the statistical results would be possible.

Problems of Estimation

The statistical models of this study have been fitted by the classical least-squares procedures. The results must, therefore, be qualified in several respects. The most obvious difficulties are caused by the presence of the lagged endogenous variable D_{-1} as an independent variable in all regression models except those of Chapter VIII. When D_{-1} is included, there are *a priori* reasons to expect a bias in the estimated regression coefficients and their standard errors.

The presence of the lagged dividend variable as an explanatory variable presents three main problems. In the first place the classical prerequisite for least-squares estimation is violated, since the error term is not independent of lagged dividends. This introduces a small sample bias of unknown magnitude into the estimate of the coefficient of the lagged dependent variable.[26] Consider the basic Lintner model as restated in (2-10):

(2-10) $$D - D_{-1} = a + crP - cD_{-1} + u$$

The estimate of the speed-of-adjustment coefficient c is presumably biased. The estimation of c is not a primary concern of this study, but

[25] "Twenty-six out of the twenty-eight companies had (or acted to a good approximation as if they had) a pretty specific value of r_1 established as a matter of policy, and twenty had reasonably definite c_1. Twenty-two of the companies considered adjusting dividends year by year and generally did so as shown in the model . . ." (Lintner, in *American Economic Review, op. cit.,* p. 108).

[26] See L. H. Hurwicz, "Least Squares Bias in Time Series," *Statistical Inference in Dynamic Economic Models,* T. C. Koopmans (ed.), Cowles Commission Monograph 10 (Wiley, 1950), Chap. 15.

the estimation of the target payout ratio r (and the function r_t) is a key objective. Since the estimate of r must be derived from the estimates of cr and c, a bias in c would also bias the estimate of r. However, this problem of small sample bias is probably not serious since the sample size (38 observations) is fairly large.

A second and more difficult problem involves the error term u in (2-10). It has been shown that if the independent variables and the error term satisfy the usual least-squares assumptions, in particular if u is not autocorrelated, the least-squares estimates of the coefficients are consistent.[27] However, if u is autocorrelated, the least-squares estimate of the coefficient of D_{-1} will be biased even in large samples.[28]

A third problem posed by the lagged dividend variable is related to the second. The Durbin-Watson test[29] applied to computed residuals is inconclusive as to whether the "true" error term u is actually autocorrelated. It has been shown that the presence of a lagged dependent variable biases the Durbin-Watson statistic toward two,[30] thus providing a misleading indication of independent errors. Durbin and Watson themselves also stated originally that even in the absence of autocorrelated error, their probability distributions were not applicable when a lagged dependent variable is included in the model.[31] Not only is the statistic presumed to be biased, but the significance tests are inapplicable in any case. Since a computed value near two connot be taken as persuasive evidence of independent errors, it cannot rule out possible inconsistency and a downward bias in standard errors.

Despite these weaknesses of the Durbin-Watson statistic, it is used in this study on the ground that, used cautiously, it is better than nothing. Two reasons for this may be mentioned. First, despite its presumed low power, it did indicate the presence of autocorrelation in some of the cruder models. This indication disappeared when the models were elaborated. For example, in Chapter IV it is shown that when the basic model is fitted to the thirty-eight observations for all

[27] See, for example, H. B. Mann and A. Wald, "On the Statistical Treatment of Linear Stochastic Difference Equations," *Econometrica*, Vol. 11, Nos. 3 and 4 (July-October 1943), pp. 173-220.

[28] See, for example, Koyck, *op. cit.*, pp. 32 ff.

[29] For a brief description of this test, see H. Theil, *Economic Forecasts and Policy* (Amsterdam: North-Holland Publishing Co., 1958), pp. 220-21.

[30] For example, see E. Malinvaud, "Estimation et Prevision dan les Modeles Autogressifs," *Revue l'Institut International de Statistique*, Vol. 29 (1961).

[31] J. Durbin and G. S. Watson, "Testing for Serial Correlation in Least Squares Regression," *Biometrika*, Vols. 37 and 38 (1950 and 1951).

corporations, Durbin-Watson statistics of 1.3-1.4 were found. When the target payout ratio is allowed to vary with individual tax rates in many different models, the statistic falls in the interval 1.8-2.0. The latter results by no means rule out autocorrelation because lagged dependent variables were present in both sets of results. However, it is worth noting that the evidence of autocorrelation in the crude models is no longer present when the tax variable is included.

A second defense of the Durbin-Watson statistic is that recent Monte Carlo studies suggest that the Durbin-Watson test may not be as weak as generally supposed. Taylor and Wilson found in most of their experiments that the test was quite powerful on ordinary least-squares residuals in models including lagged dependent variables.[32] As expected, its power was directly related to goodness-of-fit, sample size, the magnitude of the coefficient of the dependent variable, and the auto-regression coefficient of the error term.[33] Despite the lack of knowledge of these, the Durbin-Watson statistics are reported with the hope that values near two constitute at least some evidence against strong auto-correlation. However, it should be recognized that no rigorous inferences can be based on them.

As a precaution, a second test for autocorrelation was carried out for some of the key models. Taylor and Wilson concluded that in cases in which the Durbin-Watson test broke down, a standard significance test applied to the first-order autoregression coefficient estimated from the residuals worked well. These tests produced no evidence that the Durbin-Watson statistic was failing to detect autocorrelation here.

Although it is not possible to tell the extent to which the models of this study are plagued with autocorrelated error, substantial autocorrelation in conjunction with the lagged dependent variable could produce serious biases.[34] Various estimation techniques have been proposed for those cases where these two difficulties occur together, especially in distributed lag models. These include the instrumental variable ap-

[32] Lester D. Taylor and Thomas A. Wilson, "Three-Pass Least Squares: A Method for Estimating Models with a Lagged Dependent Variable," *The Review of Economics and Statistics,* Vol. 46, No. 4 (November 1964), pp. 329-46.

[33] For analysis of the relationships between the bias of the Durbin-Watson statistic and these other factors see also Z. Griliches, "A Note on Serial Correlation in Estimates of Distributed Lags," *Econometrica,* Vol. 29, No. 1 (January 1961), pp. 65-73.

[34] See G. H. Orcutt and D. Cochrane, "A Sampling Study of the Merits of Autoregressive and Reduced Form Transformations in Regression Analysis," *Journal of the American Statistical Association,* Vol. 44, No. 247 (September 1949), pp. 356-72.

proach,[35] the Klein technique[36] and other approaches.[37] However, in this study no attempt has been made to improve upon least-squares estimation by these more elaborate procedures.[38]

Another statistical problem is measurement error which would tend to produce bias and inconsistency.[39] This is considered briefly in Chapter III, where the relatively low coefficient for the official net profit variable suggests that the measurement error in this series is greater than in the other income measures. However, some measurement error is present in these other variables. The extent of the possible bias in their coefficients depends on the unknown magnitude of this error. The stress in Chapters IV and V on more general models based on official net profits requires explanation in this connection. If these models, which include depreciation liberality explicitly in the target function, are valid, the problem of measurement error should not be present in the way it is in the simple net profit model of Chapter III. Under the behavioral hypothesis of the generalized model, the measurement error in the tax return profit series is recognized by firms and allowed for by adjusting the target payout ratio based on this series. This behavior may seem less plausible than basing dividends on corrected profits or cash flow, but at least the estimation is not subject to the same bias produced by unrecognized measurement error in the simple model.

While the various estimation difficulties discussed above are not the only ones, they are probably the most important. The small sample bias associated with the lagged dependent variable is probably minor and there is no way of appraising the measurement error that persists in the better income variables. The main problem is the question of autocorrelation. It is impossible to assess accurately the seriousness of the risk that autocorrelation is present. In the first place, the serious-

[35] See, for example, N. Liviatan, "Consistent Estimation of Distributed Lags," *International Economic Review,* Vol. 4 (January 1963).

[36] L. R. Klein, "The Estimation of Distributed Lags," *Econometrica,* Vol. 26, No. 4 (October 1958), pp. 553-65.

[37] See, for example, Johnston, *op. cit.,* pp. 193-94, and Taylor and Wilson, *op. cit.* Taylor and Wilson appear to have achieved a definite improvement over ordinary least-squares estimation.

[38] See Malinvaud, *op. cit.,* for a defense of the use of least-squares techniques. On the basis of Monte Carlo studies with samples of twenty he found the performances of the instrumental variable and Klein approaches to be inferior to ordinary least-squares. This suggests that the complicated techniques should only be used for very large samples.

[39] For a discussion of the consequences of "errors in variables," see Johnston, *op. cit.,* Chap. 6.

ness of the problem depends in part on corporate behavior in setting dividends. Here, alternative types of corporate behavior are relevant. If corporate officials behave according to the directly specified speed-of-adjustment model (2-2), there is no *a priori* reason to suspect autocorrelation in the error term u. If they adjust dividends on the basis of P and D_{-1} in that model and then allow for special factors, then u will presumably be a random variable distributed independently of P and D_{-1} as required for consistent estimation.

On the other hand, if they base dividends on a weighted average of profits in all years, as in the distributed lag model (2-3), and only then take account of special factors, then the disturbance term v would presumably be random. However, the transformation then used to reach the estimating equation (2-5) induces autocorrelation by producing the composite error term $v - b_2 v_{-1}$.[40] Similarly, under the adaptive expectations behavior described in relations (2-6) and (2-7), the error term w in (2-6) would presumably be random. Again, the composite error term in the resulting transformed estimating equation (2-9) would be autocorrelated.

Thus, if the basic distributed lag or the adaptive expectations approach gives the correct description of corporate behavior, the estimating equations applied in this study may be expected to produce inconsistent estimates. This problem would not exist if corporate officials set dividends according to the directly specified speed-of-adjustment model. This reasoning, of course, provides no indication of which is the more accurate description, but the seriousness of autocorrelation in the models depends on the unknown nature of this behavior.

The composite error term which may be present is not the only possible source of autocorrelation. If the hypothesis that the target payout ratio varies substantially over time is correct, the simple models with fixed target ratios may be expected to contain autocorrelated errors. The Durbin-Watson statistics showed fairly strong evidence of this. When the target ratio was allowed to vary, this evidence disappeared. If the Durbin-Watson test is of low power, these statistics do not establish the absence of autocorrelation. They at least suggest, however, that the remaining autocorrelation is less than before the hypotheses concerning the variability of the target ratio are taken into account.

The findings of Taylor and Wilson provide some grounds for opti-

[40] When v is not autocorrelated, $v - b_2 v_{-1}$ generally will be. See, for example, Koyck, *op. cit.*, pp. 32-35.

mism with respect to any remaining autocorrelation. They showed that autocorrelation could generally be detected either by the Durbin-Watson test or by a direct test of the autoregression coefficient. The results of these tests in this study are encouraging.

Finally, perhaps the best defense of the time series estimates is that the estimating technique used in the pooled time series and cross-section analysis, while recognizing two additional variables, otherwise confirmed the general magnitude of the influence of the factors studied earlier. This technique dispensed with the troublesome lagged dependent variable and thus eliminated the *a priori* expectation of autocorrelated error and bias. Confirmation of the results of the time series analysis by this alternate method is impressive evidence that the lagged dependent variable produced no serious estimation problem because of autocorrelated error.

CHAPTER III

The Effect of Liberalized Depreciation Allowances

AFTER-TAX CORPORATE INCOME is usually assumed to be the primary current determinant of dividend payments. This seems reasonable, given the prevalence of references by corporate officials to their payout ratios, with income taken as the base or source of funds from which dividends are paid. This study adheres to that emphasis on income, but evaluates alternative income measures as indicators of the capacity to pay.

Inadequacy of Tax Return Profit Measures

The income measure adopted in Lintner's application of his basic model was net earnings (after taxes and capital consumption allowances) as reported in the national income accounts.[1] The series used was that estimated by the Office of Business Economics (OBE) of the Department of Commerce.[2] The analysis was carried out with profit series before and after the inventory valuation ad-

[1] John Lintner, "Distribution of Incomes of Corporations Among Dividends, Retained Earnings and Taxes," *American Economic Review,* Vol. 46, No. 2 (May 1956).

[2] However, see the footnote at the beginning of Chapter I where a 1965 re-

justment. Interviewed firms had reported that net earnings were the key determinant of dividends,[3] and they seem plausible as a measure of corporate ability to pay during the interwar period to which Lintner applied his model. However, the frequent liberalization of tax provisions concerning depreciation since the beginning of World War II has injected an arbitrary element into the official profit series. Accelerated depreciation[4] saves taxes for the corporations, but it artificially reduces their after-tax profit estimates reported on tax returns.[5] It also distorts the regular profit series appearing in the national income accounts where the tax return depreciation allowances are accepted without adjustment. This reduction of measured profits appears to call for a curb on dividends, but dividend payments tripled between 1946 and 1962 while officially measured profits rose only 70 percent.

This chapter represents a preliminary assessment of the effect of depreciation policy on corporate dividends. It is based primarily on OBE data and is a highly aggregative time series analysis. The over-all study is based on thirty-eight annual observations during the period 1920-60. The years 1936-38 are omitted to avoid complications produced by the effect of the undistributed profits tax levied during these years.[6] However, the timing of the two factors to be stressed in the dividend model suggested that in this preliminary analysis the interval be split into two halves. The 1942-60 period includes the first major changes in depreciation practices and is a period of generally high individual tax rates. This permits the depreciation factor to be studied in relative isolation, free from the confusing impact of the sharp increase in individual tax rates that occurred earlier. There were some additional rate increases up to

vision of the OBE data is mentioned. Some of the empirical work of this study was redone with the new data, as reported in Appendix G. However, it was found that the revisions did not alter the basic findings to be presented here.

[3] The corporation reports of net earnings to stockholders and for tax purposes are different from those in the national accounts—a problem which will be considered later.

[4] Here and elsewhere the word "depreciation" refers to the sum of depreciation and amortization.

[5] Profits reported to stockholders will be similarly depressed if accelerated depreciation is also used in company reports.

[6] The substantial influence of this tax is interesting in its own right, since it imposed a temporary penalty on retention alongside the continuing income tax penalty on distribution. Attempts to treat the two factors simultaneously in the same model proved unsuccessful.

1944 and a strong upward trend in total individual tax payments after that because of rising incomes, but the major part of rate increases had occurred by 1942.[7]

Two aspects of the effect of depreciation liberalization on profits will be considered here. In the first place, liberalization depresses tax return profits because the recorded increase in cost is about double the resulting tax saving (at postwar rates). However, insofar as the increased cost is an accounting rather than an economic charge, "true" profits are actually increased by the amount of the tax saving.

The first basic hypothesis of this study is that corporations recognize the illusory nature of tax return profits and take account of liberalized depreciation by basing dividend payments either on their total cash flow, or on some conception they may have of their "true" earnings. If this is the case, the effect of liberalization on dividend policy should be reflected in an improved explanation of dividend payments achieved by (1) substitution of income variables adjusted for variations in depreciation policy, and (2) explicit inclusion of the depreciation factor in the statistical models.

The Rapid Postwar Rise of Depreciation Charges

The most dramatic and steady rise in depreciation charges occurred after World War II.[8] Total depreciation charges by corporations rose from $4.3 billion to $23.4 billion between 1946 and 1960. In 1946, they were less than one-third of net profits,[9] but by 1960 they exceeded profits.

Economic Factors

The sharp rise in depreciation charges was because of economic factors as well as accounting liberalization. It is difficult to separate

[7] A related tax factor which may also confuse the profit estimates is the sharp postwar increase in research and development expenditures charged as expenses. These may also have artificially depressed net profits. However, this factor will not be treated here.

[8] There had been substantial amortization during the war, but this liberalization had been reversed by 1946.

[9] The net profit series referred to is the OBE estimate after taxes and depreciation, before the inventory valuation adjustment, and excluding the "rest of the world" component.

TABLE 3. Alternative Measures of Nonagricultural Corporate Depreciable Assets, 1945–60[a]

(In billions of dollars)

Year	Gross Value		Net Value[b]	
	Goldsmith	Internal Revenue Service	Goldsmith	Internal Revenue Service
1945	140.4	132.5	74.2	80.2
1946	147.7	142.5	81.6	87.6
1947	160.0	156.6	93.4	98.6
1948	175.6	172.7	106.9	111.3
1949	189.2	186.6	117.3	120.6
1950	205.6	199.8	129.3	128.9
1951	224.9	218.0	142.8	142.7
1952	244.6	233.3	157.8	152.7
1953	264.2	249.2	172.3	162.7
1954	283.2	265.6	184.6	172.9
1955	302.0	287.2	197.5	185.1
1956	325.4	314.2	215.2	202.5
1957	n.a.	342.5	n.a.	219.8
1958	n.a.	368.2	n.a.	233.8
1959	n.a.	395.0	n.a.	248.5
1960	n.a.	423.1	n.a.	264.0

n.a. Not available.

[a] Source, Raymond W. Goldsmith, *The National Wealth of the United States in the Postwar Period* (Princeton: Princeton University Press, 1962), p. 84. Goldsmith's estimates are derived by the "perpetual inventory" method. The IRS figures for 1945–53 were revised by Goldsmith to remove depletable and intangible assets. The 1958–60 figures are taken from U. S. Internal Revenue Service, *Statistics of Income*. Values are in terms of original cost. Cumulations are for the end of each year.

[b] Net of accumulated depreciation:

these two influences, but there are at least three possible economic explanations. In the first place, there was a large postwar increase of depreciable assets (plant and equipment), however evaluated. Various measures of this are given in Table 3. The Goldsmith estimates are by the "perpetual inventory" method[10]; the Internal Revenue Service (IRS) figures are book value, except for minor effects of write-ups or write-downs.

The two methods show similar postwar trends in the gross stock. The Goldsmith series increased 132 percent between 1945 and 1956 compared to the 137 percent rise indicated by the IRS. Net stocks increased even more, with Goldsmith estimating a 190

[10] This method derives the stock of a given category of assets by cumulation of past expenditures on that category of asset depreciated on a straight line basis in accordance with the average length of life of the asset.

TABLE 4. Depreciation and Amortization Charges As Percentage of Corporate Depreciable Assets, 1946–60[a]

Year	Percent of Gross Assets		Percent of Net Assets	
	Goldsmith	Internal Revenue Service	Goldsmith	Internal Revenue Service
1946	2.96	3.10	5.48	5.08
1947	3.43	3.53	6.03	5.67
1948	3.78	3.85	6.33	6.04
1949	3.96	4.02	6.44	6.23
1950	4.00	4.09	6.41	6.33
1951	4.24	4.37	6.70	6.72
1952	4.44	4.62	6.94	7.06
1953	4.72	4.98	7.29	7.63
1954	5.00	5.32	7.67	8.16
1955	5.47	5.79	8.38	8.94
1956	5.60	5.85	8.52	9.07
1957	n.a.	5.92	n.a.	9.20
1958	n.a.	5.82	n.a.	9.12
1959	n.a.	5.78	n.a.	9.15
1960	n.a.	5.71	n.a.	9.12

n.a. Not available.

[a] Source, Table 3. Depreciation and amortization charges are taken from *Statistics of Income*. Percentages are based on original cost. The asset base was estimated as the midpoint between end of year values in Table 3 and represents midyear values.

percent increase compared to 152 percent in the IRS figures.[11] This growth of assets against which depreciation may be charged accounts for a large part of the great postwar rise in these charges. However, it explains only about half of the trend. The "rate of depreciation" estimates in Table 4 show that other forces are at work.

The depreciation rates in Table 4 show a strong upward trend because postwar depreciation charges rose even faster than depreciable assets. Part of the trend in depreciation rates is because of the growing proportion of short-lived equipment with comparatively high depreciation rates relative to structures. Thus, even assuming no changes in useful lives in each category, an upward trend appears in the rate of depreciation because of changes in the rate mix of assets. The order of magnitude of this effect may be indicated by

[11] Other studies, not limited to the corporate sector, have shown similar trends. See, for example, George Terborgh, *Sixty Years of Business Capital Formation* (Machinery and Allied Products Institute, 1960); and George Jaszi and others, "Expansion of Fixed Business Capital in the United States," *Survey of Current Business*, Vol. 42, No. 11 (November 1962), pp. 9-18.

a crude illustration based on OBE estimates,[12] although they are not restricted to the corporate sector. On certain simplifying assumptions,[13] the depreciation rate for nonresidential structures averaged about 2.7 percent of gross stocks, compared to 7.1 for equipment. In the 1946-60 interval, gross stocks of these structures rose less than threefold compared to a fivefold increase in equipment stocks. This changing mix accounts for a rise in the depreciation rate from 4.4 percent of gross stocks to 5.1 percent for the two categories in combination. While not strictly comparable to the estimates of Table 4, this suggests that the rising relative importance of equipment accounts for a significant part of the upward trend in the rates.

A third possible economic factor in the rise of depreciation charges is a general decline in useful lives, although it is difficult to find evidence on this point. Goldsmith stated in 1961 that there is "no evidence that the length of useful life of comparable types of structures and equipment has generally shortened—and sharply so after 1954 . . ."[14] In any case, even if some evidence did appear, it would be difficult to separate the economically relevant changes from those caused by greater administrative liberality on the part of the tax authorities.

Legal and Administrative Liberalization

While economic factors may have had a substantial role in the postwar trend in depreciation charges, there is evidence that liberalization of depreciation regulations by accounting and procedural changes also had a major impact. It is this liberalization that is relevant to this study, in that it may account for the sharp postwar growth of dividends relative to measured net profits. The extent of the liberalization is difficult to measure since no one knows what the "true" depreciation really was. However, some light can be shed on this by comparing actual charges with available independent estimates of depreciation. There are several published depreciation series that are consistent throughout and free from the influence of accounting changes. These series can be used for statistical estima-

---

[12] The data used are unpublished, but available in OBE sourcebooks. They are the data that underlie George Jaszi and others, *op. cit.*

[13] That is, IRS Bulletin F lives, straight line depreciation, original cost.

[14] Goldsmith, *op. cit.*, pp. 85-86.

tion without delving into the theoretical issue of which is "correct." Before considering the data, the reasons for expecting noneconomic growth of depreciation allowances should be briefly considered.

One possible factor in the rise of depreciation allowances is faster writeoffs arising from greater liberality by tax authorities in approving corporate estimates of service lives. Although the useful lives specified in IRS wartime Bulletin F[15] were intended only as guidelines, there were complaints that in the early stages some Revenue agents sought rigid conformity to these standards. However, the designation of the useful life of a piece of property is to a large extent a matter of judgment, and the attitude of such agents may have mellowed over time. In fact, increased leniency would conform with the postwar philosophy favoring accelerated depreciation as an investment incentive.

The more liberal attitude toward depreciation charges was also supported by statute as in the case of the issuance of wartime "certificates of necessity" to encourage emergency construction considered essential to the war effort. These certificates authorized five-year amortization of some part of an asset's cost, regardless of its expected life. Furthermore, while the burden of proof of the reasonableness of an estimated service life has rested with the taxpayer since 1934, the Treasury now challenges an estimate only if it has a "clear and convincing reason." Finally, the review of depreciation claims was officially liberalized in 1953 by Revenue Rulings 90 and 91. The suggestion of a trend toward more liberal appraisal of service lives is speculative, but there can be no doubt that newly approved acceleration formulas, such as the "declining balance" method and the "sum-of-the-years'-digits" method permitted under the 1954 Code, offered substantial opportunity for increasing depreciation charges.

Adoption of the acceleration formulas was widespread among large firms. A study of 450 firms on the 1961 *Fortune* list of the 500 largest industrial corporations[16] showed 393, or 87 percent, using accelerated depreciation in 1961.[17] Between 1954 and 1956

[15] U. S. Internal Revenue Service, Bulletin F, *Tables of Useful Lives of Depreciable Property* (1942).

[16] "The Fortune Directory," *Fortune* (July 1961), pp. 163-84. Size is determined by a combination of sales, labor force and assets.

[17] Richard Lindhe, "Accelerated Depreciation for Income Tax Purposes," *Journal of Accounting Research*, Vol. 1, No. 2 (Autumn 1963), p. 144.

the percentage of total depreciation computed by the straight line method dropped from 89 to 74 and was down to 58 by 1960.[18] Another indication of the extent of adoption of acceleration formulas is a change in the depreciation rate. The over-all depreciation rate for all corporations was 4.3 percent in 1953, but it was 7.4 percent on assets acquired in 1954-56.[19] While some of this increase could reflect shortened lives, the rapidity of the change suggests that the new rules must have played a large part.

Although adoption of acceleration is sufficiently prevalent to affect aggregate depreciation charges, it is surprising that as many as 58 percent of charges were still computed on a straight line basis in 1960. However, there were many reasons for rejecting the acceleration—some valid and some spurious.[20] Some corporations did not wish to depress reported profits artificially, and were opposed to the tactic of avoiding this by keeping separate books for reports to stockholders. Others feared higher taxes later, higher bookkeeping costs, and revocation of approval of their liberal service life estimates. Some utilities and oil and mining companies had special reasons. However, perhaps the most prevalent reason was that many corporation officers believe that acceleration makes little difference in the long run, since it does not raise the total amount that can be charged for a given asset.

Many companies apparently failed to realize that they could achieve a net tax saving through acceleration, and that the greater their growth rate, the greater their gain. This can be shown by a few hypothetical examples, using the "sum-of-the-years'-digits" method (SYD).[21] Assume that a company can earn 10 percent on

[18] *The Federal Revenue System: Facts and Problems,* Staff Report of the Joint Economic Committee, 88 Cong. 2 sess. (1964), p. 100. The decline in the percentage of *assets* depreciated by the straight line method would probably be somewhat less sharp. The higher depreciation rate under acceleration affects this trend.

[19] *The Federal Revenue System, op. cit.,* 1961 edition, p. 83.

[20] For detailed discussions of these see Richard Lindhe, *op. cit.,* pp. 144-48; and Leonard E. Morrissey, "The Many Sides of Depreciation," *Tuck Bulletin 23* (Dartmouth: The Amos Tuck School of Business Administration), pp. 15-16.

[21] The figures cited are from Morrissey, *op. cit.,* pp. 10-13, and this method of acceleration and the "declining-balance" method are summarized there on p. 9. For a thorough analysis of the relation between growth rates and the gains achievable through accelerated depreciation, see Robert Eisner, "Effects of Depreciation Allowances for Tax Purposes," *Tax Revision Compendium,* House Ways and Means Committee, 86 Cong. 1 sess. (1959) and his other papers cited there.

capital and pays a 50 percent tax rate. The use of SYD in depreciating a $1,000 asset with a life of ten years produces a net tax gain of $43 in present value terms over the ten-year period. In this example, there is no change in the total tax or depreciation charges; the small tax gain is achieved by deferral of the payments. However, for the growing firm, the picture is entirely different. Taking the same example as above, assume the firm buys a new $1,000 asset each year. It then achieves a net tax saving over nine years with present value of $476, and a net excess of $1,600 in depreciation charges above the $4,500 that would be charged under straight line methods. Finally, the gains in both excess depreciation and tax saving are much greater than this if the firm increases its investment each year.[22] Thus, for growing firms, acceleration can produce not only a permanent tax saving, but also a continual rise in depreciation charges. The essence of the process is that for growing firms lower depreciation on its older assets is always more than offset by higher charges on its new assets.

The Extent of Depreciation Liberalization

Some individual firms state explicitly the gains achieved by accelerated depreciation.[23] However, for the present purpose, more aggregative evidence is required. It is available in various independent estimates of depreciation that utilize the same depreciation formulas year after year. The value of these is that they abstract from variations in legal and administrative practice and provide alternative estimates of the breakdown of cash flow into two components—net profits and depreciation.

[22] Among firms utilizing acceleration, there was clear awareness of the net gains achievable. Rejecting designation of the tax saving as "liability for deferred income tax," the 1958 S. S. Kresge annual report said: "We continue to believe that the liability is more a contingent liability than a real one. . . . For a company such as this one, where a continuing relatively level capital-expenditure program is a necessity, it is unlikely that any substantial amount . . . if any at all, will require liquidation." The attractiveness of acceleration during the period studied was also enhanced by the existence of preferential capital gains taxation. The (measured) profits earned and taxes paid during the early life of an asset were reduced, but higher profits were recorded later because of declining depreciation charges; the asset could then be sold for a capital gain at a low rate of taxation. The provisions with respect to such transactions were changed in 1962 so that gains up to original cost are taxed as ordinary income.

[23] See, for example, Morrissey, *op. cit.,* pp. 12-13.

The Goldsmith perpetual inventory estimates in Table 3 offer one such indication of the noneconomic effects on depreciation charges. Although IRS gross stocks grew slightly faster than indicated by the Goldsmith estimates, the IRS net stocks rose only 152 percent between 1946 and 1956, compared to a 190 percent rise shown by Goldsmith. The difference between the two reflects higher depreciation accumulation in the IRS series; the increase in depreciation reserves was 114 percent in the IRS series against only 66 percent for the consistently measured perpetual inventory series. Goldsmith interprets the differences between the two series as resulting from changes in tax legislation and corporate accounting practices. Therefore, the difference would represent a rough measure of the excessive depreciation taken for tax purposes.

A second measure of depreciation liberalization[24] is obtainable from the work of George Terborgh for the Machine and Allied Products Institute (MAPI).[25] He uses an accelerated depreciation formula, writing off two-thirds of the investment over the first half of the service life of equipment, and 60 percent over the first half-life of plant. Depreciation is estimated on a replacement cost basis, and the series differs from straight line depreciation for this reason as well as acceleration. Thus, the Terborgh estimates are not an indicator of purely legal or administrative liberalization. While they may be controversial, the estimates are constructed consistently over time and provide one measure of changes in "true" depreciation. Terborgh's results suggest that actual charges were little more than half of his estimated "realistic depreciation" charges in 1947, but actual annual charges had come close to closing the gap by 1960.

Two other alternative depreciation series were utilized. The Office of Business Economics had produced estimates of depreciation based on different formulas for all corporations and for manufacturing establishments. Each of the formulas was applied consistently over time.[26] A fourth depreciation series, at least partially

---

[24] As indicated in Appendix A, the technique used to derive this series was an approximation. However, it is shown there that the approximation was a good one.

[25] Terborgh, *op. cit.*

[26] As in the case of the Terborgh series, the OBE estimates do not differ from straight line depreciation because of acceleration alone. For example, some series are on a replacement cost basis rather than historical cost.

CHART 1. Comparison of Tax Depreciation with Alternative Depreciation Estimates, All Corporations, 1920–60

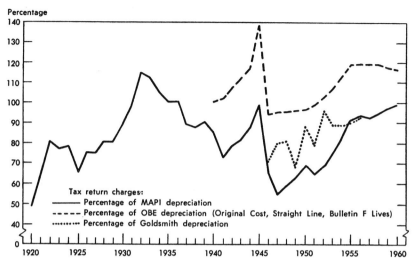

Source: See Appendix A. The MAPI and OBE series have been adjusted and carried back to early periods.

independent of tax return charges, is given by the Federal Trade Commission (FTC) and Securities Exchange Commission (SEC) quarterly series based on a sample of corporations believed to be representative of the entire manufacturing sector, except newspapers. These estimates closely follow the data provided in company reports, rather than tax return information. Both the OBE and FTC-SEC series show a smaller postwar rise in depreciation than the tax return charges, although the discrepancy is less than indicated by Terborgh's figures.

A number of the alternative series described above were used to construct the indexes of depreciation liberality that appear in Charts 1 and 2. These charts show tax return depreciation charges for all corporations and for manufacturing corporations expressed as percentages of the various alternative estimates of depreciation. It was necessary to process the underlying series in a number of ways and the figures for the twenties manufactured for this study warrant little confidence.[27] However, the postwar rise in all of the ratios is so strong that inadequacies of the data cast little doubt on

---

[27] See Appendix A.

the indicated trend. For all corporations and for manufacturing, whether the methods use original cost or current cost, whether they use straight line or fast early writeoffs, consistent application of a given formula shows depreciation rising much less rapidly than tax return charges. The OBE has also presented many other series for all corporations using lives shorter or longer than the Bulletin F schedule, and a similar trend appears in all of those series.

MAPI has long contended that depreciation allowances were inadequate. It is not surprising, therefore, to find that the postwar liberality index based on MAPI is the lowest in Chart 1; however, the 1946-60 increase from 55 percent to 98 percent is the sharpest of the three. The other two series also indicate a substantial liberalization—on the order of 30 to 40 percent.

In the case of manufacturing in Chart 2, the two OBE series agree in indicating a liberalization of between 50 and 60 percent. Since the OBE estimates assume no change in the useful lives of given types of plant and equipment, they overstate the degree of liberalization to the extent that a general shortening of lives has taken place. However, this possibility appears to be at least partially discounted by the FTC-SEC depreciation and depletion series be-

CHART 2. Comparison of Tax Depreciation with Alternative Depreciation Estimates, Manufacturing Corporations, 1920–60

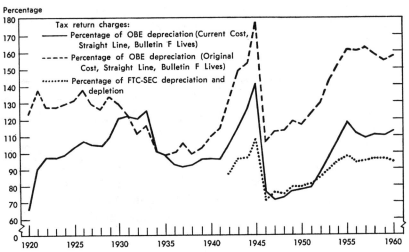

Note: The underlying series have been adjusted and extended.
Source: See Appendix A for data and adjustments.

TABLE 5. Manufacturing Depreciation Plus Depletion Recorded on Tax Returns and in FTC-SEC Survey, Selected Years[a]

(*Dollar amounts in billions*)

Year	Depreciation Plus Depletion		Ratio of Tax Return to FTC-SEC Depreciation Plus Depletion
	Tax Returns	FTC-SEC	
1946	$2.45	$2.77	88%
1948	3.88	3.72	104
1955	9.30	7.62	122
1960	12.51	10.91	115

[a] Source: See Appendix A.

lieved to be representative of all manufacturing. This series is not strictly comparable with IRS data for manufacturing in that the firms included may differ because of differences in reporting requirements, but in both series, service lives are variable. Nevertheless, it is interesting to note that the FTC-SEC series also rose much less rapidly than actual charges, although the discrepancy is less than suggested by the OBE data.

Since depletion charges cannot be separated from depreciation in the FTC-SEC series, this ratio in Chart 2 has a downward bias. However, the indicated postwar changes over time are meaningful. As a supplementary indicator, Table 5 presents data with tax return depletion charges included along with depreciation. A similar trend appears, with actual tax return charges growing faster than the accounting charges in the company reports from which the FTC-SEC obtains its data. In these annual reports, companies are free to report higher depreciation based on any assumed shortening of useful lives. Yet the accounting reports of depreciation and depletion lagged behind the tax return figures, tending to confirm the net liberalizing effect of new tax return practices.

Insofar as it is comparable with IRS manufacturing data, the FTC-SEC survey information reflected in Chart 2 and Table 5 is the most direct evidence that many corporations recognize a non-economic element in the postwar rise in depreciation charges. The comparisons in Table 5 suggest that, in terms of actual practice, allowed depreciation plus depletion charges were inadequate after the war but were 15-20 percent excessive later on. Even this is almost certainly an understatement of corporate opinion on the extent of liberalization. It reflects only firms reporting different charges for taxes than for their annual reports. There is evidence that most corporations actually taking advantage of the liberalizing effect of acceleration did not report less depreciation to shareholders.[28] This was probably more because of the complication and confusion consequent to keeping two sets of books than a failure to recognize the gains. If all corporations using accelerated methods made two reports, it is possible that the liberalization trend portrayed by the FTC-SEC data might approach that indicated by the OBE series in Chart 2.

Prior to the postwar trend, the series illustrated in Charts 1 and 2 all show a sharp liberalization with the five-year amortization plan of World War II, and then a sharp curtailment of allowances in 1946. The results for the twenties are more mixed, depending considerably upon whether depreciation is evaluated at historical or at current cost.

The Effect on Profits

The explanation of the relationship of profits and dividends is improved by revisions of the profits series to take direct account of changing tax provisions concerning depreciation,[29] and by relying on cash flow as an alternative explanatory variable. Between 1946 and 1960, cash flow increased at an average rate of 6 percent per year.[30] Several alternative estimates of the breakdown of this growth rate into rates of change in net profits and depreciation are summarized in Table 6. In all series examined—including many not reported here—the rise in estimated depreciation was considerably slower than the 13 percent annual increase in allowances reported for tax purposes (and repeated in the national income accounts). The corresponding revised net profit series, therefore, rose more rapidly than the official series.

The largest revision of the series for all corporations was that based on MAPI depreciation. It suggests that the tax return data

---

[28] For data on this, see George H. Sorter and others, "Corporate Personality As Reflected in Accounting Decisions," *Journal of Accounting Research*, Vol. 2, No. 2 (Autumn 1964), pp. 183-96. These writers also analyze this accounting decision.

[29] See Appendix A for the derivation of these revised profits series.

[30] Based on least-squares trend lines fitted to logarithms of the observations.

TABLE 6. Annual Rates of Change in Various Depreciation Estimates and Corresponding Revised Net Profits Series, 1946–60[a]

Basis and Coverage of Estimate of Depreciation	Annual Percentage Rate of Increase[b]	
	Depreciation	Net Profits
(A) Actual allowances, all corporations (OBE)	12.9	2.0
(A₁) Original cost, straight line, Bulletin F lives, all corporations (OBE)[c]	10.6	3.6
(A₂) "Realistic depreciation," all business (MAPI)[d]	8.2	4.1
(A) Actual allowances, all manufacturing corporations (OBE)	13.1	2.4
(A₃) Original cost, straight line, Bulletin F lives, manufacturing establishments (OBE)[e]	8.3	4.6
(A₄) Same as (A₃), except current cost[e]	8.8	4.2
(A₅) FTC-SEC, manufacturing[f]	10.9[g]	3.7[h]

[a] For derivation of the underlying series see Appendix A.
[b] Based on least-squares trend lines fitted to logarithms of annual data.
[c] From data underlying Murray Brown, "Depreciation and Corporate Profits," *Survey of Current Business* (October 1963), Vol. 43, No. 10, p. 5–12.
[d] Derived from data on net stocks and capital expenditures underlying *Sixty Years of Business Capital Formation*, George Terborgh (Machinery and Allied Products Institute, 1960). Reduced to corporate basis by means of estimates in Raymond W. Goldsmith, *A Study of Saving in the United States.*
[e] *Survey of Current Business* and Supplements; adjusted to exclude unincorporated enterprise, but not converted from establishment basis to corporate basis.
[f] Based on data in *Economic Almanac.*
[g] Growth rate of FTC-SEC depreciation plus depletion as adjusted by subtraction of IRS depletion.
[h] Growth rate of revised profits (based on depreciation described in note g).

overstate the growth rate of depreciation by 57 percent, and the revised profits series shows a growth rate double that of the official series. The Goldsmith estimates for all corporations are not given in the table since they are available only through 1956. However, the magnitude of the revision is somewhat smaller than that indicated by the 1946-60 OBE revision given in the table. The OBE estimates indicate that the growth rate for depreciation is overstated 23 percent by tax return allowances; the corresponding growth rate for revised profits is 80 percent higher than for the unrevised OBE profit series.[31]

The revisions in the manufacturing profit series based on OBE data are of about the same magnitude as the MAPI-based revision

[31] More recent OBE data show a continued widening of the gap between measured and adjusted profits. In terms of after-tax profits, "the National Income version shows an increase of 39 percent between 1948 and 1963, while standardized straight-line current costs depreciation methods would have shown corporate profits increasing by 74 percent." (Richard H. Holton, "The Record of Corporate Profits," *Financial Analysts Journal*, Vol. 20. No. 4 [July-August 1964], p. 47.)

for all corporations. The adjustments based on the FTC-SEC data are somewhat smaller, partly because of the decision of many corporations taking accelerated depreciation to report the same depreciation to stockholders as on tax returns. Given this fact, the gap between the FTC-SEC trends and those of the unrevised OBE series seems substantial (assuming the two series are reasonably comparable).

Cash Flow and the Capacity to Pay Dividends

Some of the revised net profit series show growth rates double that of the official OBE series, and should come closer to explaining the big postwar gains in dividends. These revised profit growth rates of about 4 percent still fail to match the 5.8 percent average annual growth of dividends, however. On the other hand, the growth rate of dividends is equaled by that of cash flow, which was 6 percent for manufacturing as well as for all corporations. These trends are shown for all corporations in Chart 3. One hypothesis suggested by these time series is that cash flow may have influenced dividends more strongly in this period than either tax return profits or company profit estimates that allowed for liberalization of depreciation.

There are several hypotheses that might explain an observed tendency of dividends to follow cash flow, although the particular reasons may vary from firm to firm. In its most general form, the behavioral proposition is that most firms are aware of the misleading effect of liberalized depreciation on their indicated ability to pay dividends. To allow for this, some revise their profits on reporting to stockholders so that the justification for higher dividends will be apparent. Most do not, however, but they may feel that the higher "quality" of their reported earnings should be recognized in the dividend decision.[32] In that situation, the gross measure—cash flow—may be as handy a measure as any, and can be justified on several grounds.

[32] This is akin to a point made by Darling. Firms may tend to pay more dividends out of a given level of net profits when depreciation charges are relatively high. The greater certainty of the latter component of cash flow justifies higher payout. Paul G. Darling, "The Influence of Expectations and Liquidity on Dividend Policy," *Journal of Political Economy*, Vol. 65, No. 3 (June 1957), p. 216.

CHART 3. Postwar Corporate Dividends and Various After-Tax Corporate Income Measures, 1946–60

Ratio Scale

Billions of Dollars

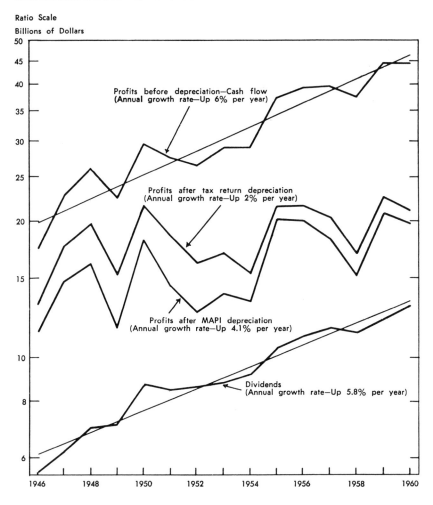

In the first place, firms may think of depreciation as a purely accounting charge not affecting their current ability to pay. Cash flow (after taxes) is viewed as a source of funds to be allocated between dividends and gross retentions without taking account of depreciation. This is perfectly rational in the short run, at least on the part of those corporate officials who seek to optimize for owners. These officials can accomplish this objective by increasing dividend payments out of cash flow only insofar as the marginal (after-tax)

benefit of dividends to stockholders remains above the marginal benefit to them of retentions. Judging the optimum payout ratio in this fashion does not require the breakdown of cash flow into net profits and depreciation. In other words, the comparison of the internal and external rates of return obtainable from the investment of a given amount of cash flow is made independently of the depreciation charged in the past against that cash flow.[33]

A second rationale for cash flow as a determinant of dividends is that, while recognizing depreciation as a cost, firms may regard stability or steady growth of dividends as a primary responsibility to be met before capital requirements. This could follow from the assumption that, in practice, dividends have a direct influence on stock prices, rather than being a "mere detail," theoretically independent, as suggested by Modigliani-Miller.[34] This might in turn lead them to determine dividends by cash flow, with any excess of gross investment (including replacement) over gross retentions to be financed out of excess liquidity, or externally.[35] In the postwar period, when most investment could be financed internally, the existence of such a policy would not be surprising.[36]

Finally, with the introduction of varying depreciation practices, it is possible that firms might base their dividends on adjusted net profits utilizing consistent depreciation rules. For simplicity, how-

[33] Future depreciation must, of course, be taken into account in appraising the internal rate of return, and depreciation will, therefore, influence dividends in the long run.

[34] F. Modigliani and M. H. Miller, "The Cost of Capital, Corporation Finance and the Theory of Investment," *American Economic Review*, Vol. XLVIII, No. 3 (June 1958), p. 266.

[35] A *Management Record* survey reports: "Because most companies prefer to maintain a consistent dividend record, reduced earnings affect reinvestment funds much more quickly than they do funds available for dividends. Instead of cutting into the dividend, some executives believe that it is better to turn to other sources of growth funds, such as bank loans. A food company executive states, for example: 'It is our philosophy that the stockholders are entitled to dividends which constitute a fair proportion of the earnings realized and which should not be unreasonably withheld to accumulate funds for future growth. We feel that if, after a reasonable payout, the remaining earnings are insufficient for growth, the best interests of the stockholders are served by obtaining additional funds by means of borrowing.'" (National Industrial Conference Board, *Management Record*, Vol. XXV, No. 1 [January 1963], p. 35.)

[36] Actually, even if capital requirements should have priority, the same link between dividends and cash flow could show up if the capital required tends to be proportional to cash flow.

ever, they may use cash flow as a proxy to represent the pattern of change in adjusted net profits. In other words, firms might base dividends on true net profits, but measure trends in that variable by gross profits, lowering the fraction paid out proportionately. This is analogous to the current tendency of national income specialists to reject the theoretically preferable "national income" series in favor of the GNP as a measure of economic growth.

Statistical analysis does not point to any one of these behavioral patterns as typical. It does suggest, however, that firms may be influenced by some of these considerations.

Tests of Alternative Income Variables

Alternative income variables were substituted for the official profit series to test their ability to improve the explanation of 1942-60 dividend behavior.[37] The objective was to show that removal of noneconomic changes in depreciation allowances would provide a better explanatory basis. In order to provide a more direct measure of the impact of these accounting developments, measures of depreciation liberalization were also tested explicitly as explanatory variables.

The starting point was the basic Lintner model.[38] A general income variable Y was substituted for net profits P in the Lintner model. Multiplying out the right-hand side, the relations estimated were of the form:

(3-1) $$D - D_{-1} = a + b_1Y + b_2D_{-1} + u$$

It seemed preferable to leave the model in this first difference form as Lintner originally stated it,[39] rather than transpose the D_{-1} to the right-hand side. Such a transposition would yield the same regression coefficients, but the coefficient of multiple determination

---

[37] In evaluating these and all other regression results, the statistical qualifications outlined in the second technical note following Chapter II should be kept in mind. Also, see the footnote at the beginning of Chapter I where a 1965 revision of the OBE data is mentioned. Some of the empirical work of this study was redone with the new data, as reported in Appendix G. However, it was found that the revisions did not alter the basic findings to be presented here.

[38] Relation (2-2), see p. 19.

[39] See John Lintner, "Distribution of Incomes of Corporations Among Dividends, Retained Earnings and Taxes," *American Economic Review*, Vol. 46, No. 2 (May 1956), pp. 97-113.

TABLE 7. Regression Results for Alternative Corporate Income Variables Tested in the Basic Model, 1942–60
(Constant term in billions of dollars)

Income Measure (Y)	Regression Coefficients[a]			Coefficient of Determination[b] (R^2)	Durbin-Watson Statistic (D–W)	Target Payout Ratio[c] (r)	Dividend-Income Ratio, 1942–60 (D/Y)
	Constant Term (a)	Income (Y)	Lagged Dividends (D_{-1})				
All Corporations							
Official net profits	−.583 (.293)	.132 (.027)	−.147 (.045)	.610 (.561)	1.79	.90	.498
Revised net profits[d]							
(P_1) Series	−.472 (.229)	.162 (.025)	−.249 (.048)	.728 (.694)	2.12	.65	.464
(P_2) Series	−.326 (.201)	.166 (.023)	−.203 (.038)	.766 (.737)	1.82	.82	.580
Cash flow	.285 (.168)	.158 (.020)	−.540 (.074)	.801 (.776)	1.90	.29	.297
Manufacturing Corporations							
Official net profits	−.201 (.170)	.141 (.026)	−.217 (.051)	.648 (.604)	1.85	.65	.465
Revised net profits[d]							
(P_3) Series	−.037 (.125)	.167 (.022)	−.379 (.057)	.775 (.747)	2.22	.44	.396
(P_4) Series	−.146 (.132)	.170 (.023)	−.298 (.049)	.768 (.739)	2.20	.57	.461
(P_5) Series	−.061 (.146)	.148 (.024)	−.290 (.056)	.701 (.664)	2.01	.51	.432
Cash flow	.146 (.114)	.158 (.020)	−.536 (.072)	.794 (.769)	1.97	.30	.300

a Figures in parentheses are the standard errors of the coefficients.
b Figures in parentheses are the coefficients of multiple determination adjusted for the number of degrees of freedom consumed by the regression ($\bar{R}^2$).
c For derivation of this ratio, see p. 57.
d These revised profits series are adjusted according to the corresponding depreciation concepts listed in Table 6, p. 51.

R^2 would approach unity because of mutual trends in the variables. The first difference form produces a lower R^2, but the result is probably a clearer measure of the fraction of dividend variation explained by the model in its own right without the aid of these mutual trends.

In addition to tests of the official OBE net variable P and the gross variable, cash flow C, net profit series reflecting the various depreciation measures were substituted for P in the basic Lintner model. The revised profits variables, distinguished by subscripts corresponding to those of the appropriate depreciation concept as listed in Table 6, are defined as follows:

> P_1 = profits revised by OBE depreciation, all corporations, based on original cost, straight line, Bulletin F lives (variable 2, Table 6).
>
> P_2 = profits revised by "realistic depreciation," all business (MAPI) (variable 3, Table 6).
>
> P_3 = profits revised by OBE depreciation, manufacturing establishments, based on original cost, straight line, Bulletin F lives (variable 5, Table 6).
>
> P_4 = profits revised by OBE depreciation, manufacturing establishments, based on current cost, straight line, Bulletin F lives (variable 6, Table 6).
>
> P_5 = profits revised by FTC-SEC data (depreciation and depletion, adjusted by subtraction of IRS depletion), all manufacturing corporations except newspapers (variable 7, Table 6).

Evaluation of the Income Measures

Least-squares regression estimates with the various income measures in the basic model are given in Table 7. The regression coefficients given for income and lagged dividends are the values of b_1 and b_2 obtained in the basic estimating equation (3-1). However, they may also be used to derive the coefficients for the same basic model stated in the speed-of-adjustment form as:

$$D - D_{-1} = a + c(rY - D_{-1}).$$

The estimated speed-of-adjustment coefficient c in this model and later models is $-b_2$. The target payout ratio r presented in Table 7 is estimated by b_1/c.

Several features of these results point to cash flow as the best explanatory variable in this simple model, at least for the 1942-60 period. First, according to the coefficient of determination, the substitution of any of the seven alternative income variables for the official profit series improves the explanation of dividend behavior during this period when tax provisions concerning depreciation changed. The substitution of the cash flow variable for the original net profits series provides the best results. It increases the fraction of variance explained from 61 percent to 80 percent, reducing the unexplained variance by 49 percent for all corporations. The reduction of residual variance is 42 percent in the case of manufacturing.[40]

Although the five revised profit series achieve a smaller improvement than cash flow, a clear pattern emerges from their results. The three best explanatory improvements among the five were accomplished by P_2, P_3, and P_4. As shown in Table 6, these were the profit series based on the least growth in depreciation—only 8 to 9 percent per year—compared to the 13 percent rate shown by the official series. The other two series, P_1 and P_5, were based on a faster growth of depreciation and made a smaller improvement in the explanation of dividend changes. These figures suggest that (within this range of adjustment at least) the greater the downward adjustment in the trend of depreciation the better the explanation of dividend behavior.

The varying results for the different profit measures may also be viewed in another way. Any measurement error introduced into the official net profits variable P by the liberalization of depreciation would produce a downward bias in the profit coefficient.[41] That is, insofar as firms base dividends on some other profit measure, the regression on P will tend to yield a regression coefficient that is biased downward as a measure of the response of dividends to changes in "true" profits. In this light, the relative magnitude of the various profit coefficients in Table 7 may, in part, reflect the degree of measurement error. For example, the coefficient for official net profits for all corporations is about 20 percent lower than those for the two adjusted profit measures. Although other factors may be

[40] These improvements in explained variance are easily significant at the 0.1 percent level on the F test. In this test and in all tests of significance used here, the phrase "significant at the 0.1 percent level" refers to the area in the tails outside the critical region of the distribution of the statistic.

[41] For a discussion of this "errors in variables" type of bias see J. Johnston, *Econometric Methods* (McGraw-Hill, 1963), Chap. 6.

causing this, it at least suggests that the adjusted profit series, though certainly not free of measurement error, are less subject to it than the official series.

A comparison of the size of the coefficient for cash flow to those for profits is also of interest. Unless corporations ignore depreciation, they would be expected to pay out a smaller fraction of cash flow in dividends than they would pay out of profits. The regression coefficient (the estimated short-run marginal propensity to pay dividends) would therefore be smaller for cash flow, if there were no measurement error in any of the series. As shown in Table 7, however, the coefficient for cash flow for all corporations is well above that for official profits and only slightly below those for adjusted profits. These results might suggest that cash flow (as a determinant of dividends or as a proxy) is the least subject to measurement error of the four income measures given.

The Performance of the Cash Flow Variable

The regression results in Table 7 show additional reasons for regarding cash flow as the more influential determinant of dividends in this period. Only the cash flow regressions yield the positive constant term anticipated by *a priori* theory[42] and found by Lintner for the interwar period. With respect to this and other features of the results, the cash flow models for both manufacturing and all corporations are remarkably consistent. The constant term a allows for reluctance to cut dividends and can be viewed as the estimated annual upward drift of dividends that would take place in the absence of a discrepancy between the target level of dividends and the dividend payments of the previous year. The estimate of this coefficient based on cash flow is $146 million for the manufacturing sector, or 51 percent of the amount indicated by the coefficient for all corporations. This seems consistent with the fact that manufacturing represents about half the corporate aggregate and paid out 53 percent of all dividends over the nineteen-year period.

The other coefficients for the aggregate and for manufacturing are also surprisingly close in the cash flow models. The coefficient

---

[42] The constant term is expected to be positive for reasons discussed in Chapter II, p. 19. It should be recognized, however, that if the relationship is not linear, the fitted model could yield a negative constant term even if the true intercept were positive.

of C, the short-run marginal propensity to distribute dividends, is 0.158 for both sectors, indicating an annual dividend response of 15.8 percent of any change in cash flow.[43] The long-run target payout ratios are 29 percent for all corporations, 30 percent for all manufacturing. Not only are these about the same for both sectors, but they are practically equal to the observed 30 percent over-all payout ratios (listed in the table as the over-all dividend-income ratio, in this case D/C). These short-run and long-run propensities to pay dividends are linked by the speed-of-adjustment coefficient c, which is 54 percent in both cases. In summary, both the aggregate and the manufacturing sectors were found to be aiming at a target payout ratio of about 30 percent, but they adjust only 54 percent of the way toward the target each year so that the short-run marginal propensity to pay dividends is 0.54 times 0.30, or about 16 percent.[44]

Results for Net Profits Variables

In contrast to the results achieved with the cash flow variable, the other income measures yielded implausible results in addition to the negative constant terms. A second, and related, peculiarity is that in all cases the over-all payout ratio D/Y is short of the estimated target ratio. This discrepancy is greatest in the Lintner model based on the official profit series which produced a 90 percent target payout ratio in the face of an over-all observed payout ratio of only 50 percent during 1942-60; in fact, the highest payout ratio for any year was only about 67 percent (in 1958).[45] Cast in the original form of the Lintner model this regression equation is:

$$(3\text{-}2) \qquad D - D_{-1} = -.583 + .147(.90P - D_{-1})$$

[43] This response is over and above the upward drift portrayed by the constant term.

[44] It is possible that the equal payout ratios based on cash flow for all corporations and manufacturing are a coincidence which really reflects the basing of dividends on net income. For example, utilities charge relatively greater depreciation than the manufacturing sector. Utilities also appear to aim at higher payout ratios based on net profits than does the manufacturing sector. Because of its higher depreciation the utility sector may achieve its higher payout ratio out of net income but exhibit a payout ratio based on cash flow no different from that in manufacturing. Thus an equality of the cash flow ratios for the two sectors would not necessarily reflect a failure to take depreciation into account.

[45] With dividends responding to profit increases with a lag, a lag of actual payout ratios behind the target ratios is to be expected. However, the persistence and magnitude of the postwar lag cast doubt on the estimated target payout ratio itself.

The estimated target level of dividends is 0.90P, and the expression in parentheses gives the gap between this and actual payments in the previous year. This gap is very large, as shown in Table 8, with the theoretical target often more than double the dividend payments of the year before and of the current year. While this gap between desired and actual payout tended to be chronically large, the speed-of-adjustment coefficient was only 14.7 percent. Thus, the model has the corporate sector moving only very slowly toward a very distant target.

TABLE 8. The Gap Between the Target Level of Dividends Estimated by the Lintner Model and Observed Previous-Year Dividends, Selected Years

(In billions of dollars)

| Year | Profits (P) | Dividend Level | | Estimated Target (rP) | Gap $(rP - D_{-1})$ |
| | | Actual | | | |
		Current (D)	Previous (D_{-1})		
1942	9.2	4.2	4.3	8.3	4.0
1946	13.0	5.6	4.6	11.7	7.1
1947	17.6	6.2	5.6	15.8	10.2
1950	21.8	8.7	7.1	19.6	12.5
1955	21.5	10.5	9.2	19.3	10.1
1959	22.7	12.4	11.4	20.4	9.0
1960	21.1	13.0	12.4	19.0	6.6

It is apparent that the Lintner model is being strained by the requirement to explain rapidly rising dividends by means of profit estimates that were very sluggish from 1947 on. Since the constant term is negative, the model can only call for a rise in dividends if rP tends to stay well above D_{-1}. However, since D_{-1} was rising very rapidly and P was sluggish, rP could stay ahead only with the help of a very high value of the target payout ratio r. It is very difficult to accept an estimate of the target payout ratio of 90 percent for a nineteen-year period during which the actual ratio for each year was in the 35 to 70 percent range and was 50 percent over all. When the model is fitted to the 1946-60 interval only, it produces even worse results. A target payout ratio of 1.46 is required to get booming dividends out of stagnant profits, and the target level of

TABLE 9. Regression Results for Alternative Corporate Income Variables Tested in the Basic Model, 1920–41 (Excluding 1936–38)

(Constant term in billions of dollars)

Income Measure (Y)	Regression Coefficients			Coefficient of Determination (R^2)	Durbin-Watson Statistic (D–W)	Target Payout Ratio[a] (r)	Dividend-Income Ratio, 1920–41 (D/Y)
	Constant Term (a)	Income (Y)	Lagged Dividends (D_{-1})				
All Corporations							
Official net profits	.311	.157	−.237	.818	1.68	.66	.93
Lintner net profits[b]	.106	.145	−.212	n.a.	n.a.	.68	n.a.
Revised net profits[c]							
(P_1) Series	.314	.156	−.237	.816	1.67	.66	.93
(P_2) Series	.364	.179	−.243	.820	1.92	.74	1.12
Cash flow	−.027	.160	−.292	.827	1.75	.55	.51
Manufacturing Corporations							
Official net profits	.196	.155	−.283	.797	1.71	.55	.76
Revised net profits[c]							
(P_3) Series	.215	.152	−.312	.788	1.63	.49	.69
(P_4) Series	.232	.162	−.317	.793	1.69	.51	.75
Cash flow	.074	.154	−.342	.801	1.74	.45	.47

n.a. Not available.

[a] For derivation of this ratio, see p. 57.

[b] Derived from slightly different data for the period 1918–41 (excluding 1936–37). See John Lintner, "Distribution of Incomes of Corporations Among Dividends, Retained Earnings and Taxes," American Economic Review, Vol. 46, No. 2 (May 1956), p. 109.

[c] These revised profits series are adjusted according to the corresponding depreciation concepts listed in Table 6.

dividends is as much as five times the actual level of dividends in some years. In this context, a paraphrase of Hume is appropriate: "No evidence is sufficient to establish an implausible result unless the unreliability of the evidence would be more remarkable than the result which it endeavors to establish."[46] It has been suggested that the stagnant profit series is partly a statistical illusion associated with the liberalization of depreciation. In this case, therefore, a finding that the profit variable, or the model, is defective would seem far less remarkable than these 90 percent and 146 percent target payout ratios.

The inference that the poor explanation of dividends by net profits results from the vagaries of depreciation allowances since 1941 is supported by fitting the same regression equations to the 1920-41 period, when tax provisions concerning depreciation underwent little change. All income measures performed about as well for this period as cash flow for the 1942-60 period and almost as well as cash flow in the early period. Table 9 reports some of the results for 1920-41, including a Lintner estimate that was fitted to slightly different data and years, but is roughly comparable. All the coefficients of determination for the profit variables are around 0.82 for the corporate aggregate and 0.79 for manufacturing. The cash flow variable explains dividend variation only slightly better in each case. The constant terms for the net profit variables are large and have the expected positive sign, while those for cash flow are close to zero.

The income series for this earlier interval, including the Lintner equation, all yield plausible b_1 and b_2 coefficients that are reasonably stable from model to model and from sector to sector. The speed-of-adjustment coefficients are much more in agreement than before. Instead of lagging far behind the targets as in the later period, the actual payout ratios for the profit variables are well above the target ratios. This is to be expected in a period that includes 1921 and the Great Depression when profits even became negative during four years. Dividends held up well enough in the face of poor profits to produce a 93 percent aggregate payout ratio for the nineteen years. Despite the crudity of some of these early data, these

[46] Richard Goode, "Rates of Return, Income Shares and Corporate Tax Incidence," Symposium on Business Taxation, Wayne State University (unpublished, March 11, 1964).

alternative profit series did a creditable job of explaining dividends in a period relatively free of the distortions produced by the liberalization of depreciation.

Other Problems of Income Measurement

Another income measurement problem involves the proper treatment of the inventory valuation adjustment (IVA). It was thought possible that before applying a target payout ratio firms would first, at least informally, adjust profits to remove the erratic inventory appreciation component in order to have a more stable payout base. A similar assumption was implied by the use of the OBE profit series from which other capital gains are removed. Lintner fitted his model to interwar data using net profits including the IVA, as well as the unadjusted series which underlies his result given in Table 9 above. He found that the adjusted profits variable produced better projections beyond the period of fit, but it performed about the same as the unadjusted profits according to the standard error of estimate and less satisfactorily according to the Durbin-Watson statistic and the coefficient of determination R^2. Because the transposition of lagged dividends to the right-hand side of the model produced R^2 values near unity, the difference between the two series in that respect appeared to be minor. However, the multiple correlation coefficients of 0.976 and 0.967 which Lintner reports[47] for the unadjusted and adjusted series, respectively, are substantially different. The unexplained variance is 27 percent lower in the model using the unadjusted series.

In the present study, evidence of the superiority of the unadjusted profits variable is even more convincing. A series of regressions was run using various income measures plus IVA. In all cases, including the overall 1920-60 fit and separate fits to the first and second halves, the adjustment yielded a coefficient of determination substantially lower than the corresponding models using unadjusted income, and in many cases the Durbin-Watson serial correlation statistic was intolerably low.[48]

Some of the models for manufacturing illustrate the deteriora-

[47] Lintner, in *American Economic Review, op. cit.,* p. 109n.

[48] It should be recognized that even a Durbin-Watson statistic of a magnitude near two does not necessarily establish independence of the error terms. See the technical note on problems of estimation following Chapter II, for qualifications of this test.

tion of estimates when the IVA is included. In the 1920-41 period, which the basic model explained well[49], substitution of the adjusted series for P reduced the coefficient of determination R^2 from 0.80 to 0.64, cut the Durbin-Watson statistic from 1.71 to 0.89, and yielded a target payout ratio of only 38 percent in a period when the other profits series showed it to be around 50 percent. Both P and P + IVA did a poor job for the 1942-60 period, but the addition of IVA to P cut R^2 from 0.65 to 0.29. The best income variable in this period was cash flow, but when the IVA was added to it, R^2 dropped from 0.79 to 0.38.

Inclusion of the IVA as a separate variable added to the simple model, as well as to more complex ones, was no more successful. Including it with the first four manufacturing income variables in Table 9 not only produced no significant coefficient, but reduced the adjusted coefficient of determination $\overline{R}^2$. A final attempt was made to utilize the IVA by lagging it. Some evidence was found of the expected positive impact on dividends in the postwar period, but this was not confirmed by the 1920-41 or 1920-60 regressions, whether the lagged IVA was used to adjust profits or included separately.

These negative findings seemed sufficient to warrant dropping the IVA from the analysis. One interpretation of the finding is that the IVA is an example of a meaningful economic concept that is either not recognized or else is regarded as inappropriate for corporate decisions. Certainly corporations make few if any such adjustments on their own books, although they often do exclude other capital gains which are usually of a smaller magnitude. It appears likely that the dividend policies of corporations are generally guided by what their books show, except in the case of such striking developments as the postwar inflation of depreciation charges. In any case, there appears to be little inclination to separate inventory appreciation from other income in weighing the ability to pay dividends.

Another income measurement problem considered was the possibility that current income in each single year might not be regarded as an adequate basis for setting the level of dividends. To some extent, the constant term in the model takes care of this possibility by allowing for reluctance to cut dividends because of a tem-

[49] See the sixth equation, Table 9.

porary lapse of profits. However, a more elaborate formulation might be effective if firms tend to think in terms of normal or previous peak profits, or some kind of permanent component of corporate income. Attempts were made to test for this by inclusion in the model of an income variable measuring the relation of current income to its previous peak, or to the peak up to and including the current level. However, no significant improvement was achieved over the simple constant term.

Explicit Depreciation Variables in the Models

A more direct measure of the impact of liberalization of depreciation during the 1942-60 period was sought by including actual charges, measures of "excess depreciation," and indexes of depreciation liberality in the models.

Results Using Depreciation Charges

Inclusion of actual depreciation charges A in the aggregate model using the official series as an income measure yielded equation (3-3).

$$(3\text{-}3) \qquad D - D_{-1} = .117 + .162P + .136A - .495D_{-1}$$
$$\phantom{(3\text{-}3) \qquad D - D_{-1} = } (.276) \quad (.021) \quad (.034) \quad (.094)$$

$$\bar{R}^2 = .771 \qquad D\text{-}W = 2.06 \qquad r_t = .326 + .274\,A/P$$

The new variable is highly significant, differing from zero in the expected direction by 4 standard errors, and its presence raised the adjusted coefficient of determination $\bar{R}^2$ from 0.56 to 0.77. Furthermore, the short-run propensity to pay out of profits is only about 20 percent higher than that for depreciation allowances, suggesting that the propensity to pay dividends out of the depreciation component of cash flow is not far below that for the profit component. The model apparently achieves no gain over the use of cash flow and, in fact, the $\bar{R}^2$ (which is corrected for the additional lost degree of freedom) is down slightly from that achieved by C alone.

The A term can be regarded simply as a linear addition to the basic model, or the P and A terms can be combined in a target function r_t representing a variable long-run propensity to pay dividends out of net profits.[50] The implied long-run r_t is given in (3-3). It fits into the entire model as indicated in relation (3-4).

(3-4) $D - D_{-1} = .117 + .495[(.326 + .274 \, A/P)P - D_{-1}]$

This is equivalent to (3-3), but it shows how the basic Lintner model (2-2) may be generalized by allowing the target payout ratio to vary over time with A/P. This target ratio moved up sharply in the postwar period—from 41.6 percent in 1946 to 63.0 percent in 1960.

The manufacturing results are almost the same, as shown in (3-5). Again the $\bar{R}^2$ is slightly lower than for C alone.

(3-5) $D - D_{-1} = .069 + .162P + .133A - .496D_{-1}$
$\phantom{(3-5)   D - D_{-1} = }(.154)\quad(.021)\quad(.039)\quad(.091)$

$\bar{R}^2 = .762 \qquad \text{D-W} = 2.16 \qquad r_t = .328 + .267 \, A/P$

While the constant term is smaller than for all corporations, as expected, the other coefficients, including those of the target function, are extremely close to those of (3-3). Here, too, the target ratio rises sharply, and the propensity to pay dividends out of depreciation is not far below that for profits. The similarity of the two sets of results suggests that a fit to nonmanufacturing would show the same behavior.

Inclusion of Excess Depreciation

As an alternative to the inclusion of actual depreciation charges, estimates of "excess depreciation" implied by the alternative profit series were included with P. Two measures of excess depreciation were defined for both sectors as:

All Corporations	*Manufacturing*
(1) $E_1 = A - A_1 = P_1 - P$	(3) $E_3 = A - A_3 = P_3 - P$
(2) $E_2 = A - A_2 = P_2 - P$	(4) $E_4 = A - A_4 = P_4 - P$

Regression results including these E's are given in Table 10. The E variables all have positive coefficients that are significant at the one

[50] The target payout function implied by relation (3-3) is obtained by dividing the terms between the constant term and the lagged dividend term by cP. The target functions throughout the study will be derived similarly.

TABLE 10. Regression Results for Excess Depreciation Variables Added to the Basic Model, 1942–60

(Constant term in billions of dollars)

| Excess Depreciation Measure[a] | Regression Coefficients[b] | | | | Adjusted Coefficient of Determination ($\bar{R}^2$) | Durbin-Watson Statistic (D-W) |
	Constant Term (a)	Income (P)	Excess Depreciation[c] (E)	Lagged Dividends (D_{-1})		
Difference between official net profits and:						
		All Corporations				
(P_1) Series	−.380	.165	.223	−.279	.687	2.21
	(.259)	(.026)	(.082)	(.061)		
(P_2) Series	−.419	.168	.139	.203	.731	1.97
	(.235)	(.024)	(.042)	(.039)		
		Manufacturing Corporations				
(P_3) Series	−.001	.166	.191	−.397	.733	2.20
	(.155)	(.023)	(.065)	(.074)		
(P_4) Series	−.148	.170	.167	−.297	.721	2.20
	(.144)	(.024)	(.060)	(.052)		

[a] These revised profits series are adjusted according to the corresponding depreciation concepts listed in Table 6.
[b] Figures in parentheses are the standard errors of the coefficients.
[c] Excess depreciation is measured by the amount by which revised net profits exceed official (OBE) net profits

percent level or better. However, these models do not fit as well as the cash flow model, and the E variables improve the basic model less than actual depreciation charges did in relations (3-3) and (3-5). The separate inclusion of the excess depreciation variables even produced a lower adjusted coefficient of determination than the simple models based on the corresponding profit variables (Table 7).[51]

The excess depreciation models are interesting in one respect. It might have been expected *a priori* that dividends would be more responsive to excess depreciation than to actual charges. The coefficient for E in the first equation is higher than the depreciation

[51] These equations containing E, particularly the two for the corporate aggregate, are also suspect for their negative constant terms and the correspondingly high implied target payout ratios. The P_1 model with E included shows this ratio rising from 58 percent to 72 percent between 1946 and 1960. The comparable P_2 model (based on MAPI depreciation) shows a rise from 70 percent to 82 percent. All of these are well above the observed payout ratios.

TABLE 11. Results for Alternative Indexes of Depreciation Liberality, 1942–60

(Constant term in billions of dollars)

Depreciation Liberality Index (A_L)[a]	Regression Coefficients[b]				Adjusted Coefficient of Determination $(\bar{R}^2)$	Durbin-Watson Statistic (D-W)
	Constant Term (a)	Net Profits (P)	Depreciation Liberality $(A_L P)$	Lagged Dividends (D_{-1})		
All Corporations						
Ratio of official depreciation to:						
(A_1) Series	−.552	.043	.116	−.231	.647	2.21
	(.263)	(.047)	(.052)	(.055)		
(A_2) Series	−.378	.084	.115	−.267	.740	2.06
	(.233)	(.025)	(.033)	(.049)		
Manufacturing Corporations						
(A_3) Series	−.099	.078	.063	−.299	.679	2.09
	(.160)	(.037)	(.029)	(.060)		
(A_4) Series	−.180	.100	.070	−.286	.697	2.09
	(.149)	(.028)	(.029)	(.053)		

[a] These revised depreciation concepts are detailed in Table 6.
[b] Figures in parentheses are standard errors of the coefficients.

coefficient in (3-3), but the coefficient for MAPI excess depreciation[52] (based on P_2) was about the same. Similarly, in manufacturing, dividends showed only about 25 to 45 percent greater sensitivity to excess depreciation than to actual charges. This may reflect estimation difficulties, particularly in the measures of the excess, but if not, it tends to support the cash flow hypothesis. While recognizing depreciation as a cost, and the recent existence of excess depreciation, firms may still find cash flow a convenient measure of changes over time in their ability to pay dividends.

Results Using Depreciation Liberality

An additional set of models containing target payout functions that vary with ratios measuring depreciation liberality was also tested. These liberality ratios, A_L, are measured by the ratios of

[52] MAPI "excess depreciation" was negative throughout but approached zero by 1960.

actual charges to the various depreciation series. The fixed target payout ratio r was replaced by $r_t = \alpha + \beta A_L$. Substituting for r in the basic model and multiplying out the expression yields (3-6).

$$(3\text{-}6) \qquad D - D_{-1} = a + c\alpha P + c\beta A_L P - c D_{-1}$$

The results appear in Table 11. Again, the depreciation variables are all significant—positive by at least two standard errors. However, in no case is the fit as good as in the simple model with cash flow substituted for net profits.

Forecasting Ability of the Models

Table 12 presents projections of the 1942-60 regressions for three years beyond the period of fit—years that had seen further liberalization of depreciation under the 1962 IRS guidelines. "Forecasts" are given for all corporations and for manufacturing using three equations—the original net profit model, the cash flow model, and a model using net profits and depreciation explicitly. The forecasting errors are compared to those made by a naive model based on changes duplicating those of the previous year.[53] The cash flow model yielded the best forecast in five of the six cases and was surpassed only by the 1962-63 naive forecast for all corporations. Equations (3-3) and (3-5) performed nearly as well, and, like the cash flow equations, were superior to the basic net profit model in every case. The very low forecasts of dividend change for these years by the net profit series is further evidence of the importance of cash flow in the dividend decision.

Despite its clear success relative to the other forecasting models, the cash flow equation produced a forecasting error for manufacturing in 1961-62 that was double the standard error of estimate and a forecasting error for all corporations in 1962-63 triple the standard error of estimate. This suggests the possibility of structural change. The most conspicuous indication of this was the case of the finance, insurance, and real estate industry to which about 60 percent of the 1962-63 error can be traced.[54] Cash flow rose only 7

[53] A second-order autoregressive equation will be used in addition to this naive model in testing the forecasting ability of the more elaborate models in Chapter V.

[54] A fit of the cash flow model to data for this industry gave a 1962-63 forecast that understated the actual change by $449 million, or 60 percent of the error made by the aggregate equation.

TABLE 12. Forecasts of Dividend Changes by Models Fitted to 1942–60 Data, 1960–63

(In millions of dollars)

		Forecasting Model					
		All Corporations			Manufacturing		
Date of Forecast		Net Profits	Cash Flow	Equation (3–3)	Net Profits	Cash Flow	Equation (3–5)
Standard error of estimate (adjusted)		335	239	242	212	162	164
1960–61	Actual change	+310	+310	+310	+20	+20	+20
	"Forecast"	+62	+106	+70	−145	−30	−66
	Error, 1942–60 fit	−248	−204	−240	−165	−50	−86
	Error, naive[a]	+500	+500	+500	+280	+280	+280
1961–62	Actual change	+1200	+1200	+1200	+880	+880	+880
	"Forecast"	+390	+938	+851	+126	+553	+481
	Error, 1942–60 fit	−810	−262	−349	−754	−327	−399
	Error, naive[a]	−890	−890	−890	−860	−860	−860
1962–63	Actual change	+1530	+1530	+1530	+520	+520	+520
	"Forecast"	+446	+774	+719	+126	+379	+334
	Error, 1942–60 fit	−1084	−756	−811	−394	−141	−186
	Error, naive[a]	−330	−330	−330	+360	+360	+360
Root-mean-square forecasting error	1942–60 fit	794	477	528	500	208	259
	Naive model	619	619	619	562	562	562

[a] The naive model used here forecast the same change as in the previous year.

percent while dividends rose an unprecedented (and implausible) 40 percent.[55] Obviously these income-oriented models cannot explain a dividend change of that magnitude. This could be evidence of structural change. More likely, however, it indicates errors in the data. The OBE estimates for 1962 and 1963[56] are based on a sample of corporations, rather than *Statistics of Income* which offers fuller coverage but which is available only after a two- or three-year lag.

[55] These dividends are net of dividends paid out of gains by investment trusts.
[56] *Survey of Current Business,* Vol. 66, No. 7 (July 1964), pp. 31-32. Dividends paid out of capital gains by investment trusts were excluded from these estimates.

Tentative Conclusions

To sum up, every measure of depreciation and the liberalization of allowances improved the basic model's explanation of dividend change in the 1942-60 period. Even so, none of these variables, whether used to adjust profits or included separately, improved on the simple cash flow model for this period. This is substantial support for the general hypothesis that depreciation influences dividends and the particular hypothesis that cash flow is a good measure of ability to pay.

If firms really do follow cash flow in their dividend policy, a rise in depreciation charges broadens the payout base, because the resulting tax saving is relevant to the dividend decision, and the (greater) fall in measured profits is not. The effect on dividends may be suggested by a hypothetical exercise. For the corporate aggregate, the ratio of depreciation allowances A to net profits P rose from 33 percent in 1946 to 110 percent in 1960. If the ratio A/P had remained at its 1946 level (other things remaining equal), 1960 allowances would have been $6.9 billion instead of $23.4 billion, and taxes would have been $8.6 billion higher. According to the cash flow model, this amount of tax saving led to a target level of dividends $2.5 billion higher than it would otherwise have been.[57] The tax cut arising from the relative increase in depreciation allowances thus appears to have given a boost to 1960 dividends on the order of 25 percent.

Although the superior explanatory performance of cash flow can be given no definite behavioral interpretation, a few additional observations are in order. First, a short-run determination of dividends by cash flow (as a liquidity variable) is undoubtedly more plausible than cash flow as a long-run determinant. In the long run, "true" economic depreciation will generally be interpreted by firms as a charge against the flow from which dividends are paid. Thus the conclusion here that the cash flow measure provides the best statistical explanation of dividends in the 1942-60 period carries no implication that corporate officials either ignore economic depreciation or reject the economist's view that it constitutes a cost. They

[57] Based on the target payout ratio for the cash flow model for all corporations, Table 7.

may only regard depreciation reported for tax purposes as a poor measure of that cost. If so, there are two reasons to expect their dividend payments to be linked statistically to cash flow. In the first place, some firms may wish to pay out a certain fraction of "true" net profits, but they have no reliable measure of depreciation; as a substitute they pay out a (smaller) fraction of cash flow on the ground that a relative change in this indicator is the best available estimate of the relative change of "true" net profits. Secondly, other firms may substitute alternative depreciation estimates for tax depreciation and base dividends on adjusted net profits; however, insofar as their depreciation estimates remain a stable fraction of cash flow, dividends will still follow the latter closely. Both types of dividend policy recognize depreciation, but neither accepts officially measured net profits as the payout base. It may be concluded tentatively that the superior explanation of dividends by cash flow, as compared to official net profits, reflects these two behavioral patterns, as well as the direct impact of cash flow on dividends in the short run.[58]

[58] A possible qualification of this conclusion should be mentioned. Since cash flow is a relatively stable dividend measure compared to official net profits, this may account in part for its better explanation of the relatively stable dividend series. However, within the speed-of-adjustment framework the greater volatility of net profits is accommodated by a smaller speed-of-adjustment coefficient than that applied to cash flow. Also it may be noted that the net profit series adjusted for depreciation changes also improved the explanation given by the official profit series, even though the adjusted series are no less volatile.

CHAPTER IV

The Effect of Individual
Income Tax Rates

IT IS IMPROBABLE that any simple model describing the behavior of dividends during the 1942-60 period could also accurately describe the entire 1920-60 period because of the substantial change in the corporate environment beginning with World War II. Lintner applied his equation, fitted to interwar data, to the 1946-54 period and found that it gave a better explanation of postwar dividends than other models.[1] Further statistical tests suggest, however, that the changes in relationships require a more general model. The second basic hypothesis of this study is that in addition to an upward postwar trend in the payout ratio because of liberalized depreciation, a downward pressure on dividends was expected because of generally higher rates of individual taxation. This hypothesis was tested by generalizing the basic model to allow for variations in the long-run payout propensity. Depreciation liberalization has already been interpreted as exerting an upward influence on the (variable) target ratio. Here, the impact of individual tax rates on changes in payout ratios will be estimated.

The ability of the aggregate 1920-41 net profits equation (Table

[1] John Lintner, "Distribution of Income Among Dividends, Retained Earnings and Taxes," *American Economic Review,* Vol. 46, No. 2 (May 1956).

9) to explain postwar dividends was tested to demonstrate the need for elaboration of the basic Lintner model. The standard error of estimate of this equation applied to 1946-60 was $645 million; this was slightly larger than the $611 million figure obtained by Lintner when he applied his 1918-41 regression to the 1946-54 period. These estimating errors are small relative to total dividends, as Lintner pointed out, but by other criteria they are large. They are double the standard error of estimate of the same model fitted to the 1942-60 period, and triple that of the cash flow model fitted to that same period. The postwar annual increase in dividends estimated by the interwar equation is too large every year and averages over $1 billion or double the actual average. This upward bias is primarily the result of the application of the high prewar target payout ratio of 66 percent to the later period when actual payout was much lower.

More detailed tests for structural change showed that whatever income variable is substituted for official net profits in the basic model, the 1920-60 fit (excluding 1936-38) is distinctly inferior to those of equations fitted to the first and second halves of the interval. This suggests a changed relationship and/or the omission of an important factor in dividend policy.

A Statistical Test for Structural Change

The regression coefficients for the first and second halves of the 1920-60 period of observation were given in Tables 9 and 7, respectively. Despite the lower observed postwar payout ratios, the estimated target payout ratios for the profit variables were somewhat higher in the 1942-60 equations than in the 1920-41 period. Associated with this were large negative constant terms. In contrast, cash flow models produced target payout ratios of about 30 percent in the second half, compared to 55 percent and 45 percent for the aggregate and manufacturing, respectively, for the early period. The constant terms and speed-of-adjustment coefficients in the cash flow models were also higher in 1942-60 than previously.

Inspection of Tables 7 and 9 suggests a change in relationships between the two periods. If the changes in coefficients are statistically significant, it is probable that structural change has occurred. One approach to this is a comparison of the goodness-of-fit of each model when fitted to the entire period with its performance when

TABLE 13. Comparison of Regression Results for Simple Models Fitted to the Entire 1920–60 Period and to Two Halves Separately (Excluding 1936–38)

Income Measure	Coefficient of Determination (R^2)			Standard Error of Estimate (SEE)[a]			1920–60 Durbin-Watson Statistic	F Ratio
	1920–60	1920–41	1942–60	1920–60	1920–41	1942–60		
All Corporations								
Official net profits	.637	.818	.610	.355	.262	.308	1.35	5.78
Revised net profits[b]								
(P_1) Series	.677	.816	.728	.334	.263	.257	1.41	6.94
(P_2) Series	.727	.820	.766	.307	.260	.238	1.39	5.52
Cash flow	.702	.827	.801	.321	.256	.220	1.33	8.63
Manufacturing Corporations								
Official net profits	.662	.797	.648	.197	.149	.194	1.50	3.18
Revised net profits[b]								
(P_3) Series	.725	.788	.775	.177	.152	.155	1.57	3.51
(P_4) Series	.725	.793	.768	.177	.150	.158	1.56	3.41
Cash flow	.741	.801	.794	.172	.147	.148	1.52	3.84

[a] In billions of dollars.
[b] These revised profits series are adjusted by the corresponding depreciation concepts listed in Table 6.

fitted to the first and second halves. If the latter are significantly better than the former, some kind of structural change is indicated. Such comparisons are made in Table 13. The coefficients of determination R^2 for the entire period are 8 to 14 percent below the average of those for the separate halves, and standard errors of estimate are correspondingly higher.

Another indication that structural change is plaguing these models when fitted to all thirty-eight years is the indicated autocorrelation of residuals, especially in the aggregate models. Tests for the whole period produced Durbin-Watson statistics of only 1.3-1.4 compared to values near two for the separate halves. All equations tended to underestimate prewar annual dividend changes and overestimate those of the later period. The mean prewar residuals in the aggregate models were 107, 112, 101 and 93 million dollars, while the average 1942-60 residuals were negative by the same amounts. Although cash flow was the best postwar explanatory variable and did well prewar, its explanatory power also diminished when it was used to explain the entire period. This fact, plus the low 1920-60 Durbin-Watson statistics, suggest a structural change and/or the absence of one or more important explanatory factors. Either an allowance for depreciation charges is not the only necessary generalization of the basic model, or the response to factors included in the model has changed.

Evidence of structural change is also apparent in the standard errors of estimate shown in Table 13. The cash flow model for the corporate aggregate shows an overall standard error of $321 million compared to $256 million and $220 million for the separate halves. These statistics can be used to make a more precise evaluation of the evidence; a standard analysis of covariance test was applied to test the hypothesis that the overall fit was significantly poorer than the separate ones.[2] The appropriate F ratios are given in Table 13. The discrepancies between the overall and separate standard errors of estimate are great enough for the corporate aggregate to permit the interpretation of the two sets of observations as coming from different structures (at the 0.5 percent level of significance or better).

The evidence of structural change is somewhat weaker for the manufacturing sector, but all F ratios are significant at the 5 percent level, and that for cash flow is significant at the 2.5 percent level. It is worth noting that the evidence of a changed relationship is strongest for the cash flow model. Although that income measure allows for depreciation variations and performs best in the second period, it is strained even more than the others by the requirement to explain dividend behavior in both periods with a single relationship.

Payout Ratios and Individual Tax Rates

The above tests tend to support the original comment of Tarshis[3] concerning the oversimplicity of the basic model contain-

[2] See Gregory C. Chow, "Tests of Equality Between Sets of Coefficients in Two Linear Regressions," *Econometrica*, Vol. 28, No. 3 (July 1960), pp. 591-605.

[3] L. Tarshis, "Economic Growth: Income Distribution—Discussion," *American Economic Review*, Vol. 46, No. 2 (May 1956), p. 118.

ing only profits and lagged dividends as independent variables. Whatever explanatory income variable is used in the simple model, there appear to be different structural relations present in the two time periods. One of the most likely elements in this structural change is the fact that the first period was one of relatively low tax rates, while the 1942-60 interval was one of generally high taxes. The tendency for the simple models to underestimate prewar dividend changes and overestimate them later is consistent with the hypothesis that low prewar taxes made for a higher level of dividend payments than would have been expected on the basis of income alone, and that higher rates later had a depressing effect. The use of after-tax cash flow as an explanatory variable allowed for change in corporate taxes as well as depreciation charges. Changes in the individual income tax rate structure may also be a relevant factor, however.

The Tax Shelter Hypothesis

The hypothesis was that corporate payout ratios may tend to vary inversely with the differential between tax rates on ordinary income and capital gains. Assume that there is a certain payout ratio that, under a given tax structure, optimizes for a particular shareholder. This shareholder is likely to prefer lower dividends when the differential increases, because of the tax saving (or shelter effect) afforded by corporate retention. There are several aspects of this tax advantage. If the retention leads to realized capital gains, these are taxed at lower rates than those applicable to dividend income. Even if dividends are ultimately paid, the investor has the advantage of tax deferral. Finally, capital gains unrealized at the time of an investor's death completely escape the income tax, even if they are realized by his heirs.[4]

The hypothesis that the payout ratio varies inversely with the tax differential assumes that a substantial number of owners is

[4] Higher retention in response to higher tax rates would not be popular with shareholders who are wedded to some fixed level of after-tax dividends. Under higher tax rates they would want more dividends in order to shore up disposable income. The hypothesis of this study implies, however, that this consideration is a less important long-run factor in corporate dividend policy than the tax-saving advantage of retention. The corporate decision-makers may feel that owners of the bulk of the stock are less concerned with short-run fluctuations in disposable income than with maximization of the present value of future income streams.

sufficiently sophisticated to recognize the tax saving via retention and that they expect a lag in current dividends to be more than compensated by higher dividends later, and/or by capital gains taxed at lower rates.[5] It is also necessary to assume that the interests of the owners are somehow known and respected by the corporate decision-makers. The latter must, in turn, be confident that stockholders will not interpret a dividend lag as indicative of a dark future which warrants a sell-off of the stock.

In order for the assumed stockholder desire for a tax shelter to be reflected in corporate policy, the payout ratio adopted by boards of directors must be subject to one or more of these influences: (a) the personal tax-saving possibilities of high-income owners may be recognized and directly pursued by boards (especially those of closely held companies) who seek to shelter owners, including themselves, from taxes; (b) on a more sophisticated level, firms that are trying to maximize the discounted value of all future after-tax returns recognize that a rise in personal taxes may lower the individual optimum payout ratio; (c) the preference for capital gains of high-income shareholders, as expressed in the capital market by their relative demand for securities with lower payout ratios, may move boards of directors to let payout lag when tax rates rise; and (d) officers of growing companies, especially those with low shareholdings, may seize every opportunity to reinvest earnings, and high tax rates may provide such an opportunity by blunting potential stockholder protest.

It is not reasonable to assume that such considerations affect every corporation. Even where they do, the impact is likely to be much stronger in some cases than in others. For example, the more closely held the corporation, the more likely a strong shelter effect. In any case, the hypothesis here is that this influence is sufficiently prevalent to account for a significant part of the variation of aggregate dividends.[6]

[5] The likelihood of such ultimate compensation is taken for granted here, although the effect of corporate saving on stock prices has never been satisfactorily demonstrated. It is not necessary for the saving to be fully reflected in prices in order for retention to be attractive.

[6] The policy of increasing retentions to avoid individual taxes is not without limits. Insofar as the projects financed internally by corporations produce diminishing yields, the desire to maintain the value of the corporation will limit the amount of income that is retained.

Recognition of the Shelter Effect by Corporate Officials

Explicit references to the tax saving accomplished by retention appear to be rare in corporate reports and among corporate officials. This reticence may result, in part, from the existence of the accumulated earnings tax to which a corporation is liable if it retains income for the purpose of preventing the imposition of the income tax upon its shareholders. This tax on "improper accumulation" appears to have been infrequently assessed and thus only a minor deterrent to retention, particularly in the case of widely held corporations. However, even though corporation officials may feel the need to justify low dividends, they may be reluctant to court trouble by referring to any motive of tax-avoidance. Certainly the rather general silence on the subject, except in confidential interviews such as those conducted by Lintner, should not be taken as evidence of ignorance of the advantage of retention to high-income shareholders.

Although Lintner concluded that target payout ratios of firms were more stable than indicated by the aggregative models to be described here, his field interviews did show concern with factors other than net earnings. He found major "importance attached by management to longer-term capital gains as compared with current dividend income for its shareholders"[7] in setting dividend targets. He also concluded that companies sought a pattern of action "which would both meet the company's needs most of the time and reasonably balance the longer term interests of shareholders in the company and their shorter term interests in current income."[8]

Capital Gains Preference of High-Income Groups

A tendency for high-income investors to avoid high-dividend securities and concentrate on capital gains would tend to support a hypothesis that high tax rates lead to low aggregate payout. However, evidence of this proved difficult to find. Dividends and capital gains on corporate stock, by income group, are given for 1959 in Table 14. As expected, the figures show the importance of dividends relative to capital gains to be far less for higher incomes than for low incomes. The relative share of dividends in total income re-

[7] Lintner, *op. cit., American Economic Review,* p. 104.
[8] *Ibid.,* p. 102.

TABLE 14. Dividends, Net Long-Term Capital Gains, and Gross Stock Sales by Income Group, 1959

(Dollar amounts in billions)

Adjusted Gross Income	Total Dividends[a] (D)	Net Long-Term Capital Gains[b] (G)	D / (D+G)	Gross Sales[c]
Under $10,000	$2.440	$ .642	.79	$ 3.73
10,000–50,000	4.050	1.816	.69	8.07
50,000–100,000	1.416	.776	.65	2.19
100,000–200,000	.845	.596	.59	1.51
200,000–500,000	.509	.595	.46	1.04
500,000–1,000,000	.191	.311	.38	.43
1,000,000 or more	.263	.382	.41	.50
All incomes	9.714	5.116	.65	17.47

[a] Source, total domestic and foreign dividends received, *Statistics of Income, Individual Income Tax Returns* (1959), p. 4.
[b] Source, *Statistics of Income, Supplemental Report* (1959).
[c] Source, *Ibid.*, p. 11.

alized from the two sources[9] was only about 40 percent for very high incomes compared to 79 percent for incomes under $10,000.

The predominance of capital gains among high-income groups gives superficial support to the tax shelter hypothesis, but the fact that high-income groups recorded more capital gains does not necessarily reflect a concentration in growth stocks. First, there is some evidence that high-income groups may be more active traders.[10] Secondly, they may be more successful traders. In the year 1959, a record $5 billion in net long-term capital gains was reported, and many of the high-income recipients may have been boosted to the top rank because of unusually high gains. The more stable dividend component would tend to lag behind capital gains for these income groups, especially the 784 recipients with incomes greater than

[9] Short-term capital transactions are excluded from this comparison because data are not available, but short-term sales appear to have been of minor importance in 1959. Short-term capital transactions in capital stock were listed on only one-third of returns reporting sales of capital stock, and it seems probable that losses predominate among these under a tax structure that defers realization of gains for six months.

[10] One scrap of evidence on this point is given by a survey of 199 income recipients with incomes over $20,000 in 1959-60. In the first half of 1960, 64 percent reported stock transactions. Another survey shows only 48 percent of all stockholders effecting transactions in the entire year, 1959. (G. Katona and G. B. Lansing, "The Wealth of the Wealthy," *Review of Economics and Statistics*, Vol. XLVI, No. 1 [February 1964], p. 11.)

$500,000. The ratio of gains to gross sales (available from Table 14) shows the top groups gaining 70-80 percent on sales compared to less than 20 percent for the low income groups. These exceptional trading successes by the top income groups help account for their receiving only about 40 percent of their income from stock as dividends, compared to 80 percent for low incomes. Despite these qualifications, the sharpness of the contrast of a dividend-capital gain ratio of four for low incomes against only two-thirds for high incomes is rather impressive, although by no means conclusive, evidence.[11]

Stock Ownership Concentration and Dividend Policy

A preference for low-payout stocks by high-income groups could also be expected to produce an inverse relationship between firm payout ratios and the degree of concentration of shareholdings. High-income shareholders will generally hold relatively large blocks of stock, and if they prefer low-payout securities, this should be revealed in a relatively high concentration of ownership of such securities. In a crude test of this hypothesis, data collected by W. L. Crum[12] were used to derive rough measures of the degree of concentration of shareholdings of eighteen firms in late 1951.[13] The Spearman coefficient of rank correlation between the estimated Pareto concentration measure and the 1951 payout ratio was 0.33. This represents the expected negative association since the Pareto measure is related inversely to the degree of concentration. Although the correlation is weak, it is significant at the 10 percent

[11] For some (inconclusive) evidence of preference by top income groups for low-dividend securities, see T. R. Atkinson, *The Pattern of Financial Ownership, Wisconsin Individuals, 1949* (New York: National Bureau of Economic Research, 1956), pp. 130-31. Dividend yield on traded stock declined as incomes rose, but not at high income levels. Unfortunately dividend yield is measured in relation to stock price rather than gains.

[12] W. L. Crum, "Analysis of Stock Ownership," *Harvard Business Review,* Vol. XXXI, No. 3 (May-June 1953), pp. 36-54.

[13] The concentration measure used was Pareto's α estimated on the basis of the relative frequency of shareholdings of 100 shares or more and 1,000 shares or more, respectively. The concentration slopes varied from 0.96 (high concentration) for Crucible Steel to 1.73 (low concentration) for American Telephone and Telegraph. The other firms for which this measure could be derived from Crum's data were Anaconda, Atlas Powder, Bell Aircraft, Borg-Warner, Goodyear, Inspiration Copper, Jones and Laughlin, National Gypsum, Packard, Parke Davis, Remington Rand, Tidewater Associates, Southern California Edison, Eastman Kodak, American Home Products, and U. S. Steel.

level on the one-tail test. The hypothesis that investors seeking a tax shelter might be more closely oriented to the ratio of dividends per share to stock price than to the payout ratio was also tested. The correlation of the dividend-price ratio with concentration produced a rank coefficient of 0.69. This result is easily significant at the one-tenth of one percent level.

Edwin Cox obtained similar results in an analysis of dividend payments and concentration of ownership measured by holdings of large stockholders.[14] For a cross-section of 31 firms, he correlated the payout ratio with the percentage of shares held by the top 5 percent of the stockholders, and found weak negative association. He also found strong negative association between these concentration measures and the dividend yield (dividend-price ratio). However, Cox attributes this to a preference for high dividend yield on the part of individuals who tend to have smaller holdings than other holders of record. While this is a plausible factor, some large holders such as nonprofit institutions may also prefer high dividend yield since they have no taxes to avoid.

The Cox hypothesis is essentially that his "percent of shares held by individuals" is the variable that has the basic association with dividend yield. This is undoubtedly a partial explanation of the strong negative association of dividend yield and concentration. However, it does not displace the shelter hypothesis. On the assumption that his rank correlation coefficients[15] are a fair approximation of the Pearson coefficients in this sample of 31, the partial correlation between dividend yield and concentration (given the degree of individual participation) may be estimated at $-.70$. If this coefficient is approximately correct, it indicates that even after individual participation has explained what it can of dividend yield variations, about one-half the residual variance can still be explained by concentration. The inference remains that the association of high concentration with low dividend yield is attributable, at least in part, to the desire of upper bracket investors for tax shelter through low-yield securities.

[14] Edwin B. Cox, *Trends in the Distribution of Stock Ownership* (University of Pennsylvania Press, 1963), p. 88.

[15] They are $-.78$ between dividend yield and concentration, $+.62$ between dividend yield and individual participation and $-.93$ between concentration and individual participation. (Cox, *op. cit.*, pp. 84, 88, 89.) The raw data and Pearsonian coefficients are not presented.

Derivation and Measurement
of the Tax Shelter Variable

A measure of the incentive to retain profits is necessary to test the association between dividends and individual tax rates. One such measure is based on the hypothesis that firms try to maximize the value of stockholders' future after-tax returns. Assuming equal tax rates for all shareholders, Myron Gordon derived an optimum payout ratio inversely dependent upon the ratio of individual tax rates on ordinary income to rates on capital gains (t_y/t_g).[16] The direction of the hypothetical association is in accord with the hypothesis of this study, and t_y/t_g was one of the measures used in the model.

From the point of view of relative demand of high-income security holders for low dividend stocks, it is appropriate instead to measure shareholder incentive to hold low payout securities. Martin Bailey derived the simple difference $(t_y - t_g)$ as a measure of this shelter effect.[17] A third measure might be $(1 - t_g)/(1 - t_y)$, the ratio of disposable income per dollar of capital gains to disposable income per dollar of other income.[18] Each of these three measures of the differential was tested in the model, and was expected to be inversely related to the payout ratio.

[16] Myron J. Gordon, *The Investment, Financing and Valuation of the Corporation* (R. D. Irwin, 1962), pp. 131-39.

[17] *Capital Gains and Income Taxation* (unpublished paper).

[18] Assume that the expected gross rate of return is r_y on assets yielding ordinary income and r_g on assets yielding capital gains. The tax rates on the two types of income are t_y and t_g, respectively. The third measure of the shelter effect may be derived on the assumption of equal risks associated with the two types of investment. If the expected pre-tax yield rates r_y and r_g (discounted) are different, an investor with a given amount to invest will be in equilibrium and indifferent between the two types of investment if $(1 - t_y)r_y = (1 - t_g)r_g$, or when $r_y/r_g = (1 - t_g)/(1 - t_y)$. If tax rates are changed so that $(1 - t_g)/(1 - t_y)$ increases, marginal investors will wish to substitute capital gains for ordinary income, with the equilibrium condition being restored by a resulting fall in the yield on capital gains assets relative to the yield on assets producing ordinary income. The ratio $(1 - t_g)/(1 - t_y)$ thus appears to be a plausible measure of investor incentive to seek a tax shelter via capital gains and a lower payout ratio. The same shelter measure can also be derived without the equal risk assumption. The equal sign in the equilibrium condition is replaced by an inequality but the relevant tax ratio is the same.

Additional methodological issues are involved in the actual measurement of t_y and t_g. In the first place, dividends may respond to changes in statutory rates or effective rates, or both. The former abstracts from income effects, while the latter is subject to the additional influence of changes in income levels and distribution. In a comment on a preliminary report on this study, Lintner suggested statutory rates were more relevant, objecting to "a variable which confounds changes in tax laws with the very different phenomenon of changing income distributions."[19] However, from a behavioral point of view, it appears unlikely that corporate decision-makers react differently to (1) a rise in effective marginal tax rates originating in a rise in incomes, and (2) an increase following a change in the rate structure, assuming they are equally aware of each. If they are seeking to provide a shelter, the reason for the rise in effective rates appears irrelevant, except possibly with respect to the intensity of the reaction of those being taxed.[20]

Lintner did not rule out the income effect altogether, noting that "there is interview evidence of the relevance of a company's judgments of income levels of its shareholders in fixing targets,"[21] but he regarded these as "rather static judgments." However, it is difficult to believe that companies taking account of stockholder income levels at one time would fail to consider the increase in effective tax rates during the sharp rise in incomes beginning with the war. It may be that the income effects are relatively small because of the great breadth of many income tax brackets. If so, the issue becomes academic.[22] In any case, effective rates were stressed

---

[19] John Lintner, "Problems in Taxation—Discussion," *American Economic Review*, Vol. 54, No. 3 (May 1964), p. 304.

[20] A rise in effective rates along with higher disposable income may seem less painful than higher tax rates on given incomes. On the other hand, there is a sense in which the effective rate may understate the effect of tax increases. If a high-income individual reacts to tax increases by making higher deductible charitable contributions, the measured rise in his effective rate will be held down. However, the bite of the higher taxes which moved him to greater deductions is not really escaped by such a device as it may well be by shifting toward capital gains income.

[21] *Ibid.*, p. 304.

[22] By similar reasoning, another methodological problem was dismissed as academic. The payout ratio itself affects incomes and, therefore, influences the tax variables being used to explain the ratio itself. Presumably this reverse relationship is minor.

in this study, but as a check some tests were also carried out with statutory rates.

Another measurement problem is the choice of single time series to represent t_y and t_g. Perhaps a series showing annual weighted average marginal rates on dividend income and on capital gains income would be the most appropriate. Such a measure of t_y, for example, would show the tax saving for shareholders as a whole attainable by a uniform percentage cut in dividends. On the other hand, the tax rates on very high income groups may be of greater significance because of special influence of these groups on corporate policy. For this reason, and for simplicity, an alternative to the over-all marginal rate was adopted.

In order to abstract as far as possible from inflationary effects, tax rates were not measured for a specific, constant income group. Instead, the income level used to measure taxes was allowed to vary from year to year. This varying income level was derived from time series showing the proportionate share of dividends received by income groups.[23] Cumulating the share of dividends for the highest income groups downward, the income level was derived for each year such that 10 percent of all dividends received accrued to income recipients above that level. This was an attempt to standardize the income base so as to permit annual measurement of tax rates for taxpayers at a given rank in the dividend distribution structure. Similar income series were also derived which cut off at the top of the income scale recipients of 25 percent and 50 percent, respectively, of all dividends received. The marginal values of t_y and t_g for certain family structures at these three different income levels[24] were then estimated, and the resulting time series were used as explanatory variables. To minimize the risk that the outcome of the statistical analysis could be determined by an arbitrary

[23] Daniel Holland, *Dividends Under the Income Tax* (New York: National Bureau of Economic Research, 1962), pp. 40-41. The derivation of the tax series is more fully explained in Appendix B.

[24] The family of four was stressed as a large and typical group, but at these high income levels the number of exemptions makes little difference in the trends of tax rates. Special adjustments were made, however, to take account of the major impact of income splitting beginning with 1948 (see Appendix B).

CHART 4. Measures of Marginal Statutory Individual Tax Rates on Ordinary Income, Family of Four, 1920–60[a]

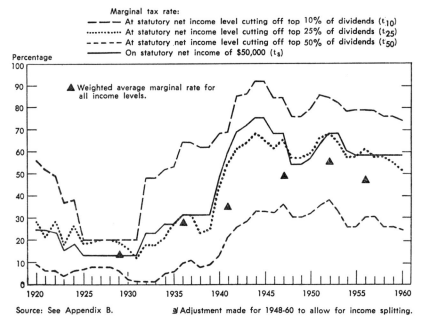

Source: See Appendix B.   [a] Adjustment made for 1948-60 to allow for income splitting.

selection of one of these measures, the three different tax rate series, for both ordinary income and capital gains taxes, were tested in the models. In addition, the marginal statutory rates for a family of four with statutory net income of $50,000 were used as the basis for a fourth measure of the tax differential. As might have been expected, the four series are closely correlated as illustrated in Chart 4. The four series for tax rates on ordinary income, labeled t_{10}, t_{25}, t_{50}, and t_s, show a downward trend in the twenties, a rise through World War II, and a slight decline since then.

Testing the Tax Shelter Variables

Since no unique measure of either the tax shelter factor or depreciation liberality can be established as the correct one, many alternative combinations of measures were used in the payout models.

Preliminary Tests of Different Measures

The basic Lintner model was generalized by substituting a target function for the target payout ratio in addition to using alternate income measures in place of the basic net profits series. Designating the shelter variable as T_i, the original relation (2-2) is revised to read:

(4-1) $D - D_{-1} = a + c[(\alpha + \beta T_i)Y - D_{-1}]$

Multiplying out the expression yields dividend change as a function of three variables:

(4-2) $D - D_{-1} = a + b_1 Y + b_2 T_i Y - c D_{-1}$

About twenty different pairs of income measures and shelter variables for the corporate aggregate were tested in relation (4-2) and about twenty more pairs for manufacturing. In all cases, the shelter variable carried the expected negative coefficient and was highly significant, with ratios of regression coefficients to standard errors that ranged from -2.50 to -4.22. The equations containing the capital gains factor gave a generally poorer performance than those excluding it.[25] This suggests that the tax rate on ordinary income alone is as good an explanatory factor as the more complex measures of the differential between income and capital gains taxes. The surprising nature of this result prompted further tests in which various measures of t_y and t_g were included separately. In all tests t_y carried the explanatory weight, and in no case did t_g demonstrate any significance; in most cases, its inclusion reduced $\bar{R}^2$.

The explanatory impotence of capital gains tax rates may reflect economic reality. It is possible that individuals and corporate officials who think in terms of tax avoidance via low payout may be unconcerned with the tax bite attending ultimate realization. They may think of retention as providing a tax shelter indefinitely for the common savings of shareholders. The capital gains tax itself can be deferred indefinitely if realization is avoided. Certainly most wealth-holders who plan to pass the securities to heirs know that the tax can be avoided completely. In fact, a study by Martin Bailey shows that in practice the tax is deferred indefinitely on a large

[25] This is true whether the criterion applied is $\bar{R}^2$, the beta coefficients, or the t-ratios.

fraction of capital gains, since about 80 percent is not realized.[26] Insofar as these considerations are operative, the level of ordinary rates becomes the basic factor in measuring the incentive to forego current income for the sake of tax avoidance. On the other hand, the failure of the capital gains variable may result from statistical difficulties. The t_g series is more stable than t_y, and this may make the influence of capital gains rates more difficult to establish statistically, but does not prove it to be nonexistent. In any case, it seemed appropriate and convenient to downgrade t_g and rely primarily on ordinary income tax rates as a measure of the incentive to provide or seek tax shelter through retention.[27]

Results of Including a Tax Shelter Variable

To show the explanatory gain achieved through generalization of the model, the two equations from each sector with the highest adjusted coefficient of determination $\bar{R}^2$ are given below.[28] Measuring the constant term in billions of dollars and the tax variable in decimal form, the two equations for the corporate aggregate are:

$$(4\text{-}3) \qquad D - D_{-1} = .47 + (.198 - .096t_{10})C - .430D_{-1}$$
$$\qquad\qquad\qquad\; (.11) \quad (.020) \quad (.019) \qquad\quad (.042)$$

$$\bar{R}^2 = .814 \qquad \text{D-W} = 1.75 \qquad r_t = .460 - .224t_{10}$$

$$(4\text{-}4) \qquad D - D_{-1} = .15 + (.240 - .179t_{25})P_2 - .200D_{-1}$$
$$\qquad\qquad\qquad\; (.11) \quad (.026) \quad (.041) \qquad\quad (.028)$$

$$\bar{R}^2 = .810 \qquad \text{D-W} = 1.82 \qquad r_t = 1.198 - .894t_{25}$$

For manufacturing the equations are:

$$(4\text{-}5) \qquad D - D_{-1} = .23 + (.188 - .097t_{25})C - .455D_{-1}$$
$$\qquad\qquad\qquad\; (.06) \quad (.022) \quad (.030) \qquad\quad (.046)$$

$$\bar{R}^2 = .785 \qquad \text{D-W} = 1.78 \qquad r_t = .413 - .213t_{25}$$

$$(4\text{-}6) \qquad D - D_{-1} = .18 + (.211 - .134t_{25})P_3 - .334D_{-1}$$
$$\qquad\qquad\qquad\; (.06) \quad (.025) \quad (.038) \qquad\quad (.038)$$

$$\bar{R}^2 = .782 \qquad \text{D-W} = 1.95 \qquad r_t = .632 - .401t_{25}$$

[26] Bailey, *op. cit.*

[27] Some additional tests of the capital gains factor were carried out, especially for the industries and firms reported in Chapters VI and VII. Capital gains rates were never found to make any explanatory contribution.

[28] These are chosen for summary purposes with no implication that they are significantly better than all others. The Durbin-Watson statistic was not considered, because it was satisfactory in all cases.

Cash flow continues to give the best explanation of dividends, but the corrected profit series do practically as well. These equations, based on cash flow and utilizing shelter variables, may be compared to results for the Lintner model for the entire period and for that model with cash flow substituted for profits. The generalization in (4-3) reduces the unexplained variance of the Lintner model by 53 percent; the addition of the shelter variable alone improves the simple cash flow model by reducing unexplained variation 43 percent. The corresponding improvements in manufacturing by (4-5) are 42 percent and 24 percent, respectively.[29] The income variables in the four equations (4-3) to (4-6) are factored out to show the estimated short-run propensity to distibute in each case; these propensities now vary with individual tax rates. The implied long-run target functions (obtained by division by the speed-of-adjustment coefficient) are also given for each equation and designated as r_t. The Durbin-Watson statistics of the four equations are consistently higher than for the simple models, and the evidence of autocorrelated errors has largely disappeared.

In the 1942-60 estimates of Chapter III, substitution of better income measures was found to reduce the residual variance by about 50 percent, but as shown in Table 13, this was not true for the entire 1920-60 period. The extent to which addition of the shelter variable has improved the ability of a single equation to explain both the first and second halves is shown by the covariance tests reported below:

	Coefficient of Determination			Standard Error of Estimate[a]			F
	1920–60	1920–41	1942–60	1920–60	1920–41	1942–60	Ratio
(4–3)	.829	.860	.801	.243	.230	.220	1.24
(4–4)	.826	.866	.768	.246	.225	.237	1.00
(4–5)	.803	.845	.795	.150	.130	.148	1.20
(4–6)	.800	.817	.793	.151	.141	.149	.62

[a] In billions of dollars.

[29] Using $\bar{R}^2$ as the criterion to allow for the degree of freedom lost with the addition of the shelter variable, the four percentage gains cited above become 51 and 41 for all corporations and 40 and 22 for manufacturing.

In all four cases, the standard errors of estimate for 1920-60 are somewhat higher than those for either the 1920-41 period or the 1942-60 period. However, the discrepancies between the standard errors for the whole period and for the first and second halves are much smaller than those for the simple models shown in Table 13. In addition, the F ratios for equations (4-3) to (4-6) are remarkably low compared to those for the simple models, and they fall far short of the 2.69 figure required for significance at the 5 percent level. Thus, generalization of the payout model to allow for the effect of changing individual tax rates provides a statistical explanation of the entire 1920-60 period not significantly inferior to its separate explanations of the first (low-tax) period and the second (high-tax) period. This does not, of course, prove that the tax shelter models are correct or complete. However, the contrast between the strong evidence of structural change in the simple models and the lack of such evidence in the models containing the tax factor is impressive.

The regression analysis also showed that the various measures of tax rates on ordinary income performed about equally well. The shelter effect was clearly discernible whether it was measured by the statutory rate series t_s (rates on \$50,000 incomes), or by effective rates t_{10}, t_{25}, and t_{50}. These last three series embody income change effects as well as statutory rate changes, but the high correlation of all four series led to roughly equal explanatory performances.

Equations (4-3) and (4-4) provide a preliminary explanation of the major decline in the aggregate payout ratio between the late twenties and the postwar period. The actual dividend-cash flow ratio dropped from 48 percent to 27 percent between 1929 and 1947. According to the target function in (4-3), the tax rate factor accounted for most of this by calling for a 15-point drop in the target ratio in the interval. The target ratio of 1960 was still 30 percent below the 1929 level, implying that the target level of dividends was \$5-\$6 billion below what it would have been at 1929 individual tax rates. The dividend-corrected profits ratio declined from 75 percent in 1929 to 42 percent in 1947. This is more than accounted for by relation (4-4) which shows tax rates depressing this long-run payout propensity by 42 percentage points. The trend in manufacturing dividends in this period can be similarly explained.

The Combined Influence of Depreciation and Tax Rates

When the shelter variable was added, the cash flow income variable generally gave the best explanation of dividends for 1920-60, although its advantage over corrected profits was slight. Models with shelter functions applied to uncorrected net profits also performed reasonably well according to their coefficients of determination $\overline{R}^2$. This suggests that further tests of the influence of depreciation liberality on dividends are called for.

Tests of Models with Both Variables

Indexes of depreciation liberality developed in Chapter III were included explicitly along with the shelter variable in the target function which was applied to the net profits income variable. Some of the results are recorded in Table 15.

The t-ratios show the shelter variables to have about the same explanatory importance as in models (4-3) to (4-6) without explicit depreciation. In the case of all corporations, a rise of one standard deviation in any shelter variable produces a fall of one standard deviation or more in the dividend change variable. The shelter coefficients range from 3.63 to 5.35 times their standard errors and are highly significant in all cases. The performances of the explicit depreciation variables are somewhat less striking, but they are generally significant at the 5 percent level or better. Despite the loss of an additional degree of freedom, each adjusted coefficient of determination $\overline{R}^2$ showed improvement over that for the corresponding equation using net profits and a shelter variable but no depreciation index.[30]

Since the target percentages of Table 15 all relate to the same income base, net profits P, they are comparable from equation to equation and can be compared to the observed payout percentages.

[30] The Durbin-Watson statistics of Table 15 are also further improved, tending to be higher and all falling in the range 1.80-2.09.

All of the equations show 1920-29, 1929-47, and 1947-60 trends in payout policy in the same direction as the observed changes, except for three of the capital gains models that behaved perversely in the 1920-29 interval. The theoretical target ratios account for the halving of the observed over-all payout ratio between 1929 and 1947 when tax rates rose and depreciation became less liberal. The models explained the 43 percent decline in the manufacturing payout ratio in the same interval even more effectively, with all ratios showing a theoretical decline in the neighborhood of 40 percent. The sharp 1947-60 recovery of the aggregate and manufacturing payout ratios was also well accounted for by all of these tax models.

The level of the estimated target percentages is implausibly high (especially for 1929 and 1947) in the models that rely on the depreciation variable A_1 for all corporations. As shown in Table 6, this depreciation series is the one which made the smallest downward adjustment in the growth rate of depreciation indicated by actual charges. Its poorer $\overline{R}^2$ performance and unrealistic target ratios parallel the 1942-60 result for the basic Lintner model, which sought to explain rising dividend-profits ratios as a continually failing effort to reach excessively high target ratios. Again it appears that the series with the slowest upward postwar trend in depreciation provides the poorest explanation of dividends.

Selection of Depreciation-Shelter Models

To summarize the influence of tax and depreciation factors on dividends three equations were selected to represent all corporations and three for manufacturing. The equations with the two highest $\overline{R}^2$ were chosen, since they also had plausible target ratios. Both were based on the tax variable t_{25}, and the depreciation variables were A/P and A/N (the ratio of actual depreciation charges to net assets). The third best fit for all corporations was by the model combining t_{25} and A/A_2. This was chosen so that one independent estimate of depreciation could be represented. The same pair of variables was used in the third equation for manufacturing. These depreciation measures are similar, though not identical.

TABLE 15. Summary Results for Regression Models Including Both Depreciation Liberality and Shelter Variables with Net Profits, 1920–60 (Excluding 1936–38)

Combination of Variables[a]		Coefficient Measures[b]				Adjusted Coefficient of Determination ($\bar{R}^2$)	Durbin-Watson Statistic (D-W)	Target Percentages[c]			
Tax Shelter	Depreciation Liberality	Shelter		Depreciation				1920	1929	1947	1960
		Beta	t	Beta	t						
All Corporations											
								(64)	(71)	(36)	(62)
t_{10} and:	A/P	−1.42	−4.70	.93	3.83	.803	1.88	52	66	38	62
	A/N[d]	−1.44	−4.68	1.41	3.67	.798	1.86	46	60	35	58
	A/A₁	−1.43	−4.20	1.41	2.20	.752	1.80	67	88	47	63
t_{25} and:	A/P	−1.49	−5.24	.70	2.96	.821	1.94	66	71	40	66
	A/N[d]	−1.52	−5.35	1.07	2.94	.820	1.95	62	67	38	63
	A/A₁	−1.58	−5.22	1.02	1.73	.792	1.91	87	96	49	70
	A/A₂	−1.29	−4.20	.91	2.84	.818	1.91	68	85	42	68
t_s and:	A/A₁	−1.24	−4.37	1.43	2.26	.759	1.91	78	85	45	62
	A/A₂	−.99	−3.85	1.18	3.80	.807	1.96	57	78	38	63
t_{25}/g_{25} and:	A/A₁	−1.68	−4.17	1.02	1.59	.751	1.87	84	72	44	63
	A/A₂	−1.36	−3.63	1.08	3.35	.800	1.95	63	67	37	63
$\dfrac{1-g_{25}}{1-t_{25}}$ and:	A/P	−1.53	−4.65	.52	2.00	.802	1.85	66	65	38	65
	A/A₂	−1.37	−4.03	.83	2.48	.812	1.91	64	73	39	67

94

Manufacturing Corporations

								(55)	(63)	(34)	(58)
t_{10} and:	A/P	−1.16	−3.17	.85	3.47	.779	1.93	46	57	36	55
	A/N[d]	−1.05	−2.84	1.27	3.48	.780	1.96	38	54	34	50
	A/A_3	−1.16	−2.89	1.02	2.14	.736	1.84	53	68	40	52
	A/A_4	−1.07	−2.69	.80	2.44	.745	1.82	50	73	41	54
t_{25} and:	A/P	−1.25	−3.54	.66	2.66	.791	2.04	55	60	37	57
	A/N[d]	−1.20	−3.39	1.04	2.84	.797	2.09	49	58	36	53
	A/A_3	−1.38	−3.75	.78	1.72	.768	2.02	66	73	42	57
	A/A_4	−1.30	−3.50	.63	1.96	.773	2.01	64	77	42	58
t_{50} and:	A/P	−.82	−2.64	.54	1.89	.763	1.99	54	57	37	56
t_s and:	A/A_3	−.96	−2.89	1.03	2.16	.736	1.94	58	65	39	51
	A/A_4	−.92	−2.87	.85	2.64	.751	1.96	56	71	40	54
t_{25}/g_{25} and:	A/A_3	−1.31	−2.98	.81	1.68	.739	1.97	63	57	39	52
	A/A_4	−1.29	−3.08	.77	2.39	.759	2.02	60	62	39	54
$\dfrac{1-g_{25}}{1-t_{25}}$ and:	A/A_3	−1.40	−3.75	.70	1.53	.768	2.07	62	62	38	56
	A/A_4	−1.34	−3.58	.61	1.91	.776	2.07	60	66	38	57

[a] For definition of shelter variables, see pp. 86-7 and Appendix B; for definition of depreciation variables, see Table 6, Chapter III and Appendix A.
[b] The beta-coefficient is the regression coefficient that would have been obtained if the measurement of each variable had been standardized by division of each observation by the standard deviation of the variable. The t-ratios are ratios of regression coefficients to their standard errors.
[c] Figures in parentheses are the observed payout percentages for these years.
[d] Net assets.

The three equations for the corporate aggregate are:

(4-7) $D - D_{-1} = .27 + (.219 + .067A/P - .180t_{25})P - .305D_{-1}$
            $(.14)\ (.023)\ (.023)\quad\quad (.034)\quad\quad (.054)$

   $\bar{R}^2 = .821\quad D\text{-}W = 1.94\quad r_t = .717 + .221A/P - .591t_{25}$

(4-8) $D - D_{-1} = .38 + (.170 + 2.11A/N - .183t_{25})P - .266D_{-1}$
            $(.17)\ (.029)\ (.72)\quad\quad (.034)\quad\quad (.043)$

   $\bar{R}^2 = .820\quad D\text{-}W = 1.95\quad r_t = .641 + 7.95A/N - .690t_{25}$

(4-9) $D - D_{-1} = .18 + (.150 + .082A/A_2 - .156t_{25})P - .220D_{-1}$
            $(.12)\ (.035)\ (.029)\quad\quad (.037)\quad\quad (.032)$

   $\bar{R}^2 = .818\quad D\text{-}W = 1.91\quad r_t = .682 + .374A/A_2 - .707t_{25}$

The equations for manufacturing were:

(4-10) $D - D_{-1} = .17 + (.217 + .080A/P - .150t_{25})P - .370D_{-1}$
             $(.08)\ (.028)\ (.030)\quad\quad (.043)\quad\quad (.061)$

   $\bar{R}^2 = .791\quad D\text{-}W = 2.04\quad r_t = .587 + .217A/P - .407t_{25}$

(4-11) $D - D_{-1} = .23 + (.160 + 2.17A/N - .144t_{25})P - .324D_{-1}$
             $(.09)\ (.037)\ (.76)\quad\quad (.042)\quad\quad (.045)$

   $\bar{R}^2 = .797\quad D\text{-}W = 2.09\quad r_t = .495 + 6.69A/N - .445t_{25}$

(4-12) $D - D_{-1} = .08 + (.178 + .048A/A_4 - .156t_{25})P - .261D_{-1}$
             $(.07)\ (.039)\ (.025)\quad\quad (.045)\quad\quad (.036)$

   $\bar{R}^2 = .773\quad D\text{-}W = 2.01\quad r_t = .683 + .185A/A_4 - .598t_{25}$

The first equation in each set shows why explicit inclusion of depreciation improves slightly the simpler model based on cash flow and the shelter variable. By combining net profits P and depreciation A into one variable, cash flow C,[31] the latter model requires their coefficients to be the same in any given year.[32] In model (4-7) the coefficient for A is $+.067$ and that for P is $+.219 -.180t_{25}$. During the low-tax period this variable coefficient for P was as high as $+.197$; even during 1942-60, when taxes were relatively high, the coefficient of net profits ranged from $+.097$ to $+.126$ and was always higher than the depreciation coefficient.

[31] This model for all corporations produced a lower $\bar{R}^2$ of 0.802.

[32] The coefficient of C varies over time with the shelter variable, but in any given year the same coefficient applies to both P and A if they are listed separately in the model.

CHART 5. Target Payout Percentages Estimated by Three Regressions, and Selected Observed Percentages, 1920–60

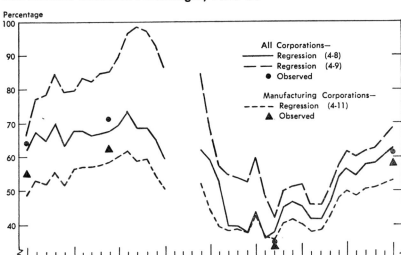

This again suggests tentatively that the truth is somewhere in between the net profit shelter model and the cash flow shelter model. Taking account of depreciation improves the explanation of dividends, but the marginal propensity to pay (short-run and long-run) appears higher for measured net profits than for depreciation. The model says that if P is stable, the short-run and long-run marginal propensities to pay dividends out of income against which depreciation is charged are 6.7 percent and 22 percent, respectively.[33]

The changing long-run payout ratios implied by equations (4-8), (4-9), and (4-11) are plotted in Chart 5. The manufacturing target ratios tend to be slightly lower than those for the aggregate (as expected from the lower actual payout), and models (4-9) has produced unrealistically high target percentages, but the patterns over time are remarkably similar.

Also included in the chart are the observed ratios for the four years best describing the main trends in payout policy.[34] These fol-

---

[33] Measured net profits can only be stable with a rise in A if gross profits rise. The model says that even if any such rise in the gross is offset by a rise in A so that the net remains stable, dividends will still tend to rise.

[34] The four years selected represent in sequence a long-term low, a high, a low and a high in the payment ratio (after exclusion of the erratic or negative ratios appearing in 1921 and the thirties).

TABLE 16. Decomposition of Changes in Target Payout Percentages into Contributions by Depreciation Index and Tax Shelter Variables, 1929–47 and 1947–60[a]

Change in Target Payout Percentage	Model Used					
	All Corporations			Manufacturing Corporations		
	(4–7)	(4–8)	(4–9)	(4–10)	(4–11)	(4–12)
Contribution by:			1929-47			
Depreciation index (A_L)	− 4	+ 2	−10	− 4	− 2	− 7
Tax shelter (t_{25})	−28	−32	−33	−19	−21	−28
1929–47 Change in payout	−32	−30	−43	−23	−23	−35
Contribution by:			1947-60			
Depreciation index (A_L)	+18	+16	+16	+14	+11	+ 8
Tax shelter (t_{25})	+ 8	+ 9	+10	+ 6	+ 6	+ 8
1947–60 Change in payout	+26	+25	+26	+20	+17	+16

[a] Derived from Table 15. The target changes in this table may disagree slightly with those indicated in Table 15 because of rounding.

low very closely models (4-8) and (4-11), which measure depreciation liberality by the ratio of charges to net assets (A/N). The aggregate payout ratios are lower than the theoretical targets in (4-9), but changes in these observed ratios are reasonably consistent with that model.

Separate Influence of Variables

Table 16 decomposes the two main trends in the theoretical target payout ratios of relations (4-7) to (4-12) into the separate contributions of the depreciation and tax shelter variables. The three equations in each set suggest the same explanation of the major trends in dividend policy since World War I. The 1929-47 reduction in payout was almost exclusively associated with higher tax rates which depressed the target ratio for all corporations about 30 percentage points.[35] Most of the subsequent 1947-60 recovery can be credited to liberalized depreciation, but tax rates also made a contribution. In fact, these models suggest that tax rates were the

[35] Models (4-9) and (4-12) show appreciable negative effect from less liberal depreciation, but it is minor compared to the tax effect.

stronger factor over the entire period. According to the target functions in both (4-8) and (4-9), the most extreme tax rate change (which was between 1931 and 1951) contributed a net depressing effect of about 40 percentage points.

Assuming actual payout tends to follow the targets, aggregate dividend payments were about $5-$6 billion lower in 1947 than they would have been under 1929 tax and depreciation conditions. Then, with liberalization, dividends paid out of given net profits were $5-$6 billion higher in 1960 than they would have been under the 1947 tax and depreciation structure. Since various measures of depreciation liberalization, tax rates, and the tax differential have produced similar results, it is probably safe to conclude that these findings are independent of the specific method of measurement of those factors.

CHAPTER V

Other Factors in Corporate Dividend Policy

THE AGGREGATIVE TIME SERIES analysis of two major features of tax policy—depreciation liberality and individual tax rates—has supported the hypothesis that these two factors influence dividend policy. The model invites further elaboration, however. Many other possible influences on the payout ratio suggest themselves, and statistical tests of their impact would be of interest. Moreover, there is the possibility that further generalization of the model may either enhance the credibility of the two tax factors or downgrade their indicated influence. The tax variables gain credibility if they remain significant in the presence of competitive explanatory variables. As Theil says:

The mere fact that a certain "maintained" hypothesis can be excluded raises the plausibility of its rivals. This can be compared to a large extent with the function of standard errors of parameter estimates. Just as the standard errors contribute to an appraisal of numerical outcomes within a certain "maintained" hypothesis, in just the same way alternative analyses of separate "maintained" hypotheses contribute to an appraisal of the hypothesis which is finally preferred.[1]

[1] H. Theil, *Economic Forecasts and Policy* (Amsterdam: North-Holland Publishing Co., 1958), p. 207.

100

Even the tests of hypotheses that are rejected are reported in this chapter along with those judged successful.

Method of Analysis

It was assumed that the initial depreciation and tax hypotheses were sufficiently well established to warrant inclusion of these variables with the rivals to be tested here. If the depreciation and tax variables should turn out to be spuriously associated with dividends or merely a coincidental proxy for some other explanatory factor, inclusion of the true variable should destroy their statistical significance in the models. On the ground that practically every measure of depreciation liberality and individual tax rates tested earlier showed the expected association with dividends, a more restricted group of these different measures was used in further analysis.

Since this study is concerned with long-run relationships, in most of the analysis the new variables were tested as components of the long-run target function, rather than simply as linear additions to the model. Thus, the income variables are multiplied by the new variables as well as by tax rates and indexes of depreciation liberalization. However, supplementary tests of the same variables, inserted as separate linear terms, did not produce any markedly different results.

Factors that appear to have a significant impact will be discussed first. Perhaps more important in the present context are a few obvious candidates that failed and, in so doing, made the tax factors more credible; these will be discussed briefly later.

Growth Rates and Dividend Policy

An additional factor found to be associated with dividends is the change in sales. A two-year sales change variable has been suggested by Darling[2] on grounds that this variable would indicate anticipated working capital needs. An alternative, and perhaps more likely, rationale for the sales change variable is tied directly to the dividend decision. It is possible that a rapid increase in sales is a

[2] Paul G. Darling, "The Influence of Expectations and Liquidity on Dividend Policy," *Journal of Political Economy*, Vol. 65, No. 3 (June 1957), pp. 209-224.

TABLE 17. Regression Results for Models Including Sales Change Variable in Target Payout Function, 1920–60 (Excluding 1936–38)

(Constant term in billions of dollars)

Depreciation Index[a] (A_L)	Regression Coefficients[b]						Coefficient of Multiple Determination ($\bar{R}^2$)	Durbin-Watson Statistic (D-W)	Target Payout Percentage[c]			
	Constant Term (a)	Net Profits (P)	Depreciation Liberality ($A_L P$)	Tax Shelter ($t_{25}P$)	Sales Change ($S/S_{-2}P$)	Lagged Dividends (D_{-1})			1920	1929	1947	1960
All Corporations												
A/P	.33 (.13)	.287 (.034)	.056 (.022)	−.152 (.034)	−.066 (.026)	−.310 (.050)	.846	1.97	(64) 58	(71) 68	(36) 35	(62) 62
A/N[d]	.42 (.16)	.246 (.041)	1.75 (.68)	−.155 (.034)	−.065 (.026)	−.276 (.040)	.845	1.95	55	65	33	60
A/A$_2$	.24 (.12)	.230 (.048)	.064 (.028)	−.136 (.036)	−.062 (.027)	−.234 (.031)	.839	1.94	59	80	36	64
Manufacturing Corporations												
A/P	.22 (.07)	.287 (.033)	.059 (.027)	−.116 (.039)	−.071 (.022)	−.371 (.054)	.838	2.19	(55) 50	(63) 57	(34) 36	(58) 54
A/N[d]	.26 (.08)	.244 (.042)	1.58 (.70)	−.113 (.039)	−.070 (.022)	−.336 (.040)	.841	2.22	45	55	35	51
A/A$_4$	.17 (.06)	.260 (.040)	.040 (.021)	−.114 (.040)	−.078 (.022)	−.298 (.032)	.834	2.18	52	65	38	53

[a] For definition of these measures of depreciation liberalization, see Chapter III, Table 6.
[b] Figures in parentheses are standard errors of the coefficients.
[c] Figures in parentheses are observed payout percentages for these years.
[d] Net assets.

102

proxy for a rapid gain in earnings which firms may feel will not be maintained. This rate-of-change factor could encourage a lag in payout in addition to that described by the speed-of-adjustment coefficient c, or it could affect c itself. This behavioral hypothesis, like Darling's, implies a negative association of dividends with sales change. Whether firms expect to need funds or are merely cautious, they are likely to adopt a conservative dividend policy during a time of rapid growth.

Tests carried out in this study tend to confirm Darling's point that a one-year sales change is less influential than longer-run comparisons. Table 17 summarizes a sample of regression models with a two-year sales change variable included in the target function.[3] The coefficients for the sales change variable are significant. They differ from zero in the expected direction by more than two standard errors in the models for all corporations and by more than three standard errors in the manufacturing models. However, the depreciation and tax rate variables remain highly significant in these new equations.

A comparison with equations (4-7) to (4-12) in Chapter IV shows that the depreciation liberalization coefficients have been cut on the order of 20 percent with the addition of the sales change variable, but they are still positive by two to three standard errors. The tax rate coefficients for all corporations have been reduced about 15 percent and the manufacturing coefficients somewhat more. The target payout percentages in Table 17 are generally somewhat below the actual ratios, as expected. The changes between years rather closely follow the actual ratios, except in the case of the models based on the depreciation measure A_2.

Although sales change is a successful explanatory rival, it takes over only a small part of the credit earned by the tax variables. Table 18 decomposes the 1929-47 and 1947-60 changes in payout targets recorded in Table 17 into the separate contributions of the different variables. A comparison of these figures with Table 16 shows that the new results confirm the earlier ones in crediting most of the 1929-47 fall in the payout ratio to rising tax rates and the 1947-60 recovery mainly to liberalized depreciation. The data sup-

---

[3] The speed-of-adjustment coefficient c was also allowed to vary with sales change and other factors, but no significant results were obtained.

TABLE 18. Decomposition of Changes in Target Payout Percentages into Contributions by Depreciation Index, Tax Shelter, and Sales Change Variables, 1929–47 and 1947–60 (Excluding 1936–38)[a]

Change in Target Payout Percentage	Depreciation Index Used[b]					
	All Corporations			Manufacturing Corporations		
	A/P	A/N[c]	A/A₂	A/P	A/N[c]	A/A₄
			1929-47			
Contribution by:						
Depreciation index (A_L)	− 3	+ 2	− 7	− 3	− 1	− 5
Tax shelter (t_{25})	−23	−26	−27	−15	−16	−18
Sales change (S/S_{-2})	− 7	− 8	− 9	− 3	− 4	− 4
1929–47 Change in payout	−33	−32	−43	−21	−21	−27
			1947-60			
Contribution by:						
Depreciation index (A_L)	+15	+12	+12	+11	+ 8	+ 6
Tax shelter (t_{25})	+ 7	+ 8	+ 8	+ 4	+ 5	+ 5
Sales change (S/S_{-2})	+ 6	+ 7	+ 8	+ 3	+ 3	+ 4
1947–60 Change in payout	+28	+27	+28	+18	+16	+15

[a] Derived from Table 17. The target changes in this table may disagree slightly with those indicated in Table 17 because of rounding.
[b] For definition of these measures of depreciation liberalization, see Table 6.
[c] Net assets.

port the interpretation of growth rates as a factor modifying dividends in the short run. This growth rate variable, while significantly improving the overall fit, appears to have had less effect on long-run trends in payout policy.

Interest Rates and Dividend Policy

Another hypothesis given some support by the time series tests was that dividends would tend to be negatively associated with the cost of debt financing. Even if the dividend decision is the primary one, rising interest rates may tend to discourage dividends by making internal finance relatively more attractive. Supporters of the "availability" doctrine might also add that rising bond yields may cause lenders to ration funds and seek reduced risk by increasing restrictions on loans at given interest rates, resulting in greater reliance by corporations on internal finance.[4]

This hypothesis was tested for all corporations by including Moody's overall bond yield series based on thirty-eight industrials, thirty-two railroads, and forty public utilities in the aggregate target payout function, and including the series for industrials in the manufacturing models. A sample of results is shown in Table 19. The interest rate variable i was of at least marginal significance in most models, and it had the expected sign. It was most successful in the first model in the table, which is based on the A/P depreciation index. In this model, interest rates made substantial contributions to the explanation of trends in payout policy, as indicated in Table 20.

According to the models, low interest rates during the war and early postwar period worked against high tax rates to encourage dividends and high rates later partially counteracted the effect of rising depreciation. As a result, including interest rates in the target function substantially increases the coefficients for both the depreciation and the shelter variables. The statistical significance of depreciation was thereby increased, but there was no similar rise in the significance of the shelter variable. Since i and t_{25} were highly correlated (with a simple correlation coefficient of -0.83), the inclusion of interest rates raised the standard error of the shelter variable.[5]

Interest rates showed greater explanatory importance in cash flow models. This payout model was greatly improved by including this series along with the shelter variable in the target function applied to cash flow. This is shown in relations (5-1) and (5-2) for all corporations and for manufacturing respectively:

[4] An alternative hypothesis is that high interest rates call for high payout so that equity yield can compete with bond yield in the eyes of investors. However, this would require that investors fail to recognize the potential capital gains and tax advantages of high retention. In any case, no evidence of positive association was found.

[5] This negative association itself is of interest. Modern fiscal and monetary policies for stabilization and growth could be expected to produce positive association. If there were such a situation it was swamped and reversed by other (possibly fortuitous) factors. For example, during the war and early postwar periods of high taxes, interest rates were kept low in support of bond prices. The negative association could also result, in part, from a tendency for the two policy instruments to be viewed as substitutes.

TABLE 19. Regression Results for Models Including Interest Rate Variable in Target Payout Function, 1920–60 (Excluding 1936–38)

(Constant term in billions of dollars)

Depreciation Index[a] (A_L)	Regression Coefficients[b]						Coefficient of Multiple Determination ($\bar{R}^2$)	Durbin-Watson Statistic (D-W)	Target Payout Percentage[c]			
	Constant Term (a)	Net Profits (P)	Depreciation Liberality ($A_L P$)	Tax Shelter ($t_{25}P$)	Interest Rates[d] (iP)	Lagged Dividends (D_{-1})			1920	1929	1947	1960
All Corporations												
A/P	.25 (.13)	.332 (.057)	.099 (.026)	−.283 (.058)	−.173 (.081)	−.328 (.052)	.838	2.06	(64) 51	(71) 72	(36) 38	(62) 65
A/A₂	.13 (.13)	.205 (.053)	.102 (.032)	−.216 (.056)	−.109 (.078)	−.206 (.033)	.823	1.93	54	92	43	69
Manufacturing Corporations												
A/P	.14 (.08)	.310 (.063)	.111 (.035)	−.240 (.069)	−.145 (.089)	−.381 (.060)	.802	2.12	(55) 45	(63) 61	(34) 37	(58) 57
A/A₄	.06 (.08)	.208 (.063)	.054 (.026)	−.190 (.071)	−.052 (.085)	−.249 (.041)	.769	2.00	60	81	43	58

a For definition of these depreciation liberalization measures, see Table 6.
b Figures in parentheses are standard errors of the coefficients.
c Figures in parentheses are observed payout percentages.
d The interest rate variable is measured in units of ten percentage points each; for example, 5 percent is measured as 0.5.

TABLE 20. **Decomposition of Changes in Target Payout Percentages into Contributions by Depreciation Index, Tax Shelter, and Interest Rate Variables, 1929–47 and 1947–60 (Excluding 1936–38)**[a]

Change in Target Payout Percentage	Depreciation Index[b]			
	All Corporations		Manufacturing Corporations	
	A/P	A/A₂	A/P	A/A₄
1929-47				
Contribution by:				
Depreciation index (A$_L$)	− 5	−13	− 5	− 8
Tax shelter (t$_{25}$)	−40	−49	−30	−36
Interest rates (i)	+12	+12	+10	+ 6
1929–47 Change in payout	−33	−50	−25	−38
1947-60				
Contribution by:				
Depreciation index (A$_L$)	+24	+22	+19	+ 9
Tax shelter (t$_{25}$)	+12	+14	+ 9	+10
Interest rates (i)	−10	−10	− 7	− 4
1947–60 Change in payout	+26	+26	+21	+15

[a] Derived from Table 19. The target changes in this table may disagree slightly with those indicated in Table 19 because of rounding.
[b] For definition of these measures of depreciation liberalization, see Table 6.

$$(5\text{-}1) \quad D - D_{-1} = .21 + (.280 - .206t_{25} - .125i)C - .368D_{-1}$$
$$\phantom{(5\text{-}1) \quad D - D_{-1} = } (.12) \quad (.031) \quad (.033) \quad (.035) \quad (.039)$$

$$\overline{R}^2 = .854 \qquad D\text{-}W = 2.04 \qquad r_t = .760 - .558t_{25} - .340i$$

$$(5\text{-}2) \quad D - D_{-1} = .12 + (.271 - .182t_{25} - .111i)C - .407D_{-1}$$
$$\phantom{(5\text{-}2) \quad D - D_{-1} = } (.08) \quad (.038) \quad (.043) \quad (.043) \quad (.046)$$

$$\overline{R}^2 = .816 \qquad D\text{-}W = 2.12 \qquad r_t = .665 - .446t_{25} - .274i$$

The measure $\overline{R}^2$ for all corporations was raised from 0.785 to 0.854, and the interest rate coefficient is nearly 4 times its standard error. The coefficient for the shelter variable for all corporations was increased to six times its standard error, and the success of the cash flow model also confirms depreciation as an important factor.[6]

[6] The Durbin-Watson statistic showed no evidence of serial correlation in the errors which would give a downward bias to these standard errors. However, since use of the Durbin-Watson statistic is questionable in this context (as discussed in the technical note following Chapter II), another test for autocorrelation is applied to these equations and others tested for reliability on pp. 123-24.

TABLE 21. Decomposition of Changes in Target Payout Percentages for Models Based on Cash Flow into Contributions by Tax Shelter and Interest Rate Variables, 1929–47 and 1947–60 (Excluding 1936–38)

Target Payout Percentages and Changes	Model Used	
	All Corporations	Manufacturing Corporations
	(5–1)	(5–2)
Target payout percentage		
1929	48	44
1947	30	30
1960	31	31
1929-47		
Contribution by:		
Tax shelter (t_{25})	−26	−21
Interest rates (i)	+ 8	+ 7
1929–47 Change in payout	−18	−14
1947-60		
Contribution by:		
Tax shelter (t_{25})	+ 7	+ 6
Interest rates (i)	− 6	− 5
1947–60 Change in payout	+ 1	+ 1

Table 21 shows the change in implied target payout ratios and the separate contributions of the shelter and interest variables for the cash flow models. One reason the contributions shown in Table 20 tend to be larger than those in this table is that they apply to the smaller payout base, net profits, rather than to cash flow. Thus, the 26-point depression of payout by the tax shelter factor shown for the 1929-47 period in Table 21 is not necessarily less in impact than the 40-point magnitude indicated in Table 20.

On the whole, the evidence on the role of interest rates is mixed, and its importance varies with the models tested. This factor will be examined in greater detail later on the basis of industry and firm data. It may be concluded here, at least, that inclusion of interest rates in the models augments the indicated importance of tax rates, and (to a lesser extent) of depreciation.

Sales Change and Interest Rates in the Same Models

The conclusions concerning the impact of growth rates and interest rates hold to about the same degree when they are tested simultaneously. Equations (5-3) to (5-8) give results for this combination with varying measures of income. These models also include measures of all factors that were persistently significant. The results for all corporations are:

(5-3) $\quad D - D_{-1} = .31 + (.364 + .082A/P - .237t_{25} - .135i - .056S/S_{-2})P - .327D_{-1}$
$\qquad\qquad\quad (.13)\ (.056)\ (.026)\qquad (.059)\quad (.079)\ (.026)\qquad\qquad (.049)$

$\bar{R}^2 = .855 \qquad \text{D-W} = 2.10 \qquad r_t = 1.113 + .252A/P - .724t_{25} - .413i - .170S/S_{-2}$

(5-4) $\quad D - D_{-1} = .20 + (.260 + .079A/A_2 - .179t_{25} - .075i - .056S/S_{-2})P - .224D_{-1}$
$\qquad\qquad\quad (.13)\ (.057)\ (.032)\qquad (.057)\quad (.077)\ (.028)\qquad\qquad (.033)$

$\bar{R}^2 = .838 \qquad \text{D-W} = 1.96 \qquad r_t = 1.165 + .352A/A_2 - .802t_{25} - .336i - .252S/S_{-2}$

(5-5) $\qquad\quad D - D_{-1} = .29 + (.308 - .197t_{25} - .126i - .025S/S_{-2})C - .393D_{-1}$
$\qquad\qquad\qquad\quad (.13)\ (.036)\ (.033)\quad (.034)\ (.016)\qquad\qquad (.041)$

$\bar{R}^2 = .859 \qquad \text{D-W} = 2.04 \qquad r_t = .785 - .501t_{25} - .321i - .062S/S_{-2}$

The most general of the successful equations for manufacturing are:

(5-6) $\quad D - D_{-1} = .20 + (.350 + .083A/P - .183t_{25} - .105i - .067S/S_{-2})P - .379D_{-1}$
$\qquad\qquad\quad (.07)\ (.058)\ (.033)\qquad (.064)\quad (.080)\ (.022)\qquad\qquad (.053)$

$\bar{R}^2 = .842 \qquad \text{D-W} = 2.24 \qquad r_t = .923 + .218A/P - .484t_{25} - .278i - .176S/S_{-2}$

(5-7) $\quad D - D_{-1} = .15 + (.282 + .044A/A_4 - .140t_{25} - .041i - .078S/S_{-2})P - .289D_{-1}$
$\qquad\qquad\quad (.07)\ (.058)\ (.023)\qquad (.063)\quad (.073)\ (.022)\qquad\qquad (.037)$

$\bar{R}^2 = .830 \qquad \text{D-W} = 2.17 \qquad r_t = .979 + .154A/A_4 - .485t_{25} - .141i - .270S/S_{-2}$

(5-8) $\qquad\quad D - D_{-1} = .18 + (.306 - .166t_{25} - .118i - .033S/S_{-2})C - .436D_{-1}$
$\qquad\qquad\qquad\quad (.08)\ (.040)\ (.041)\quad (.041)\ (.015)\qquad\qquad (.046)$

$\bar{R}^2 = .835 \qquad \text{D-W} = 2.13 \qquad r_t = .701 - .380t_{25} - .270i - .075S/S_{-2}$

The sales change variables are all significant at least at the 5 percent level in the four profit models, but less so in the cash flow models. On the other hand, interest rates perform best in the cash flow models.

The adaptive expectations interpretation of the dividend model (Chapter II, pp. 28-31) suggests a reason for the greater contribution of sales change in the net profit models than in those based on cash flow. Insofar as firms base dividends on "permanent" profits (or the expected value of profits), the change in profits may be viewed as an indication of the extent to which observed profits depart from permanent profits. It might have been appropriate on these grounds to include the change in profits in the model as a correction variable along with observed profits. Since the sales change variable is undoubtedly closely correlated with profit change, it may be performing this correction function. Because of the large depreciation component, the cash flow variable is less volatile than net profits. Thus, the correction factor may be less needed in the cash flow models.

Despite the marginal contribution of the sales change and interest rate variables in some cases, their overall performance suggests that they warrant consideration in the explanation of dividends. A comparison of (5-3), (5-4), (5-6), and (5-7) with (4-7), (4-9), (4-10), and (4-12), respectively, shows that the addition of the new variables increases the magnitude of the shelter coefficient in the target function in all cases except (5-7). The depreciation coefficient is not strengthened when these competing variables are introduced, but it averages about the same magnitude as before.

One new conclusion emerges when the models are generalized in this fashion. The cash flow models (5-5) and (5-8) perform as well as those profit models that include depreciation as a separate variable. In fact, the cash flow model for all corporations (5-5) is greatly improved by the inclusion of interest rates and has the highest adjusted coefficient of determination of all. This suggests once more the possibility that corporate officials generally do not distinguish net profits and depreciation charges in evaluating the source from which dividends can be paid. Thus these more general models support for the entire period the preliminary conclusion for 1942-60 reached in Chapter III.

The target percentages for selected years are given in Table 22 for this final set of aggregate models. All of them show two pronounced trends similar to those in the observed payout ratios. The further generalization of the payout models by including sales change and interest rates has not downgraded the indicated importance of depreciation and tax rates. In fact, omitting interest rates involved some understatement of the influence of the shelter variable since these two negatively correlated factors tend to counteract

TABLE 22. Decomposition of Changes in Target Payout Percentages into Contributions by Depreciation Index, Tax Shelter, Sales Change, and Interest Rate Variables, 1929–47 and 1947–60

Target Payout Percentages and Changes	Model Used					
	All Corporations			Manufacturing Corporations		
	(5–3)	(5–4)	(5–5)	(5–6)	(5–7)	(5–8)
Target payout percentage						
1929	69	85	45	58	68	40
1947	35	37	27	36	39	28
1960	62	65	30	54	53	29
1929–47						
Contribution by:						
Depreciation index (A_L)	− 4	−10	a	− 4	− 6	a
Tax shelter (t_{25})	−34	−37	−23	−23	−23	−18
Sales change (S/S_{-2})	− 6	− 9	− 2	− 3	− 4	− 1
Interest rates (i)	+10	+ 8	+ 7	+ 8	+ 4	+ 7
1929–47 Change in payout	−34	−48	−18	−22	−29	−12
1947–60						
Contribution by:						
Depreciation index (A_L)	+20	+16	a	+14	+ 6	a
Tax shelter (t_{25})	+10	+11	+ 7	+ 7	+ 7	+ 5
Sales change (S/S_{-2})	+ 5	+ 7	+ 2	+ 3	+ 4	+ 1
Interest rates (i)	− 8	− 6	− 6	− 6	− 3	− 5
1947–60 Change in payout	+27	+28	+ 3	+18	+14	+ 1

a No explicit depreciation variable was included in the cash flow models.

each other. Inclusion of interest rates, therefore, increased the contributions of the shelter variable over those estimated in Table 16. At the same time, the two new variables made very little difference in the estimated effect of depreciation liberalization.

The Impact of Corporate Taxation

Three possible influences of the corporate tax on dividends were considered. First, a tax increase that is not completely shifted reduces the payout base and thus undoubtedly has a depressing effect on aggregate dividends. On the other hand, such a tax increase could actually raise the after-tax payout ratio since it cuts the profitability of investment and rules out marginal projects; in this situation, dividends might be maintained without additional resort to external finance. Finally, it is possible that a large tax increase might be passed along in the form of a dividend cut by firms insistent (perhaps irrationally) upon a fixed level of saving or of reserves. The second and third of these factors appear to be insignificant or offsetting, because inclusion of aggregate corporate tax variables and tax rate measures in models using after-tax income made no contribution. Inclusion of pretax income and aggregate taxes in the same model produced positive and negative coefficients (respectively) of about the same magnitude.

Apparently, the tax reduces the *level* of dividends but not the after-tax payout ratio. This suggests that it is adequate to allow for the tax bite simply by adopting after-tax income as an explanatory variable, substantiating an early conclusion by Lintner.[7] However, any after-tax model may be used to analyze the implied impact of the corporate tax. The first and third equations in Table 19, to be labeled (5-9) and (5-10), were chosen to illustrate this. Let T denote aggregate taxes and $t_c = T/(P + T)$ the effective corporate tax rate. These rates are recorded in Table 23 for all corporations and for manufacturing. On the assumption that the tax is not shifted, the rates show (*ceteris paribus*) the percentage by which the tax depressed after-tax profits and therefore the target *level* of dividends. This indicated impact can, of course, be scaled down according to any assumption about the fraction of the tax which is shifted.

As a second measure of the impact of the corporate tax, actual profits and target dividend levels are compared with what they would have been under the low effective rate of 1929. These hypothetical profit and dividend figures are shown in Table 23 as P_{29} and rP_{29}, where r is the target ratio yielded by relations (5-9) and (5-10). Under the no-shift and *ceteris paribus* assumptions, the rise in tax rates between 1929 and 1943 depressed aggregate profits for 1943 by $10.5 billion and the target level of dividends by $4.5 billion, a reduction of both by 51 percent, as indicated in the last column of the table. Corporate tax rates were reduced temporarily in

[7] To this conclusion he adds the corollary judgment that "postwar dividends were not depressed (below normal expectations in terms of profits after tax and long-established policies) by the large tax bite out of pretax earnings." *American Economic Review*, Vol. 46, No. 2 (May 1956), p. 113.

TABLE 23. Impact of Changes in Corporate Tax Rates Since 1929 on After-Tax Profits and Target Dividend Levels, Selected Years

(Dollar amounts in billions of dollars)

Year	Effective Corporate Tax Rate	Profits P	Profits P_{29}	Target Payout Ratio[a]	Target Dividends rP	Target Dividends rP_{29}	Percentage Impact
			All Corporations				
1929	.146	$ 8.03	$ 8.03	.716	$ 5.75	$ 5.75	0
1943	.579	10.24	20.76	.429	4.39	8.91	−51
1947	.391	17.55	24.62	.384	6.74	9.45	−29
1951	.548	18.49	34.96	.429	7.94	15.00	−47
1960	.515	21.11	37.19	.648	13.67	24.10	−43
			Manufacturing Corporations				
1929	.128	4.23	4.23	.614	2.60	2.60	0
1943	.609	5.56	12.41	.427	2.37	5.30	−55
1947	.391	10.06	14.41	.368	3.70	5.30	−30
1951	.541	10.64	21.80	.398	4.24	8.68	−51
1960	.496	11.64	19.83	.573	6.56	11.36	−42

[a] Implied by equations (5–9) and (5–10), the first and third equations in Table 19.

the early postwar period, but, with later increases, they depressed the dividend target by $7 billion in 1951 and over $10 billion in 1960. The manufacturing sector shows similar patterns. These 40 to 50 percent cuts in dividend targets brought about by corporate tax increases since the twenties are of the same order of magnitude as the depressing effect of higher individual tax rates which halved the target ratio after 1929.

Also of interest is the combined effect of the two taxes. According to equation (5-9), substitution of the 1929 individual tax rate variable (19 percent) for the 1943 figure (63.8 percent) raises the 1943 target ratio from 0.429 to 0.816. Applying this to the hypothetical 1943 after-tax profit figure of $20.76 billion (under 1929, corporate tax rates) yields a hypothetical 1943 target dividend figure of nearly $17 billion. The increases in corporate and individual taxes between 1929 and 1943 cut both aggregate profits and the theoretical payout ratio in half. Thus, the two taxes together reduced the hypothetical dividend level by about 75 percent. Even though qualified by the no-shift and *ceteris paribus* assumptions, this hypothetical impact of taxes is impressive. For example, if 50 percent of the corporate tax is assumed to be shifted from profits, P_{29} would be $15.5 billion in 1943; application of the 1943 target payout function with 1929 individual tax rates shows a theoretical dividend level of $12.6 billion in 1943. According to the models, increases in the two taxes together after 1929 would cut the target level of dividends by about two-thirds in spite of a 50 percent shifting of the corporate tax.

Other Possible Influences on Dividend Policy

Various other hypotheses were tested in addition to the sales change and interest rate variables. While they failed statistically in these models, they will be summarized briefly as unsuccessful rivals of the initial hypothesis of the study.

Investment Demand

A plausible explanation of the low postwar payout ratio is that retained earnings took priority over dividends since the heavy postwar investment could be financed most cheaply from internal funds. One factor in the cost differential between internal and external financing has already been stressed—the level of individual tax rates. Insofar as new investment is financed through reinvested dividends, expanding corporations reduce their potential source of funds by distributions which are trimmed by taxes before they can be reinvested. In addition, retention also avoids the cost of selling new securities. Whatever the level of tax rates, it is plausible that the incentive to retain profits could vary with the intensity of investment demand. It was necessary to use data on actual investment expenditures as measures of investment demand.[8] The variables tested were plant and equipment expenditure with and without inventory change added. Ratios of these variables to income originating in corporations and net assets were also included in the target function. None of these variables made any significant contribution to the explanation of dividends. This finding suggests that funds are

[8] The use of plant and equipment expenditure as a measure of investment demand is open to question. Some measure of the rate of return might have been superior. However, in a cross-section analysis, Gordon found the retention rate to be negatively correlated with the rate of return. For an interpretation of this surprising finding, see Myron J. Gordon, *The Investment, Financing and Valuation of the Corporation* (R. D. Irwin, 1962), pp. 230-32.

allocated to dividends on the basis of income with modification by tax factors, but without regard for the amount of capital that must be raised externally.

This tentative indication that corporate saving is unaffected by capital requirements is interesting and surprising, although it is consistent with Lintner's earlier results.[9] However, a stronger estimation technique, involving a pooling of time series and cross-section information, strongly indicates that high investment demand does depress dividends (Chapter VIII).

Corporate Liquidity

A high degree of liquidity might be expected to encourage dividends by enabling high dividends to be paid without resort to external finance. The two measures of liquidity tested were "liquid assets" (holdings of cash plus government securities) and "working capital" (the sum of cash, government securities, inventories, and notes and accounts receivable less notes and accounts payable). These stocks are on a year-end basis, but adjacent estimates were averaged to approximate mid-year levels. The variables were expressed as ratios to net assets and to sales which were included in the target function. Although they showed some signs of significance in the simpler models, they could not meet the competition when depreciation and tax rates were included with them. However, like the investment demand variables, liquidity made an explanatory contribution in the pooled time series and cross-section analysis.

Other Possible Factors

Tests were also made of what might be called the "erosion" and "hedging" hypotheses. The erosion hypothesis is that firms may take advantage of inflation to allow erosion of payout ratios. In the words of David Walker:

Especially in the large Public Companies, Directors appear to regard the shareholders more as creditors who deserve a steady return upon their loans than as owners entitled to the profits. It is suggested that Directors though rarely prepared to make trouble with their shareholders by reducing the rate of dividend are nevertheless not seeking con-

[9] John Lintner, "Distribution of Incomes of Corporations Among Dividends, Retained Earnings and Taxes," *American Economic Review,* Vol. 46, No. 2 (May 1956), pp. 112-113.

tinuously to reward them. The rising prices and profits of recent years have enabled them to reduce the share of profits distributed to shareholders and the real value of dividends while at the same time maintaining—and in many cases increasing—the rate of dividend.[10]

As a crude test of the potentiality of such erosion, the price level was "measured" by the BLS wholesale price index for all commodities other than farm products and foods, and this variable was included in the target function. The expected negative association with the payout ratio was not found.

The hedging (or speculative confidence) hypothesis is that in a time of rising consumer good prices wealth-holders may bid up stock prices because they desire equities as a hedge against inflation. In this buoyant environment for equities, corporate officials may be inclined to allow dividends to lag since they are less essential to the maintenance of stock prices. The ratio of all stock prices (Standard and Poor's) to the consumer price index (BLS) was used as a measure of the strength of this tendency. However, inclusion of this variable in the target failed to produce any evidence of the expected negative association with payout.

Stock prices were also tested directly as a possible factor in dividend policy. In practice, dividends may have a direct influence on stock prices rather than being a "mere detail," theoretically independent, as suggested by Modigliani-Miller.[11] Corporate officials have expressed the belief that dividends do affect the market for their stock. For example, in announcing a 1964 dividend increase and stock split, the board chairman of the American Telephone and Telegraph Company stated:

The higher dividend and stock split should make A.T.&T. stock more attractive to individual investors, broaden the market for the stock, and help us raise the very large amounts of new capital that the company requires.[12]

[10] David Walker, "Some Economic Aspects of the Taxation of Companies," *The Manchester School of Economic and Social Studies,* Vol. XXI, No. 1 (England: Norbury Lockwood & Co., 1953), p. 28.

[11] Franco Modigliani and M. H. Miller, "The Cost of Capital, Corporation Finance and the Theory of Investment," *American Economic Review,* Vol. 48, No. 2 (June 1958).

[12] "The Chairman's Letter," *American Telephone Share Owners Quarterly* (Winter 1963/1964).

The belief in such a relationship might also produce a feedback impact by stock prices on dividends. The hypothesis was tested that unfavorable behavior of stock prices would be followed by increases in dividends in an effort to stimulate the price of stocks. Indexes of stock price change in the previous one-year and two-year intervals were tested as explanatory variables; the expected negative association with dividends was not found.

Other variables tested in these models were designed to allow for a "ratchet effect" in dividend policy reflecting a greater reluctance to cut dividends than to raise them. Relative income measures, such as the difference between current income and the previous peak income or the difference between current income and the peak level of the series including the current year, were substituted for the constant term or added to the model, but they made no contribution.

Labeling these hypotheses as unsuccessful is not intended to imply their outright rejection. Some of the series used in the tests were too crude to be conclusive. In fact, two of the hypotheses were successful with a change in analytical technique (Chapter VIII). However, insofar as they failed to dislodge the original hypotheses, they add credibility to them.

Several features of the capital structure of corporations should also be mentioned because of their possible relevance to dividend policy although their impact has not been studied here. First, there is some evidence that a high debt-equity ratio may have a depressing effect on payout.[13] Second, the corporate tax may affect dividends through its influence on the capital structure, in addition to its impact on income. The higher the corporate tax, the more attractive is debt financing relative to internal finance, and this could depress retentions. Third, the recently increasing tendency of firms to repurchase their own securities not only alters their capital structure, but also has a direct impact on dividends insofar as the securities are not resold.[14] Finally, the widespread adoption of stock option plans by corporations during the fifties may have had some im-

---

[13] For example, a study of electric utilities showed substantial negative correlation between payout ratios and leverage. (See F. Modigliani and M. H. Miller, "The Cost of Capital, Corporation Finance and the Theory of Investment," *op. cit.*, p. 288n.)

[14] Such stock reacquisition programs have become substantial in recent years. See, for example, "Investing in Yourself," *The Wall Street Journal*, June 30, 1965.

pact on dividend policy. Under these plans, corporate officials tend to be especially concerned with stock prices. This may lead to a more liberal dividend policy insofar as they believe this supports stock prices.

Tests of the Reliability of the Most Successful Models

Since none of the new factors discussed in the last section improved the explanation of dividends, it was tentatively concluded that the most effective time series models derived for all corporations are (5-3) and (5-5), and the best for manufacturing are (5-6) and (5-8). To evaluate the reliability of these relationships further, tests of their stability were carried out.

A Test for Structural Change

The credibility of any model is enhanced if it explains behavior over a long period as well, and in approximately the same way, as it explains subperiods. The differing explanations of the two halves of the period under study act as evidence against the simple models, although the tax rate variable was found to remedy this (Table 14). The same check was applied to the more elaborate and better fitting models of this chapter by comparing their performance for subperiods. Data for these tests are given in Table 24. The F-ratios for all corporations, while falling short of significance at the 5 percent level, are surprisingly large compared to those of models that did not include the additional variables (Table 14). This is because the standard errors of estimate for the 1942-60 period are much lower

TABLE 24. Comparison of Regression Estimates for All Corporations Fitted to Entire 1920–60 Period and to Two Halves Separately (Excluding 1936–38)

Equation	Coefficient of Determination (R^2)			Standard Error of Estimate (SEE)[a]			F Ratio
	1920–60	1920–41	1942–60	1920–60	1920–41	1942–60	
(5–3)	.878	.901	.944	.2053	.1930	.1171	2.24
(5–5)	.878	.906	.918	.2055	.1884	.1413	2.26
(5–6)	.868	.865	.923	.1231	.1211	.0910	1.11
(5–8)	.857	.875	.889	.1279	.1164	.1089	1.24

[a] In billions of dollars.

than for 1920-41 or for the entire period. Inspection of the regression equations for each half of the interval shows that sales change made a highly significant explanatory contribution in the second half, but not in the first.

To pinpoint this evidence of structural change, F-ratios were computed for models identical to (5-3), (5-5), (5-6) and (5-8) except for the exclusion of sales change. The models substituted for (5-3) and (5-6) respectively, were:

(5-9) $D - D_{-1} = .25 + (.332 + .099A/P - .283t_{25} - .174i)P - .328D_{-1}$
  $(.13)\ (.057)\ (.026)\quad (.049)\quad (.081)\quad (.052)$

  $\bar{R}^2 = .838 \qquad D\text{-}W = 2.06 \qquad r_t = 1.012 + .302A/P - .863t_{25} - .530i$

(5-10) $D - D_{-1} = .14 + (.310 + .111A/P - .240t_{25} - .145i)P - .381D_{-1}$
  $(.08)\ (.063)\ (.035)\quad (.069)\quad (.089)\quad (.060)$

  $\bar{R}^2 = .801 \qquad D\text{-}W = 2.12 \qquad r_t = .814 + .291A/P - .629t_{25} - .381i$

The cash flow models substituted for (5-5) and (5-8) were already given previously as (5-1) and (5-2). The tests for structural change are given in Table 25. Exclusion of the sales change variable produced very low F-ratios, indicating no significant difference in the relationship between dividends and depreciation, tax rates, and interest rates in the two periods.

The same tests were run on models in which sales change was included instead of interest rates. The F-ratios were easily significant at the one percent level in the models for all corporations. This supports the conjecture that the structural change may be traced to the strong role of sales change in 1942-60 in contrast to

TABLE 25. Comparison of Regression Estimates for Manufacturing Corporations Fitted to Entire 1920–60 Period and to Two Halves Separately (Excluding 1936–38)

Equation	Coefficient of Determination (R^2)			Standard Error of Estimate (SEE)[a]			F Ratio
	1920–60	1920–41	1942–60	1920–60	1920–41	1942–60	
(5–9)	.860	.900	.853	.2201	.1941	.1886	1.40
(5–1)	.869	.900	.846	.2127	.1940	.1935	1.15
(5–10)	.828	.864	.822	.1401	.1217	.1380	.70
(5–2)	.836	.865	.819	.1372	.1210	.1391	.59

[a] In billions of dollars.

TABLE 26. "Forecasts" of 1956–60 Dividend Change by Models Excluding Sales Change Fitted to 1920–56 Data

(In millions of dollars)

Forecast Year		Forecasting Model			
		All Corporations		Manufacturing	
		(5–9)	(5–1)	(5–10)	(5–2)
Standard error of estimate (Adj.)		248	228	156	151
1956–57	Actual change	+420	+420	+280	+280
	"Forecast"	+491	+514	+192	+191
	Error, 1920–56 fit	+70	+94	−88	−89
	Error, 1920–60 fit	−11	−38	−101	−109
	Error, naive	+330	+330	+120	+120
	Error, autoregression	+160	+160	+30	+30
1957–58	Actual change	−200	−200	−380	−380
	"Forecast"	+191	+139	−121	−164
	Error, 1920–56 fit	+391	+339	+259	+216
	Error, 1920–60 fit	+280	+208	+211	+185
	Error, naive	+620	+620	+660	+660
	Error, autoregression	+660	−660	+670	+670
1958–59	Actual change	+960	+960	+420	+420
	"Forecast"	+915	+1030	+445	+470
	Error, 1920–56 fit	−45	+70	+25	+50
	Error, 1920–60 fit	−137	−108	+23	+37
	Error, naive	−1160	−1160	−800	−800
	Error, autoregression	−730	−730	−300	−300
1959–60	Actual change	+660	+660	+300	+300
	"Forecast"	+783	+934	+246	+267
	Error, 1920–56 fit	+123	+274	−54	−33
	Error, 1920–60 fit	+13	+83	−83	−57
	Error, naive	+300	+300	+120	+120
	Error, autoregression	0	0	+20	+20
Root-mean-square Forecasting error	1920–56	209	226	140	120
	1920–60	156	126	124	112
	Naive	694	694	526	526
	Autoregression	499	499	368	368
F-ratio		.47	.35	.71	.54

its previous insignificance. However, it may still be concluded that there is no evidence of instability in the relationship between dividends and the other significant variables, and no indication that the two sets of observations were drawn from a different structure. It also suggests that the models excluding sales change are likely to make better forecasts, despite their slightly lower coefficient of multiple determination (R^2).

Forecasting Ability of the Dividend Models

As a second test of the validity of the models, their ability to forecast dividend changes beyond the period of fit was checked. Since the data available after 1960 were less reliable, the models were first fitted to 1920-56 data and used to "forecast" changes in the next four years.[15] The tests were carried out for equations (5-3), (5-5), (5-6) and (5-8), and also for (5-9), (5-1), (5-10) and (5-2), which are the corresponding models with sales change excluded. Although the former set performed satisfactorily, the models without sales change gave even better forecasts, as expected. The greater stability and better forecasting ability of this second set of equations are grounds for judging them the best descriptions of aggregate dividend behavior obtained in this study, despite their slightly lower coefficients of determination.

Results of the tests of the forecasting ability of these equations are given in Table 26. There are four forecasts by four different models. The sixteen forecasting errors exceeded one adjusted standard error of estimate in only five cases—the expected number.[16] It also compares favorably to the three such errors that were committed by the regression model fitted to the entire thirty-eight years. The projected models performed poorly in the recession of 1957-58, overstating dividend change by roughly 1.5 times the standard error of estimate, but the models using all observations did poorly then also. The forecasting errors by the projected models exceeded one standard error of estimate in only one of the other twelve forecasts.

---

[15] Since these 1957-60 data were available when the models were developed, this is a biased procedure insofar as they were constructed with an eye to accommodation of these later observations. However, the models grew out of *a priori* reasoning except for the recognition of a downward trend in the payout ratio through World War II and a subsequent upward swing.

[16] This is the number expected on the assumptions of normality and no structural change.

Also given in the table for each year is the error made by a "naive" forecast. Each naive forecast simply states that the change in aggregate dividends between two years will be the same as the previous change. The forecast errors made by the naive models are very much larger in most cases, and the projection is superior to the naive forecast in every one of the sixteen examples. Given the often-observed tendency for naive models to do about as well as regression equations, this result is rather impressive.[17] However, this naive model does not offer very stiff competition. It was therefore supplemented by forecasts made by a second-order autoregression equation fitted to the dividend series.[18] In the case of the 1959-60 dividend change, these forecasts improved upon those made by the theoretical models for all corporations and manufacturing. The autoregressive forecast was also the best one for manufacturing in 1956-57. However, the great superiority of the theoretical models over the autoregressive equations in the 1957-58 and 1958-59 forecasts far outweighs the other comparisons. The autoregressive model stumbled badly at the turning points, failing to take account of the recession in those years.

To sum up the performances of the four 1920-56 equations, the root-mean-square forecasting errors are given for comparison with the standard errors of estimate. The former are slightly smaller than the latter in all four cases. The root-mean-square errors in the 1920-60 models are somewhat smaller, especially in the cash flow model for all corporations, but the projections compare favorably with them, and easily outclass the naive and autoregressive models. While the autoregressive scheme performed better than the very simple naive models, its root-mean-square errors were three to four times those of the theoretical models.

[17] For an illustration of the performance of naive models see Carl F. Christ, "Aggregate Econometric Models," *American Economic Review*, Vol. 46, No. 3 (June 1956), pp. 385-409.

[18] The equation obtained for all corporations (with dividends measured in billions of dollars) was:
$$D = 0.029 + 1.3773D_{-1} - .3534D_{-2}$$
For manufacturing corporations the equation was:
$$D = 0.013 + 1.2638D_{-1} - .2285D_{-2}$$
These equations were used to obtain "forecasts" of dividends for each of the four years 1957-60 on the basis of given data for the two previous years in each case. The forecasts for each year also implied forecasts of dividend change, and the errors in these forecasts are recorded in Table 26.

On the whole the projections appear to be adequate and suggest structural stability. However, this was also tested by means of the F-ratio based on the residual variance of the 1920-56 and 1920-60 equations.[19] These F-ratios are listed at the bottom of Table 26. They are very low and therefore give no indication that dividend payments in 1957-60 were governed by a relationship different from that of 1920-56.

Forecasts for 1961-63 were also made by the same models fitted to 1920-60 data. The results were somewhat less successful, although better than those produced by the simpler 1942-60 models and reported in Table 12. The cash flow models (5-1) and (5-2) performed best in these 1961-63 forecasts, with root-mean-square errors of $288 million and $178 million for all corporations and manufacturing respectively.[20]

An Alternative Test for Autocorrelated Error

The Durbin-Watson statistic is biased toward two when a lagged value of the dependent variable is included as an explanatory variable.[21] Therefore, an alternative test for autocorrelated error was applied to the four models found to provide the best descriptions of aggregate dividend behavior. The suggestion has been advanced that a test of the coefficient of autoregression estimated from the computed residuals may reveal autocorrelation in those cases in which the Durbin-Watson statistic fails.[22] This test was applied to the residuals in the four equations with the following results:

	All Corporations		Manufacturing	
	(5-9)	(5-1)	(5-10)	(5-2)
Autoregression Coefficient	−0.035	−0.046	−0.104	−0.097
Standard Error	−0.165	−0.166	−0.168	−0.169

[19] See Gregory C. Chow, "Tests of Equality Between Sets of Coefficients in Two Linear Regressions," *Econometrica*, Vol. 28, No. 3 (July 1960), relation (31), p. 598 and p. 604.

[20] A possible reason for the inferiority of the 1961-63 forecasts compared to those for 1957-60 is the unreliability of the data, as discussed in Chapter III.

[21] See technical note following Chapter II.

[22] Lester D. Taylor and Thomas A. Wilson, "Three-Pass Least Squares: A Method for Estimating Models with a Lagged Dependent Variable," *Review of Economics and Statistics*, Vol. 46, No. 4 (November 1964), p. 338.

The autoregression coefficients differ only trivially from zero, supporting the results of the Durbin-Watson test in showing no evidence of autocorrelated error.

Conclusion on Aggregative Time Series Models

The basic dividend model had previously been generalized by the inclusion of depreciation liberality and individual tax rates. In this chapter sales change and interest rates were added as (marginally) significant factors. While improving the explanation of dividends, these variables did not undermine the role of depreciation and individual tax rates as determinants of dividends. One additional result was that the generalized cash flow models did as well as those in which depreciation was included explicitly. This tends to support the hypothesis that dividends follow cash flow, rather than adjusted profits.

The best fitting relationships between dividends and other variables (excluding sales change) were shown to be stable over time on the basis of prediction and structural change tests. Taking these tests into account, as well as goodness-of-fit, equations (5-1), (5-2), (5-9), and (5-10) appear to be the best descriptions of aggregate dividend behavior obtained in the study. In terms of the ratios of coefficients to their standard errors and contributions to trends, the depreciation and individual tax rate variables were the most (statistically) influential determinants of the payout ratio. The significance of their coefficients, the stability of these relationships and the failure of many competing hypotheses to undermine these two explanatory variables are strong evidence of their impact.[23] Finally, although the corporate tax did not affect the after-tax payout ratio, it was found to have a strong influence on the level of dividends.

[23] As pointed out in Chapter II, the significance and accuracy of these coefficients cannot be evaluated precisely because of the possibility of serial correlation in the disturbance terms and measurement error in the variables. However, it was encouraging to find that the second test for autocorrelation supports the Durbin-Watson test in yielding no evidence of autocorrelated errors in the four "best" equations listed above.

CHAPTER VI

The Dividend Policy
of Industries

THE CORPORATE SECTOR as a whole is an appropriate focus for the main task of this study which is to isolate the influence of tax laws on aggregate dividends. However, it is possible that the success of the aggregative regression models might be an "aggregation phenomenon"—valid for corporations as a whole but not for industries or firms—or even completely spurious. The hypotheses tested at the aggregate level were actually conceived as descriptive of plausible behavior by individual firms. The models have portrayed the typical corporation as appraising its income flow and regularly adjusting its payout ratio part of the way toward a variable long run goal. This framework should prove useful as long as it continues to explain and forecast aggregative behavior adequately, but the ability of the models to explain the behavior of individual industries and firms is of interest in its own right. Further, disaggregation multiplies the available information permitting many alternative estimates of the same type of coefficient (although often at the expense of less stability in the relationships and greater problems of estimation). In other words, repeated estimation of the same type of relationship at the micro level may yield substantial statistical confirmation of the results indicated by the global models.

It is possible for a model to explain various phenomena for the aggregate of firms and industries and yet fail to explain the behavior of individual units. Despite this possibility, such a ghostly macro model with no visible means of micro support would not instill great confidence, and it might be difficult to decide whether the macro relationship was real or simply statistical. One such possibility was mentioned by John Lintner in his discussion of a preliminary summary of the present study.[1] Lintner suggested that the success of the tax shelter variable might be an aggregation phenomenon, valid for macro analysis but not descriptive of the behavior of individual firms. Estimates for individual firms are needed to check this point. Even in the absence of an extreme contrast between failure at the micro level and apparent success at the macro level, it is possible to introduce bias in the macro coefficients through the process of aggregation.[2] The existence of such a bias would require building up estimates of the macro coefficients from separate estimates at the micro level.

This chapter makes some comparisons of micro and macro estimation and reports tests of dividend hypotheses for industry time series. Time series data were utilized for seventeen industries encompassing the entire economy (excluding the "rest of the world").[3] In the next two chapters, the behavior of a sample of large firms is analyzed by time series tests and by pooled time series and cross-section information. The results were mixed, and it may be useful to summarize some of them at this point. The industry analysis strongly supported the depreciation, tax shelter, and interest rate hypotheses suggested earlier. Time series tests for firms were less convincing; only about one-third to one-half of the firms behaved according to hypothesis. On the other hand, pooling of time series and cross-section data for firms indicated strong response to liberalized depreciation and a tendency to retain earnings as a tax shelter, as well as significant influences by other factors.

[1] John Lintner, "Problems in Taxation—Discussion," *American Economic Review,* Vol. LIV, No. 3 (May 1964), pp. 302-06.

[2] See H. Theil, *Linear Aggregation of Economic Relations* (Amsterdam: North-Holland Publishing Company, 1954). For a partial exposition of this work see R. G. D. Allen, *Mathematical Economics,* Chapter 20 (London: MacMillan and Co., 1957).

[3] The sources and derivation of the time series are summarized in Appendix C.

The Relationship Between Industry and Aggregate Estimates

Reconciling the previous aggregative analysis and the micro results requires considering briefly "the problem of aggregation" as it arises in the present case. If it is assumed that the only goal is the most reliable macro relationships, the choice of estimation procedure depends on whether aggregative analysis is less accurate than a summation of separate analyses for each industry. In this context, there are two related questions. First, what are the possible gains and losses through aggregation? Second, in practice, what is the best way to explain or predict aggregate dividends—by direct regression on aggregates, or by a consensus of micro regressions?

The Degree of Explanation by Industry and Aggregate Models

In an illuminating article, Yehuda Grunfeld and Zvi Griliches[4] showed that, in practice, the aggregation error discussed by Theil may be outweighed by an "aggregation gain," at least as far as "degree of explanation" is concerned. Theil assumed correctly specified micro equations—a perfect selection and arrangement of variables —and then showed that errors would result from aggregation. Grunfeld and Griliches suggest, however, that in practice not enough is known about micro behavior to be able to specify micro equations perfectly. Aggregation can reduce specification errors and produce a higher "degree of explanation." On the other hand, aggregation does not permit allowance for changing weights of subgroups. Analysis of micro behavior may be called for if such changes are important.

In order to get some indication of possible bias or loss of explanatory power through aggregation, an experiment was conducted with the data for seventeen industries.[5] A single equation was fitted

[4] "Is Aggregation Necessarily Bad?" *Review of Economics and Statistics,* Vol. XLII, No. 1 (February 1960), pp. 1-13.

[5] The selection and classification of the industries and firms will be discussed later. The data are not completely consistent with the aggregate information used earlier, mainly because no adjustments were made to reconcile the industry

TABLE 27. Comparison of Regression Results for Seventeen Industries and the Corporate Aggregate, 1920–60 (Excluding 1936–38)

Industry	Regression Coefficients[a]				Coefficient of Determination (R^2)
	Net Profits (P)	Depreciation (A)	Tax Shelter ($t_{25}P$)	Lagged Dividends (D_{-1})	
Mining and quarrying	.255	.267	−.129	−.472	.509
Contract construction	.170	.049	−.225	−.466	.518
Food and kindred products, including tobacco	.161	.073	−.067	−.375	.451
Textile mill products, apparel, and other	.136	−.020	−.073	−.344	.773
Lumber and furniture products	.202	.062	−.210	−.455	.663
Paper and allied products	.171	.172	−.020	−.563	.771
Printing, publishing, allied industries	.264	.004	−.212	−.420	.680
Products of petroleum and coal; chemical and allied products	.181	.157	−.078	−.478	.603
Rubber products	.111	.166	−.099	−.446	.290
Leather and leather products	.072	.097	−.041	−.445	.364
Stone, clay, glass products	.181	.115	−.071	−.487	.609
Metals, metal products, machinery, transportation equipment and automobiles	.254	.098	−.192	−.419	.777
Wholesale trade	.166	−.029	−.124	−.391	.704
Retail trade	.144	.074	−.086	−.445	.765
Finance, insurance, real estate	.332	−.014	−.395	−.113	.687
Transportation, communications, public utilities	.208	.141	−.209	−.345	.558
Services, hotels, and other	.145	.050	−.026	−.456	.543
All corporations	.219	.067	−.180	−.305	.840

[a] The constant term was included in each regression but is not shown in this table.

to series for each of the seventeen industries and for the corporate aggregate used previously. This equation generalized the basic Lintner model (2-2) by substituting for the fixed target payout ratio a target function taking account of the depreciation and shelter variables. This target function was

(6-1) $r_t = \alpha + \beta A/P + \gamma t_{25}.$

After substitution and multiplication the equation to be estimated became

(6-2) $D - D_{-1} = a + b_1 P + b_2 A + b_3 t_{25} P - c D_{-1}.$

The coefficients for all four independent variables along with the coefficient of determination R^2 for each regression are reported in Table 27. With three exceptions, their signs are as expected, but the coefficients show substantial variability from industry to industry, and the R^2 is lower in every case than for the corporate sector as a whole. At first glance, this suggests an improvement in explanatory power through aggregation. However, this turns out to be a statistical illusion.

In the first place, since the industries are more homogeneous than the aggregate, combining them tends to increase the variance to be explained relative to the unexplained variance. The industry regressions appear to do less well because they have less to do.[6] There is a second reason to expect a lower degree of explanation by the individual industry regressions. Although any type of single equation will often be inadequate to describe the behavior of many units at the micro level, a great deal of irregularity in the actions of even a majority of firms might be swamped by the process of aggregation so that a clear overall behavioral pattern might emerge. Finally, the variability of dividends is a special case. If Lintner is correct that firms tend to change their target payout ratio only rarely, aggregate dividends would nevertheless change continuously and could be better explained by the kind of tax variables considered in this study. Aggregation up to the industry level partially counters these difficulties but less so than complete aggregation.

---

series derived for 1919-29 with the aggregate series derived for the same period. However, the series are sufficiently consistent to attempt some reconciliation of the macro and micro equations.

[6] Reasons for this are explained in detail by Grunfeld and Griliches, *op. cit.,* pp. 4-6.

This suggests that the relative size of macro R^2 and micro R^2 is irrelevant to the judgment as to whether industry models or an aggregate model does the better job of explaining the behavior of total dividends. In order to make that comparison, the estimates of $D - D_{-1}$ in the separate industry models were added for each year and the errors in this consensus of industry estimates were compared to the residuals in the aggregate model. The result is that the consensus of industry estimates explained 84.7 percent of the variance of $D - D_{-1}$, which is practically identical to the R^2 of 0.840 yielded by the aggregate regression. Despite the striking variation of the industry coefficients in Table 27, the consensus still does as well (but no better) than the macro equation. Apparently then, the process of aggregation neither improved nor reduced the "degree of explanation" of dividends.[7]

Predictive Ability of the Industry Consensus

For the particular equation selected, the industry consensus and the aggregate model showed the same goodness-of-fit. This is the criterion stressed by Grunfeld and Griliches, but since the structural coefficients themselves are of interest here, it is necessary to consider other criteria. In the first place, the relative predictive ability of the two approaches is of interest. Unfortunately, in the case of most industries, data were available for only one year beyond the period of observation used in estimating the model. Since a comparison of predictions for one year was of little value, the consensus and industry regression estimates of dividend change were compared *within* the period of observation. The fact that the two R^2 were found to be the same does not guarantee that the two estimated changes for each year will coincide even approximately. Yet they are remarkably close, with a Spearman rank correlation of 0.96. This high correlation suggests that actual predictions made beyond the range of observation would also be very close. So it appears that neither the consensus nor the aggregate estimate of dividend change has any advantage over the other in ability to predict—a conclusion

---

[7] An analysis of factors affecting the relative explanatory power of an aggregate regression and a micro consensus is given by Grunfeld and Griliches, *op. cit.*, pp. 6-9. They conclude that the greater the disaggregation, the more likely is aggregation to produce a gain. This is because the equations for the finely divided economic units are likely to be far from correct.

that supplements their equal R^2 performance. It is probable, therefore, that a consensus of industry predictions would perform no better and no worse than the aggregate predictions appraised in Chapter V.

Implications for the Study

This experiment suggests that, insofar as we are interested only in aggregate relationships, no accuracy was lost by aggregation, and no bias appears to have been introduced. However, this conclusion should be qualified in several respects. In the first place, only one model was tested. It included the two main factors, depreciation allowances and tax rates which, added to the basic Lintner model, raised the coefficient of multiple determination $\bar{R}^2$ from 0.616 to 0.821. Not included, for example, were the interest rate and sales change variables which had further increased the aggregate $\bar{R}^2$ to 0.855.

A second point is that the study of aggregation reported above did not use the "best" model for each industry. It is likely that use of a choice of models in making up the industry consensus would produce a higher degree of explanation and better prediction than any single aggregate model. This does not downgrade the success of aggregation, however, and it does not point to any bias in the aggregate coefficients. A final qualification is that the industry information itself represents a substantial degree of aggregation. A similar test applied to firms might well yield different conclusions. However, as Grunfeld and Griliches found in their experiment, it is probable that disaggregation would yield a loss of explanatory power if carried farther.

These qualifications do not disturb the general conclusion that aggregation is apparently not to be feared in this study. The micro models to be discussed are of interest in their own right, but from the macro point of view they are of value mainly for their partial confirmation of the macro equations, rather than as a substitute.

Variations in Industry Payout Policy

The choice of an industry breakdown of Office of Business Economics (OBE) data on the corporate aggregate was constrained by the Internal Revenue Service *Statistics of Income* classification available for the 1920's. A much more detailed OBE breakdown is available for 1929-60, but it was essential to have series going back to 1919 in order to have enough information to test the tax shelter hypothesis. Earlier information was also needed in order to compare industry results with aggregate models for 1920-60. This backward extrapolation was accomplished by regressions of OBE series on *Statistics of Income* data for overlapping periods (described in Appendix C).

Reliance on the early *Statistics of Income* data produced a breakdown that was far from ideal, since some industries consisted of very broad groupings. It was not by choice that "metals, metal products, machinery, transport equipment, including autos and auto equipment" were thrown together in one group. Another sprawling industry grouping was "transportation, communications and public utilities," but at least in this case the presence of government regulation may give this group some degree of homogeneity.[8] Each of these two "industries" paid about one quarter of all dividends in 1960. Each also paid about 80 times as much in 1960 as "leather and leather products" at the other end of the size spectrum.

Although the particular disaggregation that resulted from use of early *Statistics of Income* data does not go far enough, it did yield some fairly homogeneous groups. At least the disaggregation is sufficient to show the expected variation in dividend policy from industry to industry. To illustrate this, actual payout ratios D/P in four selected years and during the entire period are given in percentage form in Table 28. The years chosen—1920, 1929, 1947, 1960—constitute, respectively, a low, a high, a low, and a high in the aggregate target payout ratios estimated in Chapters IV and V. These years were chosen with the expectation that the industries would exhibit similar variation over time. However, the main purpose of the table is to show the variation of payout ratios from industry to industry within any period.

Part of the variation arises from negative or near-zero profits for some of the firms, especially in 1920. In fact, if the 1920 figures are ignored, the percentages for each industry exhibit remarkable regularity over time. All of the payouts follow the pattern of the corporate aggregate, lower in 1947 than in 1929, and rising again

---

[8] On the other hand this common characteristic may well be outweighed by the differences between the economic fortunes of the railroads and the rest of the regulated industries.

TABLE 28. Observed Payout Percentages of Industries and Aggregates, Selected Years and for Entire 1920–60 Period (Excluding 1936–38)

Industry[a]	1920	1929	1947	1960	1920–60
Mining	55	91	38	95	78.0
Construction	35	60	15	b	37.4
Food	169	72	42	53	59.4
Textiles	128	117	24	41	52.1
Lumber	37	93	22	74	52.5
Paper	37	60	24	62	47.6
Printing	36	63	33	40	46.7
Petroleum	112	52	38	55	53.5
Rubber	b	322	29	58	43.4
Leather	b	97	33	73	67.5
Stone, glass	29	66	36	58	47.6
Metals and products	42	57	36	64	52.0
Wholesale trade	68	74	20	33	35.1
Retail trade	90	92	25	68	49.6
Finance	284	95	58	59	67.2
Public utilities	77	71	66	92	83.0
Services	74	75	36	102	65.5
All corporations	64	71	36	62	58.2
Manufacturing corporations	55	63	34	58	52.3

[a] For more detailed title, see Table 27.
[b] Negative profits.

by 1960 (except construction which had negative profits). In contrast to the similarity of trends over time, the variation among industries is substantial. For example, in 1960—the year of least relative spread of the ratios—they ranged from 33 to 102 percent. The variation within any year is partly because of differing short-run changes in profits. However, even the aggregate ratios for the entire 38 years (given in the last column) range from 35 to 83 percent, with one quarter of them 47 percent or less and one quarter 67 percent or more. These differences in payout policy among even these relatively broad industrial groupings appear sufficient to call for separate fitting of the dividend models.

No systematic effort will be made here to explain the variation of payout by industry. The possible link between payout and the degree of concentration of firm ownership sketched in Chapter IV (pp. 82-83) might also exist within industries. Another obvious hypothesis is that industries with good investment opportunities and high growth rates will tend to have small payout ratios insofar as firms wish to avoid external financing. Jacob Michaelsen has studied factors such as this for a cross-section of firms.[9] While this problem is an important one, this study will confine itself to changes in dividends over time.

Individual Industry Models

In order to assess the contribution of depreciation and tax shelter factors to the explanation of dividends by industry, a single "best" combination of explanatory variables was selected for each industry. The variables selected as candidates were those with the best explanatory contributions in the aggregate models. It should be stressed at the outset, however, that certain tests carried out at the aggregate level could not be tried for the industry data. The most important of these was the use of profit variables adjusted by more consistent depreciation factors. Data were not available for this by industry. Thus it is possible that adjusted profits would give even better explanations than the cash flow and explicit depreciation models to be reported.

Starting with the basic Lintner model which explains dividend change by means of P and D_{-1}, additional variables were built in, singly and in combination, by substituting a target function for the fixed target payout ratio r. The shelter variable t_{25} was used throughout, and cash flow was substituted for profits in some cases. Many combinations of variables were included in the target function, which was then multiplied by an income variable. From a list of seventeen frequently successful equations, a single best one was then selected for each industry. The candidate equations are described in Table 29, beginning with the basic model. An attempt was made to choose the "best" one of these by a reasonably objective set of criteria. The general purpose was to find the equation containing all variables that made an explanatory contribution and excluding those that did not. In those relatively rare cases in which a variable improved the degree of explanation but carried a theoretically unacceptable sign, the variable was not recognized as improving the basic model since it gave no support to the hypothesis being tested. Specifically,

[9] *Determinants of Corporate Dividend Policy* (unpublished Ph.D. thesis, University of Chicago, 1961).

TABLE 29. Independent Variables Used in Equations Fitted to Industry Data

Equation Number	Income Measure (Y)		Depreciation		Tax Shelter	Sales Change	Interest Rates	Lagged Dividends
	P	C	A	$(A/S)Y$	$t_{25}Y$	$(S/S_{-2})Y$	iY	D_{-1}
(1)	X							X
(2)	X		X					X
(3)	X					X		X
(4)	X				X			X
(5)	X						X	X
(6)	X		X		X			X
(7)	X		X				X	X
(8)	X			X			X	X
(9)	X				X		X	X
(10)	X		X		X		X	X
(11)	X			X	X	X	X	X
(12)	X		X		X	X	X	X
(13)		X						X
(14)		X			X			X
(15)		X				X		X
(16)		X			X	X		X
(17)		X			X	X	X	X

the depreciation variable could only be supported by a positive sign, and the tax shelter, interest rate, and sales change variables were only recognized if they had negative signs. In general, a variable was regarded as an "improvement" of the basic model if the sign of its coefficient was acceptable, and if its inclusion increased the coefficient of multiple determination $\overline{R}^2$ (adjusted for degrees of freedom consumed with the addition of new variables).[10]

Two other criteria were considered in selection of the equations. In order for the standard errors to be meaningful, no equa-

---

[10] In practice, this criterion was approximated by choosing the equation with the highest $\overline{R}^2$, subject to the requirement that no variable with a "perverse" sign helped achieve that maximum. This process ended up with a few perverse signs present but in no case significant enough for their inclusion to improve the adjusted "degree of explanation." When conveniently available, the equation without such a variable was selected. In a few cases, to avoid running another regression, a variable with a perverse sign was left in if its t-ratio was less than one. This rule of thumb was adopted as the result of a rough estimate that inclusion of a variable did not increase the adjusted R^2 unless its t-ratio exceeded unity.

tion was selected if the Durbin-Watson test showed strong evidence of serial correlation of the residuals.[11] Another problem was the relevance of the sign of the constant term. It was positive as expected in all except one of the industry regressions. However, the firm regressions produced a considerable number of negative constant terms, although few actually increased $\bar{R}^2$. These cases cast some doubt on the hypothesis stated originally by Lintner, that the sign of this coefficient should be positive. This hypothesis was not regarded as fundamental, however, and equations were not ruled out on this account.

The Best Regression Equations

The regression equations best describing the variation of dividends in each industry are recorded in Table 30, along with models for all corporations and for manufacturing. While the industry results are not unanimous, they strongly confirm the relationships shown by the aggregate models.

Of the seventeen "best" equations, fourteen contain a tax shelter variable with a negative coefficient, and in all of the fourteen cases, except petroleum, the inclusion of this variable increased $\bar{R}^2$. There is considerable variability in the tax shelter coefficients, especially if the coefficients for food, paper, and rubber are taken to be zero. However, the median coefficient is —0.193 which is very close to the estimated coefficient for all corporations.

The best income variable Y was taken to be either profits or cash flow, and the coefficient of the selected income variable is recorded in Table 30 under either (P) or (C). The support for the positive influence of depreciation is shown in two ways. In the first place, the cash flow variable was the best basis for explaining dividends in seven of the seventeen industries. Secondly, the inclusion of depreciation separately along with profits improved the ex-

[11] For a brief discussion of the Durbin-Watson test, see Theil, *op. cit.*, pp. 220-21. Since the exact distribution of the statistic is unknown, the acceptance region for the two-tailed test at the 5 percent level of significance adopted here was based on the midpoint between the upper and lower limits given by Durbin and Watson. The acceptance region so estimated varied slightly with the number of coefficients in the equation. For example, with five coefficients the Durbin-Watson statistic must fall outside the region 1.39-2.61 if the hypothesis of independence of residuals is to be rejected. For a discussion of a possible weakness of this test, see the second technical note following Chapter II.

TABLE 30. Regression Coefficients, Best Industry and Aggregate Models, 1920–60 (Excluding 1936–38)[a]

Industry and Best Model[b]	Constant Term (a)	Income Measure (Y)		Depreciation (A)	Tax Shelter ($t_{25}Y$)	Sales Change ($S/S_{-2}Y$)	Interest Rates (iY)	Lagged Dividends (D_{-1})
		(P)	(C)					
Mining (10)	−23	.735		.377	−.563	−.715		−.495
Construction (10)	9	.510		.072	−.515	−.510		−.564
Food (13)	73		.108					−.403
Textiles (4)	28	.138			−.078			−.352
Lumber (14)	18		.200		−.193			−.492
Paper (13)	4		.158					−.542
Printing (10)	12	.452		.082	−.373	−.291		−.496
Petroleum (16)	54		.223		−.050		−.034	−.522
Rubber (2)	2	.059		.169				−.466
Leather (10)	7	.385		.205	−.316	−.432		−.499
Stone, glass (17)	7		.368		−.149	−.170	−.058	−.538
Metals and products (12)	97	.508		.118	−.318	−.293	−.068	−.432
Wholesale trade (10)	38	.312		.014	−.251	−.231		−.420
Retail trade (17)	62		.214		−.140	−.106	−.001	−.467
Finance (4)	3	.332			−.399			−.125
Public utilities (14)	35		.195		−.122			−.345
Services (10)	10	.620		.074	−.438	−.662		−.542
All corporations (17)	285		.308		−.197	−.126	−.025	−.393
Manufacturing corporations (12)	196	.350		.083	−.183	−.105	−.067	−.379

[a] The unit of measurement for the constant term, dividend, income and depreciation variables is one million dollars. The tax shelter variable is measured in decimal rather than percentage form. The interest rate variable is measured in units of ten percentage points each; for example, 5 percent is measured as 0.5.

[b] For detailed industry title see Table 27.

planation in seven more industries. Although a coefficient is given for depreciation in wholesale trade, it made no contribution to $\bar{R}^2$. In fact, the adjusted degree of explanation would be improved by dropping it. Thus, all industries except textiles, wholesale trade, and finance support the depreciation hypothesis by relating dividends either to cash flow or to an explicit depreciation variable.

The interest rate variable contributed to the explanation of dividends in all nine industries for which a coefficient is given. Among the factors treated here, only sales change failed consistently although its inclusion provided a net improvement in three of the four cases in which it is given. However, it appears to be of marginal importance, as indicated by its t-ratio of only 1.51 in the aggregate equation. It was retained here only because it contributed strongly to the explanation of manufacturing dividends, particularly in the large metals group where its inclusion raised $\overline{R}^2$ from 0.799 to 0.868.

No requirements were imposed on the constant term in selection of the equations, but in all industries except mining it appeared with the expected positive sign. As in the case of the aggregative equations, this suggests that dividends tend to be maintained even in the face of factors in the rest of the model that call for a reduction. All the coefficients for D_{-1} are negative as expected. The absolute value of these represents the estimated "speed-of-adjustment coefficient." Excluding finance (which showed peculiar characteristics in other respects also), this coefficient showed considerable uniformity from industry to industry. According to the models, industries (other than finance) tend to adjust from 34 percent to 56 percent of the way toward desired dividend levels each year.[12]

Significance Tests for Added Variables*

The rule of thumb for the selection of a model for each industry was based on a concept of effectiveness. A variable was regarded as "effective," or making a contribution, if it had the expected sign and improved the coefficient of determination after allowance for the lost degree of freedom. The variables were also subjected to more stringent conventional significance tests.

Table 31 records the level of significance for each effective variable and the gains achieved by generalizing the basic model.[13] The variables that made no contribution to $\overline{R}^2$ were dropped. Some indication of the validity of applying the standard tests of significance is given by the Durbin-Watson statistics for the generalized models

---

* This section evaluates the explanatory gains achieved by generalization of the basic dividend model. It may be omitted by readers not interested in the technical details. The statistical qualifications discussed following Chapter II should also be considered in evaluating the findings reported here.

[12] One peculiarity is the tendency for the industry speed-of-adjustment coefficients to be generally higher than those in the aggregate equations. All except three fall above the coefficient for all corporations.

[13] The ratios of regression coefficients to their standard errors, used in the significance tests, are given in Appendix E.

TABLE 31. Results of Significance Tests for Effective Variables in the Best Industry and Aggregate Models, 1920–60 (Excluding 1936–38)

Industry and Best Model[a]	Level of Significance (Percent)				Durbin-Watson Statistic (D-W)	Coefficient of Multiple Determination ($\bar{R}^2$)		
	Depreciation[b] (A)	Tax Shelter ($t_{25}Y$)	Interest Rates (iY)	Sales Change ($S/S_{-2}Y$)		Basic Model	Best Model	Equation (10)
Mining (10)	0.5	5.0	5.0		2.22	.349	.514	.514
Construction (10)	0.5	0.5	0.5		2.23	.135	.561	.561
Food (13)[c]	5.0				1.76	.352	.408	.366
Textiles (4)		5.0			2.11	.736	.750	.738
Lumber (14)[c]		0.5			2.41	.514	.665	.639
Paper (13)[c]	0.5				2.21	.598	.755	.739
Printing (10)	d	0.5	5.0		2.25	.500	.664	.664
Petroleum (16)[c]	0.5			d	2.61	.441	.570	.547
Rubber (2)	5.0				2.40	.103	.210	.180
Leather (10)	0.5	5.0	d		2.51	.307	.323	.323
Stone, glass (17)[c]	0.5	5.0	5.0	5.0	2.05	.490	.647	.631
Metals and products (12)	0.5	0.5	0.5	0.5	2.58	.614	.868	.799
Wholesale trade (10)		5.0	d		1.70	.642	.685	.685
Retail trade (17)[c]	0.5	0.5	5.0		1.74	.525	.761	.754
Finance (4)		0.5			2.33	.467	.659	.647
Public utilities (14)[c]	0.5	0.5			1.68	.348	.511	.460
Services (10)	0.5	5.0	5.0		1.53	.251	.559	.559
All corporations (17)[c]	0.5	0.5	0.5	d	2.04	.616	.859	.838
Manufacturing corporations (12)	5.0	0.5	d	0.5	2.24	.643	.842	.802

[a] For detailed industry title, see Table 27; for equation corresponding to model number, see Table 29. Although constant terms were included in all regressions, the results of their significance tests are not reported in this table. They were significantly positive at the 5 percent level in twelve of the industries.

[b] The level of significance for the explicit depreciation variable A was tested for all of the industries even though some of them used cash flow as the income variable in their best model. In such cases C was replaced by A and P.

[c] Models for these industries used cash flow as the best income variable; in addition, however, A and P were substituted for C in order to determine the level of significance of the explicit depreciation variable.

[d] These variables were not significant at the 5 percent level, but they were effective in improving $\bar{R}^2$ for the model.

in Table 31. It was decided that evidence of autocorrelation of the residuals was not sufficient to warrant an adjustment of the number of degrees of freedom.

The tax shelter variable (tP or tC) improved the model and was also significant at least at the 5 percent level on the one-tail test in thirteen industries. In seven of these thirteen industries, the shelter variable was significant at the 0.5 percent level or better. In four cases, the coefficient for this variable differed from zero by four or more standard errors. Even in the four industries for which the shelter variable was not significant, there was no indication of a perverse (positive) association.

The significance tests for the depreciation hypothesis were carried out differently. In ten cases, the best equation used profits as the income variable and a separate depreciation variable A. This variable was significant at the 5 percent level or better in six industries, and in five of these variable A was significant at the 0.5 percent level. In the other seven industries, C turned out to be the most effective income variable. While it is possible to apply an F-test for the significance of the improvement in R^2 through the substitution of C for P, a simpler test was adopted. Variables P and A were substituted for C in the best model, and the significance of A was tested. All except one were significant at the 5 percent level, and five were significant at the 0.5 percent level or better. Thus, in only five industries—textiles, lumber, printing, wholesale trade, and finance —did taking account of depreciation fail to significantly improve the explanation of dividends, and in these five cases there was at least no evidence of perverse association. Among the twelve industries in which depreciation appears to be a significant determinant of dividends, there were ten cases with coefficients for variable A that were highly significant at the 0.5 percent level or better.

Considering the tax shelter and depreciation factors together, Table 31 indicates that at least one of them improves the basic model significantly for every industry. Both factors are significant at the 5 percent level or better in eight of the industries. This overall industry evidence gives strong support to the conclusions on the influence of these two factors suggested by the aggregate models.

The inclusion of interest rates improved the explanation of dividend change in nine industries, and in seven of these, the coefficient was significant at least at the 5 percent level. The weaker sales change variable improved only three models and was significant in just two at the 5 percent level. This coefficient for the large metals group was four times its standard error, however. The income and lagged dividend variables were highly significant in almost all cases, as expected. The sixteen positive constant terms also strongly supported the hypothesis about resistance to dividend cuts, with twelve of them significant at the 5 percent level or better.

As a measure of the over-all gain through generalization of the basic model, the adjusted coefficients of determination for the basic and the various generalized models are also given in Table 31. The gains were slight in textiles, leather, and wholesale trade, but they were large in construction, retail trade, services, and metals. In the important case of metals, generalization of the model reduced the (adjusted) unexplained variance by 66 percent. A further comparison is provided between the basic model and equation 10, which was the most successful single generalization, having been selected for six industries. This model includes depreciation, tax shelter, and interest rate variables in the target function. The improvement in $\bar{R}^2$ for equation 10 is only slightly less than that for $\bar{R}^2$ for the best equation in those eleven industries for which equation 10 was not selected as best. The coefficients of equation 10 were checked for each industry to make certain that these values of $\bar{R}^2$ were not achieved with the aid of variables carrying coefficients with perverse signs. There were a few such signs, but in no case was the coefficient of sufficient magnitude for the variable to improve $\bar{R}^2$.

As a further test of the validity of the models, the ability of the models to explain dividends beyond the period of observation was checked.[14] The seventeen best equations were used to forecast the 1960-61 dividend change. These generalized models gave forecasts markedly superior to those of the basic model and to "naive" forecasts.

Trends in Industry Payout Policy

The long-run relationships between dividends and tax variables can be clarified by deriving from the best models for each industry the implied target functions explaining variations in target payout ratios.[15] A single income base—net profits P—was used throughout in order to achieve comparability from industry to industry. The equations were selected as before, but an equation including

---

[14] Details of the tests are reported in Appendix F.

[15] These target functions are implied by the underlying fitted equations in that they are the functions that must be substituted for r in the basic model in order to produce the "best" equations in Table 30. The coefficients of the target functions are derived by dividing all coefficients in Table 30, other than those of the constant term and lagged dividends, by the speed-of-adjustment coefficient c.

TABLE 32. Target Payout Percentages Implied by Best Industry and Aggregate Models, Selected Years

Industry and Best Model[a]	Target Payout Percentages				Payout Percentage, 1920–60[b]	
	1920	1929	1947	1960	Basic Model Target	Actual
Mining (10)	57	98	54	101	81	78.0
Construction (10)	9	35	10	c	25	37.4
Food (2)	43	36	32	43	43	59.4
Textiles (4)	33	35	25	28	26	52.1
Lumber (10)	24	53	16	47	25	52.5
Paper (2)	37	49	33	62	53	47.6
Printing (10)	31	51	28	36	30	46.7
Petroleum (2)	44	40	37	53	56	53.5
Rubber (2)	c	133	27	63	42	43.4
Leather (10)	c	34	18	41	13	67.5
Stone, glass (12)	16	54	30	53	45	47.6
Metals and products (12)	37	56	40	56	48	52.0
Wholesale trade (10)	17	35	20	20	19	35.1
Retail trade (10)	24	40	22	53	32	49.6
Finance (4)	177	205	56	100	67	67.2
Public utilities (6)	68	72	62	102	175	83.0
Services (10)	12	58	33	88	52	65.5
All corporations (12)	48	69	35	62	59	58.2
Manufacturing corporations (12)	43	58	36	54	49	52.3

[a] For detailed industry titles, see Table 27; for equation corresponding to model number, see Table 29. Models using the cash flow variable are not included here.
[b] Data for 1936–38 are excluded.
[c] Omitted because of negative profits.

depreciation A explicitly with P was substituted for those using cash flow C in Table 30. This limited the selection to the first twelve of the seventeen equations in Table 29. The number of the equation selected for each industry is given in Table 32. The implied target functions were used to derive the theoretical target ratios reported in Table 32. As in Table 28, the years 1920, 1929, 1947, and 1960 were selected to represent the main trends in aggregate corporate dividends. Two questions are of interest here. First, to what extent do the theoretical targets explain the trends in the actual payout percentages? Second, what were the respective roles of the different factors—especially depreciation liberalization and individual tax rates—in the variations of the target percentages?

The validity of the estimated target payout percentages does not depend on their being followed closely by actual payouts; considerable lags and rigidities in the latter are expected. On the other hand, the absence of any discernible association between observed payout and long-run targets would cast doubt on the estimates of the targets. The aggregative analysis raised no such doubts, but some industry results were less satisfactory—especially for 1920 and 1929. The problem is that the depreciation liberality measure A/P, a major variable in the target payout function, tends to blow up as profits approach zero or become negative. Owing to this methodological difficulty, the negative or low profits of some industries obscured the relationship between observed and target ratios in those years. Despite this, actual 1920-29 changes in these ratios were in the same direction as that indicated by the theoretical long-run ratios in twelve of the fifteen industries with positive profits. The association is so tenuous, however, as to discourage any further analysis of long-run changes in industry dividend policy in the twenties.

The later results inspire more confidence in the estimated target ratios. A comparison of Tables 28 and 32 shows that the observed ratios for the corporate aggregate followed the targets very closely in 1929, 1947, and 1960, with observed ratios averaging one percentage point above the targets and differing by a maximum of two. The association in manufacturing, though not as close, showed no discrepancies greater than five points, and the observed ratio averaged only two points above the targets. Although industry dividends showed less adherence to the estimated targets, the behavior was fairly consistent. For every industry, the payout ratio followed the target ratio in a decline between 1929 and 1947. However, the target ratios for most industries started from generally lower levels than observed payouts in 1929 and showed smaller declines in fifteen of the industries.

The estimated payout propensities for 1947 and 1960 appear to be more reliable. The median observed ratio was slightly higher than the median target in each year, as expected because of resistance to cuts in dividends. The 1947-60 changes were 33 to 59 in the median observed percentages and 30 to 53 in the median targets. The individual industry ratios moved up together in all cases, except wholesale trade for which the target was unchanged. Finally the rank correlations of the observed and target ratios were 0.84 in 1947 and 0.73 in 1960.

In Table 32, fixed target percentages estimated by means of the

TABLE 33. Decomposition of Changes in Target Payout Percentages into 1929–47 and 1947–60[a]

Change in Target Payout Percentage	Mining	Construction	Food	Textiles	Lumber	Paper	Printing	Petroleum	Rubber
Contribution by:									
Depreciation index (A/P)	−25	− 4	− 4		−11	−16	− 2	− 3	−106
Tax shelter (t_{25})	−53	−43		−10	−39		−35		
Interest rates (i)	+34	+21			+13		+14		
Sales change (S/S$_{-2}$)									
	—	—	—	—	—	—	—	—	—
1929–47 Change in payout	−44	−26	− 4	−10	−37	−16	−23	− 3	−106
Contribution by:									
Depreciation index (A/P)	+58	b	+11		+30	+29	+ 9	+16	+ 36
Tax shelter (t_{25})	+16	b		+ 3	+12		+10		
Interest rates (i)	−27	b			−10		−11		
Sales change (S/S$_{-2}$)									
	—	—	—	—	—	—	—	—	—
1947–60 Change in payout	+47	b	+11	+ 3	+32	+29	+ 8	+16	+ 36

[a] Derived from Table 32. The target changes in this table may disagree with those indicated in Table 32 because of rounding. This table does not include models using the cash flow variable.
[b] Omitted because of negative profits in 1960.

basic Lintner model are listed along with the variable targets. These relate rather closely to the ratios of aggregate dividends to aggregate profits for the entire period, also given in the table. As might be expected, the estimated constant payout ratios usually fall between highs and lows in the variable ratios. For example, omitting construction, all of the variable targets show 1947-60 increases, and the target payout ratio in the basic model falls within the range of the early and late values in twelve of the sixteen cases. However, among the seventeen industries, the median 1947-60 change in the variable target ratio was 26 percentage points. The size of this change reemphasizes the explanatory gain through recognition of variations in the target.

Contribution of Several Variables for Best Industry and Aggregate Models,

Leather	Stone, Glass, etc.	Metals and Products	Whole-sale Trade	Retail Trade	Finance	Public Utilities	Services	All Corporations	Manufacturing Corporations
− 6	−11	− 1	− 1	− 8		+17	−16	− 5	− 4
−33	−21	−34	−28	−20	−149	−28	−38	−34	−23
+23	+15	+16	+13	+10			+29	+10	+ 7
	− 6	+ 3						− 6	− 3
───	───	───	───	───	───	───	───	───	───
−16	−23	−16	−16	−18	−149	−11	−25	−35	−23
+32	+24	+20	+ 2	+34		+32	+66	+20	+14
+10	+ 6	+10	+ 8	+ 6	+ 44	+ 8	+11	+10	+ 7
−18	−12	−13	−10	− 8			−23	− 8	− 5
	+ 5	− 2						+ 5	+ 3
───	───	───	───	───	───	───	───	───	───
+24	+23	+15	0	+32	+44	+40	+54	+27	+19

The Contribution of Various Factors

Long-term changes in the target payout ratios of Table 32 can be decomposed in order to measure the influence of different factors presumed to affect them. Table 33 records the 1929-47 and 1947-60 changes in these theoretical targets and isolates the roles of depreciation liberality, individual tax rates, interest rates and sales change in producing the target payout trends. The contributions of these variables are derived by applying the coefficient for each variable in the target functions to the data for the variable; the contributions add, by definition, to the over-all change in the target ratios. For example, the model says that the 44 percentage point decline in the theoretical payout ratio for mining between 1929 and 1947 is the net result of (1) a 25 point depression arising from less liberal depreciation allowances, (2) a 53 point drag imposed by higher individual tax rates and (3) an offsetting 34 point increase through a lowering of interest rates.

If the fitted models are a good guide, three factors influencing payout policy—already shown to be statistically significant in a majority of cases—have a surprisingly large numerical impact. The most influential factors again appear to be the depressing effect on dividends of tax rate increases after the twenties and the stimulating effect of depreciation allowances on the payout ratio since the war. In the 1929-47 interval, the median impact of higher tax rates for the seventeen industries is a 28 percentage point cut in the target payout percentage; this is not far below the 34 point figure indicated by the aggregate model. Similarly, the median postwar boost in the payout ratio associated with depreciation liberalization is 24 points, checking well with the 20 point figure derived from the aggregate model.

The median contribution of the 1929-47 fall in interest rates was a 13 point increase in dividend targets, and the subsequent rise in interest rates was associated with a median decline of 8 points in the target payout ratio. In each period, the influence of interest rates was on the order of one-half that of the dominant factor. In both of the two periods chosen, it happens to work against the other two major factors. As noted in Chapter V, this offsetting statistical influence of interest rates tends to enhance the measured impact of individual tax rates and, to a lesser extent, of depreciation liberality. However, since the rate of interest is a rather suspect variable, especially in view of the tentative rejection of investment expenditure as a factor, another test was in order.

It is possible that a fortuitous association of dividends with interest rates spuriously enhanced the statistical significance of depreciation liberality and tax rates. Tests were applied to the best equation among those adding only one, both, or neither of these two variables to the basic model. In practically every case, the exclusion of interest rates from the models where it was effective somewhat weakened the performance of depreciation and tax rates as measured by the t-ratios given in Appendix E. The depreciation variable without benefit of interest rates remained significant at the 5 percent level in eleven industries and at the 0.5 percent level in seven cases. This was true for individual tax rates in nine cases at the 5 percent level and in six at the 0.5 percent level. It is clear, therefore, that the interest rate variable (whether spurious or not) was not responsible for the indicated significance of the depreciation and tax factors. They stand on their own feet with only slightly diminished influence.

Industry Dividend Policy: Conclusions

Detailed tests based on data for industries have produced descriptions of their behavior that are remarkably consistent with the findings for the aggregates reported in Chapters III to V. As shown in Table 31, the stimulating effect of depreciation liberalization on the payout ratio appeared significant at the 5 percent level or better for twelve of seventeen industries. As an indication of their importance, these twelve earned 79 percent of the profits and paid 81 percent of all dividends during the thirty-eight years studied. The effect of individual tax rates was significant for thirteen of the industries which earned 77 percent of the profits and paid 79 percent of the dividends.

If the rate of interest were barred from the models, this picture would be altered slightly, but the depreciation variable would lose its significance, at the 5 percent level, only in the leather industry. The percentages of profits earned and dividends paid by industries other than leather would drop only half a point. The tax rate variable would lose its significance in mining, leather, stone, and services. The hypothesis would remain significant, at the 5 percent level or better, for nine industries that earned 69 percent of overall profits and paid 69 percent of the dividends.

This confirmation of the two hypotheses by industries comprising the bulk of all corporate activity indicates that the findings for the corporate aggregate were not aggregation phenomena. The aggregate models were simply reflecting the sum of the generally consistent behavioral patterns of the seventeen industries.

CHAPTER VII

The Dividend Policy of Firms: Time Series Analysis

THE TIME SERIES ANALYSIS of industry dividend behavior was repeated in part for a sample of large firms. The firms were not selected so as to be representative of the corporate whole, and the available data were not adjusted for reconciliation with the economic definitions underlying the industry data. No general conclusions can be drawn therefore from an analysis of this group of firms. Still, a study of their dividend behavior is at least illustrative and may shed some further light on the depreciation and tax hypotheses.

Comparison of Sample and Aggregate Characteristics

The sample was limited to large firms selected from the *Fortune Magazine* list of the 500 largest industrial corporations (July 1963) and its list of the largest nonindustrial firms (August 1963). The number of firms selected from each industry was in rough proportion to the amount of dividends paid by the industry. Only firms in existence in 1920 and with data available for the entire 1919-60 period were admitted to the sample so that the analysis would be comparable with that for industries. To achieve as much continuity of identity as possible, preference was given to firms with the least merger activity during the period.

A list of the forty corporations selected in this way is given in Table 34 along with data on their actual payout ratios for selected years.[1] It is immediately apparent that these firms do not constitute a representative sample. In the first place, the payout ratios for all of them taken together (given at the bottom of the table) showed far less pronounced trends than the corporate aggregate. The 1929-47 decline was very slight in contrast to the halving of the aggregate payout ratio, and the 1947-60 recovery in the ratio for the forty firms was 10 percentage points compared to a 26-point rise in the aggregate ratio.

Part of the disparity between the observed behavior of these forty firms and the corporate aggregate arises from the definitional differences discussed in Appendix D. However, the differences are of such magnitude that it is likely that other factors are responsible. One clue is that the selected group of large firms is much more prosperous and grew much faster during good times than the corporate whole. Table 35 compares the dividends, profits, and sales of the sample and the corporate aggregate for selected years. A rough indicator of profitability is the profits-sales ratio. This ratio is higher for the sample in all years and strikingly higher in 1929 and 1960. After a rapid rise in profits during the twenties, the sample earned 13.5 percent of sales in 1929; profits for all corporations moved slowly in the twenties, and they earned less than 6 percent of sales in 1929. The profits of the sample of large corporations lost ground in the 1929-47 period but almost tripled after that, in contrast to a 20 percent gain for the aggregate. By 1960, the sample was earning 8 percent on sales compared to less than 3 percent for the aggregate. The share of the sample in total corporate profits rose from 10 percent in 1947 to 24 percent in 1960.

The comparisons above must be qualified by the lack of comparability of the two sets of data. A more direct comparison is available. Data for the twenty-eight manufacturing corporations in the sample are taken by Moody's from annual company reports.

---

[1] The data are taken from Moody's Investors Service. The differences between the underlying definitions used there and those used for the industry data are discussed in Appendix D.

TABLE 34. Observed Payout Percentages of Sample Firms, Selected Years and Entire 1920–60 Period (Excluding 1936–38)

Firm	1920	1929	1947	1960	1920–60
Allis-Chalmers Manufacturing Company	22	58	74	129	55.4
American Telephone & Telegraph Co.	84	61	117	60	75.9
Anaconda Company	233	77	59	59	68.1
Babcock and Wilcox Company	68	80	45	43	43.4
Baltimore and Ohio Railroad	56	53	0	59	22.7
Bethlehem Steel Corporation	21	37	35	90	48.0
Blaw-Knox Company	98	60	49	62	45.4
Borden Company	61	49	55	55	61.5
Burroughs Corporation	61	89	52	72	68.7
Consumer Power Company	64	64	59	68	60.2
Detroit Edison Company	106	63	74	76	77.2
Du Pont (E.I.) de Nemours & Company	43	69	74	81	74.6
General Electric Company	73	56	46	88	67.1
General Motors Corporation	47	64	46	59	63.1
International Harvester Company	34	30	44	38	48.3
Loew's-MGM	0	37	73	32	58.0
Montgomery Ward and Company	0	78	43	83	51.3
Owens-Illinois Glass Company	43	65	63	62	58.0
Peoples Gas Light & Coke Company	0	72	56	57	61.3
Pepperell Manufacturing Company	5	77	27	56	56.3
Phillips Petroleum Company	0	65	30	52	51.6
Pittsburgh Plate Glass Company	61	55	55	47	56.4
Procter and Gamble Company	85	52	68	51	62.0
Republic Steel Corporation	24	11	37	89	49.9
R. J. Reynolds Tobacco Company	34	79	62	46	62.8
St. Regis Paper Company	31	60	9	66	45.5
Sears, Roebuck and Company	61	36	' 41	53	52.4
Simmons Company	63	70	35	71	57.4
Sinclair Oil Corporation	0	89	31	87	50.2
S. California Edison Company	43	34	43	49	50.0
Studebaker Corporation	24	68	58	0	571.4
Sun Oil Company	41	16	16	25	20.9
Swift and Company	232	92	56	71	78.8
Texaco, Inc.	82	59	25	44	48.7
Union Carbide Corporation	113	59	50	69	67.5
Union Pacific Railroad	72	45	41	55	48.2
U. S. Rubber Company	30	0	32	41	29.9
U. S. Steel Corporation	23	32	36	53	44.3
White Motor Company	83	39	19	51	59.4
Youngstown Sheet and Tube Company	30	25	38	68	42.2
All 40 firms	51	55	51	61	60.7

TABLE 35. A Comparison of Data for the Sample of Firms and the Corporate Aggregate, Selected Years

(Dollar figures in billions)

Year	All Corporations[a]				Sample[b]			
	Dividends	Profits	Sales	Profits/ Sales (Percent)	Dividends	Profits	Sales	Profits/ Sales (Percent)
1920	2.98	4.65	102	6.1	.242	.474	7.14	6.6
1929	5.72	8.03	139	5.8	.806	1.465	10.86	13.5
1947	6.24	17.55	348	5.0	.916	1.782	26.08	6.8
1960	13.05	21.11	763	2.8	3.055	5.002	63.02	7.9

[a] Source, see Appendix A.
[b] Moody's Investors Service.

This is the basic source used also by the Federal Trade Commission and Securities Exchange Commission (FTC-SEC) estimates of dividends, profits, depreciation and depletion for all manufacturing except newspapers. These estimates are based on a sample believed to be representative of the manufacturing sector and may be appropriately compared to the Moody's data for individual firms. Table 36 gives the estimates for 1947 and 1960. A comparison of profit changes in that interval tells substantially the same story as the earlier comparison of the sample with the Office of Business Economics aggregate. The twenty-eight large manufacturing firms nearly tripled their profits while other firms gained only about 25 percent; the sample's share of the total rose from 12 to 21 percent. Each group raised its payout ratio, but the firms in the sample near-

TABLE 36. A Comparison of Dividends and Profits for Twenty-eight Large Manufacturing Firms to Estimates for All Manufacturing Corporations

(In billions of dollars)

Year	All Manufacturing[a]		Sample[b]		Nonsample (Difference)	
	Dividends	Profits	Dividends	Profits	Dividends	Profits
1947	3.80	10.58	.57	1.27	3.23	9.31
1960	8.28	15.20	2.00	3.24	6.28	11.96

[a] Data taken from *Economic Almanac*, with adjustments (see Appendix A
[b] Moody's Investors Service.

ly quadrupled dividends while the others were doubling their payments.

Differences between the profit trends of the sample and the aggregates could very well account for the different trends in payout ratios. The 1920-29 rise in the sample payout ratio was small relative to the corporate aggregate and probably reflects a lag in dividend increases behind the relatively rapid growth of profits. Similarly, the sample ratio held up relatively well between 1929 and 1947 as dividends were maintained while the profit-sales ratio was cut in half. Finally, the relatively small 1947-60 rise in the sample payout ratio was associated with a relatively rapid rise in profits. The general point is that factors making for changes in the aggregate payout ratio were partially offset for the sample firms by differing profit trends of these firms. This distinctly divergent behavior of profits of the sample and of the aggregate is relevant to an appraisal of the analysis of firm dividend policy.

Variations in Payout Policy

In Table 34, the actual payout ratios of the firms were reported for four years, selected to illustrate trends. The firms show trends that are far less regular and consistent in these intervals than do the industries. About half of the firms increased their payout ratios during 1920-29, twenty-five declined during 1929-47, and thirty-one out of forty increased between 1947 and 1960. One of the difficulties here is that payout policies of individual firms are subject to their own special disturbances. The officers of American Telephone and Telegraph Company, for example, have indicated that their policy is to pay a fairly stable fraction of their profits in dividends. However, their payout ratio soared to 117 percent in 1947 as they maintained dividends despite inroads against profits made by the strike of that year.

This variation in behavior from firm to firm is an obstacle for explanatory models that stress factors external to the firm, such as the depreciation regulations and individual tax rates. On the other hand, the fact that the payout ratios for individual firms were generally more variable over time than those for all forty firms taken

TABLE 37. Frequency Distributions of Actual Payout Percentages, Firms and Industries, Selected Years[a]

Payout Percentage	Forty Firms				Seventeen Industries			
	1920	1929	1947	1960	1920[b]	1929	1947	1960[c]
0–19	6	3	4	1	0	0	1	0
20–39	10	8	10	3	5	0	13	1
40–59	6	9	18	18	2	2	2	7
60–79	9	16	7	11	3	8	1	5
80–99	5	4	0	6	1	5	0	2
100 and over	4	0	1	1	4	2	0	1
1st Quartile	24	38	35	51	37	63	24	54
Median	45	60	46	59	68	74	33	61
3rd Quartile	73	70	59	71	101	93	38	69

[a] Derived from Tables 28 and 34.
[b] Rubber and leather excluded because of negative profits.
[c] Construction excluded because of negative profits.

together should offer some scope for models with varying theoretical long-run payout ratios. These variations are summarized in the frequency distributions of Table 37, where firm and industry behavior may be compared. Industry payout ratios were concentrated in the high intervals in 1929, the low in 1947, and the high again in 1960. Although the trends among the firms were less clear cut, twenty firms paid 60 percent or more in 1929, only eight did so in 1947, and eighteen reached that level again in 1960. The median payout percentages for firms in those years were also indicative of the variation in payout trends, dropping from 60 to 46 and rising again to 59.

The variation in payout among firms in a given year was substantial, and generally the payout percentages for firms appear somewhat more spread out than those for industries. The over-all payout ratios (Table 34) for the entire thirty-eight years show somewhat less variation among firms than the ratios for the single years; even so, one-quarter of the firms paid less than 48.3 percent and one-quarter paid more than 62.0 percent. These differences among firms, like those among industries, lend themselves to explanation by individual models.

TABLE 38. Regression Coefficients, Best Firm Models, 1920–60 (Excluding 1936–38)[a]

Firms and Model Number[b]	Constant Term (a)	Income Measure (Y) (P)	Income Measure (Y) (C)	Depreciation (A)	Tax Shelter ($t_{25}Y$)	Interest Rates (iY)	Sales Change ($S/S_{-2}Y$)	Lagged Dividends (D_{-1})
Allis-Chalmers (3)	.083	.206					−.043	−.247
A. T. & T. (5)	7.844	.236				−.207		−.170
Anaconda (19)	.142	1.113			−.894	−.759		−.526
Babcock & Wilcox (6)	.170	.429		−.029	−.391			−.495
Baltimore & Ohio (16)	−2.054		.470		−.494		−.075	−.505
Bethlehem Steel (6)	−3.642	.425		.031	−.482			−.150
Blaw-Knox (10)	−.012	.855		.169	−.753	−.698		−.520
Borden (10)	−.046	.433		.096	−.268	−.272		−.373
Burroughs (6)	.885	.455		.130	−.442			−.627
Consumer Power (1)	−1.532	.778						−1.124
Detroit Edison (2)	−.253	.279		.133				−.426
Du Pont (4)	−5.692	.830			−.244			−.872
General Electric (10)	−4.879	.874		.857	−.933	−.682		−.618
General Motors (10)	1.157	.924		.408	−.614	−.866		−.610
Int'l. Harvester (7)	.710	.175		.164		−.178		−.415
Loew's-MGM (1)	−.093	.184						−.296
Montgomery Ward (1)	.010	.105						−.182
Owens-Illinois (7)	.850	.284		.325		−.487		−.485
Peoples Gas Light (9)	−.278	.673			−.301	−.408		−.484
Pepperell (10)	.128	.547		.380	−.252	−.665		−.576
Phillips (1)	−.059	.169						−.267
Pittsburgh Glass (5)	1.629	.335				−.220		−.556
Procter & Gamble (5)	2.380	.391				−.124		−.661
Republic Steel (16)	−1.048		.198		−.090		−.026	−.235
Reynolds Tobacco (4)	.128	.236			−.162			−.219
St. Regis (10)	−.323	1.021		.190	−1.077	−.773		−.371
Sears Roebuck (1)	−.624	.182						−.297
Simmons (4)	.068	.302			−.181			−.399
Sinclair (15)	−1.558		.280				−.091	−.590
S. Calif. Edison (5)	−.298	.186				−.139		−.161
Studebaker (10)	.384	1.056		.125	−1.164	−.921		−.602
Sun Oil (2)	.182	.024		.085				−.502
Swift (1)	1.092	.119						−.254
Texaco (1)	4.216	.219						−.497
Union Carbide (2)	2.038	.277		.156				−.571
Union Pacific (16)	.257		.243		−.119		−.045	−.368
U. S. Rubber (1)	−.738	.224						−.557
U. S. Steel (3)	−.188	.250					−.055	−.382
White Motors (2)	−.710	.039		1.900				−.704
Youngstown (2)	−.035	.081		.042				−.231

[a] For units of variables, see Table 30.
[b] For more detailed titles, see Table 34. For equations corresponding to model numbers, see Table 29.

The Best Regression Equations for Each Firm

A single equation that best described the dividend policy of each firm was selected on the basis of the same criteria as those applied to industries. Coefficients of these equations, along with one aggregative equation, are given in Table 38. Of the forty best equations, eighteen utilize the tax shelter variable with the expected negative coefficient. This variable makes a contribution to the "degree of explanation" (measured by the adjusted coefficient of determination $\bar{R}^2$) in all of these cases except Republic Steel, where it is marginal.[2]

The positive influence of depreciation allowances on individual firms is similarly confirmed in two ways. The coefficient of the selected income variable is given in Table 38 under the heading of either (P) or (C). The cash flow variable C, which includes depreciation allowances, improved the explanation of dividends of four of the firms. Secondly, the inclusion of depreciation along with profits improved the explanation of dividends for fifteen of the seventeen firms in which depreciation appears as a separate variable A with the expected sign. Thus, according to the $\bar{R}^2$ criterion, nineteen of the forty firms give some support to the depreciation hypothesis. Interest rates contributed to the degree of explanation of dividends for all fifteen firms for which a coefficient is given. On the other hand, the sales change variable was successful for only six firms.

No requirements were imposed on the constant term in selection of the equations. As pointed out in Chapter II, positive constant terms were expected to be less frequent in the models for firms than in those for industries and aggregates. Even so, the twenty negative constant terms in Table 38 are a surprise. In the case of thirteen of these twenty firms, inclusion of the unexpected negative constant terms raised $\bar{R}^2$, and it was significantly negative at the 5 percent level in seven cases. The positive constant terms were significant for only six firms in a one-tail test. The total of thirteen significant cases may be compared with the four that would be expected by chance

---

[2] Inclusion of the tax variable there reduces the residual variance only by an amount that is offset by allowance for the lost degree of freedom.

TABLE 39. Frequency Distribution of "Speed-of-Adjustment Coefficients," Obtained From Best Regression for Each Firm[a]

Coefficient	Number of Firms
.000– .199	4
.200– .399	14
.400– .599	14
.600– .799	6
.800–1.200	2

[a] Source, Table 38.

even if the underlying "true" coefficients were zero. However, these results obviously give no evidence about the sign of the constant terms.

The infrequency of positive constant terms in these firm models may result, in part, from the relatively high profitability of most firms in the sample. In the absence of a plateau or decline in profits, firms cannot demonstrate the tendency to hold up dividends in the face of adversity. Nevertheless, the presence of a number of significant constant terms but no consistent signs may provide some support for a suggestion by Edwin Kuh.[3] Since the presence of a positive constant term yields target payout ratios generally lower than the average of realized ratios, he suggested that it be omitted. On the other hand, if Lintner's original point concerning resistance to cutting of dividends is correct, the observed ratios would be expected to average higher, and the fact that they do so offers no evidence in favor of exclusion of the constant term.[4]

The speed-of-adjustment coefficients (absolute value of the uniformly negative coefficients for D_{-1}) for the firms showed somewhat greater variability than those for industries. Table 39 summarizes the distribution of these estimated coefficients. All but one fall in the expected interval between 0 and 1, with extremes of 0.150 and 0.872. The median is 48.5 percent, and thirty-six fall in the range from 15 to 63 percent. According to the models, the great majority

[3] Edwin Kuh, *Capital Stock Growth: A Microeconometric Approach* (Amsterdam: North-Holland Publishing Co., 1963), pp. 309-14.

[4] As indicated in Table 34, over the entire period of thirty-eight observations, Studebaker paid out in dividends nearly six times its reported profits. However, an estimated target ratio far below this would not be suspect. The company presumably attained the high payout ratio by seeking to maintain dividends during the bad times of the thirties and adversity since the war.

of corporations, like industries, tend to adjust from 20 to 60 percent of the way toward desired dividend levels each year.

Generalization of the basic models was less effective for these firms than it was for industries. Nevertheless, it improved the explanation of dividends for thirty-two of the forty firms; and in twenty-nine of these cases, at least one among the depreciation, tax rate, and interest rate variables made a contribution.

Significance Tests for the Added Variables*

Table 40 reports the results of significance tests for each variable that made an effective contribution to the explanation of the dividend policy of each corporation.[5] It also illustrates the gains achieved through generalization of the basic Lintner model and records the Durbin-Watson statistic for each equation.[6]

The tax shelter variable (tP or tC) was significant at the 5 percent level or better in the case of sixteen of the firms. In eight of these, the coefficient was significant at the 0.5 percent level or better.

There were ten firms for which depreciation was significant at the 5 percent level when it was included along with profits; half of these were also significant at the 0.5 percent level. In those four cases in which cash flow C turned out to be the best explanatory income variable, net profits P and depreciation charges A were substituted for C and the coefficient of A was tested. Two of these were significant at the 5 percent level, making a total of twelve firms showing depreciation significant at least at that level. Interest rates were significant at the 5 percent level for eleven of the forty firms, and

---

* This section evaluates the explanatory gains achieved by generalization of the basic dividend model. It may be omitted by readers not interested in the technical details. The statistical qualifications discussed following Chapter II should also be considered in evaluating the findings reported here.

[5] The t-ratios underlying the tests are recorded in Appendix E.

[6] The Durbin-Watson statistic was not used as a criterion in the selection of models. As a result, the selected equations for United States Steel and Studebaker were admitted despite the fact that they fell outside the 5 percent critical region of 1.39-2.61 discussed in the last chapter. However, Durbin-Watson statistics for these firms are not far outside this region, and they only slightly qualify the significance tests. Also, even if there were no autocorrelation of the error terms, the expected number of firms for which the statistic would fall outside the 5 percent region would be the same two out of forty.

TABLE 40. Results of Significance Tests for Effective Variables in Best Firm Models, 1920–60 (Excluding 1936–38)

Firm and Best Model[a]	Level of Significance (Percent) Depreciation[b] (A)	Tax Shelter ($t_{25}Y$)	Interest Rates (iY)	Sales Change ($S/S_{-2}Y$)	Durbin-Watson Statistic (D-W)	Adjusted Coefficient of Determination $\bar{R}^2$ Basic Model	Best Model	Equation (10)	Number of Dividend Changes
Allis-Chalmers (3)				d	1.98	.202	.214	.133	29
A. T. & T. (5)			0.5		1.79	.689	.765	.752	32
Anaconda (19)		0.5	5.0		2.12	.723	.819	.813	24
Babcock & Wilcox (6)		5.0			1.59	.423	.483	.482	32
Baltimore & Ohio (16)[c]	5.0	0.5		5.0	1.74	.297	.714	.656	15
Bethlehem (6)	d	0.5			1.70	.543	.666	.653	24
Blaw-Knox (10)	d	5.0	d		2.45	.257	.294	.294	33
Borden (10)	d	0.5	5.0		2.16	.663	.743	.743	29
Burroughs (6)	5.0	5.0			1.99	.369	.458	.450	32
Consumer Power (1)					2.16	.569	.569	.545	36
Detroit Edison (2)	d				1.91	.598	.616	.647	35
Du Pont (4)		5.0			2.13	.927	.936	.933	37
General Electric (10)	0.5	0.5	5.0		2.15	.331	.496	.496	35
General Motors (10)	0.5	0.5	0.5		2.00	.786	.829	.829	32
Int'l. Harvester (7)	5.0		d		1.82	.375	.444	.428	30
Loew's-MGM (1)					2.14	.308	.308	.269	29
Montgomery Ward (1)					1.95	.210	.210	.175	18
Owens-Illinois (7)	5.0		0.5		1.86	.293	.456	.439	31
Peoples Gas Light (9)		5.0	5.0		1.88	.616	.642	.643	28
Pepperell (10)	5.0	d	5.0		1.89	.520	.627	.627	27
Phillips (1)					1.51	.590	.590	.564	30
Pittsburgh Glass (5)			5.0		2.07	.638	.661	.644	38
Procter and G. (5)			d		1.95	.642	.643	.625	31
Republic Steel (16)[c]	d			d	2.38	.531	.537	.498	26
Reynolds Tobacco (4)		5.0			1.88	.400	.489	.476	28
St. Regis (10)	5.0	0.5	0.5		1.74	.426	.601	.601	26
Sears (1)					1.48	.634	.634	.633	33
Simmons (4)		5.0			2.52	.586	.619	.613	25
Sinclair (15)[c]	5.0			5.0	2.15	.318	.458	.387	30
S. Calif. Edison (5)			d		1.75	.305	.339	.320	32
Studebaker (10)	d	0.5	5.0		2.76	.171	.617	.617	24
Sun Oil (2)	0.5				2.38	.289	.436	.406	35
Swift (1)					2.00	.214	.214	.148	22
Texaco (1)					2.19	.604	.604	.582	32
Union Carbide (2)	0.5				2.34	.466	.553	.533	31
Union Pacific (16)[c]		5.0		5.0	1.77	.384	.425	.370	11
U. S. Rubber (1)					2.56	.511	.511	.515	20
U. S. Steel (3)			d		2.75	.704	.716	.680	20
White Motors (2)	0.5				2.26	.206	.332	.293	26
Youngstown (2)	d				1.91	.365	.389	.438	25

[a] For detailed title, see Table 34; for equation corresponding to model number, see Table 29.
[b] The level of significance for the explicit depreciation variable A was tested for all of the firms even though some of them used cash flow as the income variable in their best model. In such cases C was replaced by A and P.
[c] Models for these firms used cash flow as the best income variable; in addition, A and P were substituted for C in order to determine the level of significance of the explicit depreciation variable.
[d] These variables were not significant at the 5 percent level, but they were effective in improving $\bar{R}^2$ for the model.

sales change for three. The income and lagged dividend variables were significant in all cases as expected.

It is the performance of the depreciation and tax shelter variables that is of most consequence for this study. The models for twenty-three of these firms include at least one of the two variables, significant at the 5 percent level or better. Although seventeen of the forty firms showed no significant influence from either depreciation allowances or individual tax rates, the frequent significance of these variables is impressive in light of the relative stability of the aggregate payout ratios for this group of firms. A reasonable, if not rigorous, conjecture might be that a sample of firms whose profit experience and aggregate payout ratios followed more closely the corporate whole would, like the industries, show a higher fraction of the firms sensitive to the tax and depreciation variables.

The number of successful significance tests as well as the overall goodness of fit (as measured by the adjusted coefficient of determinations $\bar{R}^2$ for the best models) are also surprising in view of the variety of circumstances faced by the firms and the presumed stickiness of their dividend policy. The median value of the $\bar{R}^2$ for the firms is 0.561, which compares favorably with the median of 0.647 for the best industry models.

The dividend policy of several of the largest corporations is especially well described by the models. In the case of Du Pont, the tax shelter variable significantly improved the basic model, yielding an $\bar{R}^2$ of 0.936, highest of any in the study. Depreciation, tax rates, and interest rates were all significant for General Motors, and $\bar{R}^2$ was 0.829. The explanation of United States Steel dividends was aided slightly by sales change, yielding an $\bar{R}^2$ of 0.716. Interest rates were significant for two of the five utilities, especially A. T. & T., for which the $\bar{R}^2$ was 0.765. These four giants, with $\bar{R}^2$ greater than 0.7, paid 56 percent of the aggregate dividends declared over the thirty-eight years by the sample corporations.

While the goodness of fit of the best models for firms is impressive, the gain achieved by generalizing the basic model was less than in the case of the industries and aggregates. Even so, the median $\bar{R}^2$ was increased from 0.446 to 0.561; this may be compared to the greater improvement of the industry median from 0.467 to 0.631. The $\bar{R}^2$ for equation (10) is included so that a single generalized equation including depreciation, tax rates and interest rates may be compared with the basic model. This particular model improved on the basic one for twenty-eight of the firms and raised the median $\bar{R}^2$ from 0.446 to 0.539.[7] Although the basic model does a relatively better job for these firms than for aggregates, this comparison shows again the importance of the three public policy variables.

Forecasting Ability of the Models

The validity of the selected models was also checked by using them to forecast the 1960-61 change in dividends. This test is reported in detail in Appendix F and the general conclusion is that the forecasts were satisfactory. However, unlike the case of the industries, the forecasting ability of the generalized models was found to be no better than that of the basic model, or of a naive model that was also tested.

As was true of the industries, very large forecasting errors, and/or evidence of structural change or highly erratic behavior is concentrated in a few cases. The errors made by the general models were more than two standard errors of estimate in the case of five firms, instead of the two such errors to be expected under the assumption of normality. All three models forecast practically no 1960-61 dividend change for General Motors, but the company raised dividends by 25 percent—an increase of $143 million—which it did not explain in its annual report. All three models missed this by about 5 standard errors of estimate. The fitted models failed because the decline in both net earnings and cash flow of General Motors did not portend a rise in dividends. Part of the rise of the dividends stemmed from an increase in shares outstanding with the exercise of stock options, but most resulted from a last quarter boost in the dividend rate. Apparently, the company was sufficiently encouraged by a rapid rate of recovery from the recession to discount the decline in earnings for the year in deciding the dividend rate. The three models presumably failed to reflect this because the use of annual data suppressed the evidence of recovery.

[7] This comparison should be qualified slightly because of the presence of some perverse signs in the general models. None of the negative depreciation coefficients improved the $\bar{R}^2$, but there was one significant positive tax coefficient and two significant positive interest coefficients. Thus, the meaningful improvement by the Equation (10) generalization is slightly exaggerated.

This forecasting error for General Motors alone accounted for about one-half of the sum of the absolute errors made by the forty models.[8]

Trends in Long-Run Payout Policy

The years 1920, 1929, 1947, and 1960 were selected to illustrate trends in the theoretical long-run payout ratios of industries. The observed payout ratio for the firm sample total (Table 34) showed far less variation between those years than did the corporate aggregate. However, for consistency, the same years were chosen to try to bring out trends in the theoretical ratios for firms. These theoretical ratios are derived from the target functions implied by the best equations. Table 41 is comparable to Table 32 in Chapter VI. It gives the number of the equation used (as described in Table 29) and the implied target ratios for the four years.

The behavior of nine of the forty firms is best described by equation 1—the basic model, since additional variables made no significant improvement. In other words, no significant explainable changes were found in the long-run payout ratio for those firms. The over-all observed payout ratio for the thirty-eight years is also given for each firm in the last column. These are expected to be greater than the payout ratios of the basic model because of maintenance of dividends in bad times; however, some differences are large. Swift paid out 79 percent over all compared to the 47 percent theoretical ratio. More surprisingly, Republic Steel did the reverse of what was theoretically expected and paid out only 50 percent compared to the 78 percent long-run theoretical ratio. United States Rubber and Consumer Power also paid out substantially less over the thirty-eight years than the theoretical ratio. Part of these peculiarities may be because of the domination of the over-all ratio by the larger magnitudes since the beginning of World War II.

---

[8] An enormous forecasting error (relatively) appeared to be made for Southern California Edison. The company reported a temporary 88 percent increase in dividends in 1961 for no reason discernible in the behavior of the explanatory variables of this study. The general model appeared to commit an error 29 times the standard error of estimate, and other models also failed.

In this case, however, the model showed the data to be wrong. A check of the company's 1961 annual report revealed that dividends had apparently doubled only because a stock dividend had been evaluated and added to cash dividends. (This error was corrected in the forecasting tests given in Appendix F.)

TABLE 41. Target Payout Percentages Implied by Best Firm Models, Selected Years and Entire 1920–60 Period

Firm and Best Model[a]	Target Payout Percentages				Payout Percentage, 1920–60	
	1920	1929	1947	1960	Basic Model Target	Actual
Allis-Chalmers (3)	68	60	71	66	67	55.4
A. T. & T. (5)	47	75	104	81	109	75.9
Anaconda (9)	55	104	59	55	57	68.1
Babcock & Wilcox (6)	59	71	34	43	38	43.4
Baltimore & Ohio (6)	62	69	31	153	66	22.7
Bethlehem Steel (6)	214	230	83	130	100	48.0
Blaw-Knox (10)	38	74	39	53	37	45.4
Borden (10)	64	74	58	58	60	61.5
Burroughs (6)	54	61	29	67	47	68.7
Consumer Power (1)	69	69	69	69	69	60.2
Detroit Edison (2)	72	83	87	88	91	77.2
Du Pont (4)	87	90	77	81	78	74.6
General Electric (10)	82	84	54	91	75	67.1
General Motors (10)	34	68	64	59	62	63.1
Int'l. Harvester (7)	18	30	39	66	63	48.3
Loew's-MGM (1)	62	62	62	62	62	58.0
Montgomery Ward (1)	58	58	58	58	58	51.3
Owens-Illinois (7)	−6	32	50	55	56	58.0
Peoples Gas Light (9)	58	83	74	67	67	61.3
Pepperell (10)	1	41	38	52	44	56.3
Phillips (1)	63	63	63	63	63	51.6
Pittsburgh Glass (5)	30	40	49	42	46	56.4
Procter & Gamble (5)	45	49	54	50	52	62.0
Republic Steel (1)	78	78	78	78	78	49.9
Reynolds Tobacco (4)	87	94	59	69	68	62.8
St. Regis (10)	53	124	36	78	72	45.5
Sears Roebuck (1)	61	61	61	61	61	52.4
Simmons (4)	63	67	46	52	48	57.4
Sinclair Oil (2)	48	70	42	96	55	50.2
S. Calif. Edison (5)	50	71	91	75	77	50.0
Studebaker (10)	16	62	16	156	14	571.4
Sun Oil (2)	22	16	15	26	41	20.9
Swift (1)	47	47	47	47	47	78.8
Texaco (1)	44	44	44	44	44	48.7
Union Carbide (2)	58	54	54	71	74	67.5
Union Pacific (6)	58	62	47	55	49	48.2
U. S. Rubber (1)	40	40	40	40	40	29.9
U. S. Steel (3)	51	49	48	50	51	44.3
White Motors (2)	117	107	44	56	22	59.4
Youngstown (2)	49	42	44	54	51	42.2

[a] For detailed firm title, see Table 34; for equation corresponding to model number, see Table 29.

The variable theoretical ratios for the other thirty-one firms appear erratic in many cases, partly because of the volatile nature of the profit base. The presence of the depreciation factor in the form A/P in many of the target functions leads to sharp increases in the target percentage whenever profits approach zero. While not much can be read into these estimates for any single firm, a summary of their behavior may give some idea of their validity. The 1920-29 rise in the observed payout ratios for the sample total was consistent with the rise in the theoretical ratios for twenty-five of these thirty-one firms. The 1929-47 decline in the total ratio is in line with the decline for twenty-one of the thirty-one firms for which the ratio changed. The 1947-60 rise in the observed total ratio paralleled the twenty-two out of thirty positive changes in the long-run ratios.

A more direct comparison may be made between changes in the observed ratios (Table 34) and theoretical ratios (Table 41) for each firm. As was the case with the industries, the 1920-29 comparison showed such a lack of correspondence that no further attempt was made to analyze changes in firm dividend policy during the twenties. However, in the 1929-47 interval, the observed ratios moved in the same direction as the theoretical ratio for twenty-two of the twenty-nine firms in which both changed. The corresponding figures for the 1947-60 interval were twenty parallel moves out of twenty-nine.

These rough checks are hardly adequate for an appraisal of the estimated theoretical long-run ratios in Table 41. The rather weak correspondence between observed (short-run) ratios and the theoretical (long-run) ratios does not necessarily invalidate the latter. On the other hand, the behavior of the long-run ratios is sufficiently erratic to qualify the estimates shown of the contribution of different variables to changes in this ratio over time. In any case, the changes themselves do seem of sufficient magnitude to justify the attempt to attribute them to individual variables.

Contribution of Various Factors to Payout Trends

Changes in the theoretical ratios are decomposed in Table 42 (comparable to Table 33 in Chapter VI) to measure the influence of the various factors included among the independent variables. The contributions of depreciation, tax rates, interest rates and sales change to the indicated 1929-47 and 1947-60 changes in the target

Firms[b]	1929–47				1947–60			
	Change in Target Payout	Contributed by:			Change in Target Payout	Contributed by:		
		Depreciation Index (A/P)	Tax Shelter (t_{25})	Interest Rates (i)		Depreciation Index (A/P)	Tax Shelter (t_{25})	Interest Rates (i)
Allis-Chalmers	+11[c]				−4[c]			
A. T. & T.	+29			+29	−23			−23
Anaconda	−45		−79	+34	−4		+23	−27
Babcock & Wilcox	−37	0	−37		+9	−2	+11	
Baltimore & Ohio	−39	+25	−64		+123	+104	+19	
Bethlehem Steel	−147	+3	−150		+47	+3	+44	
Blaw-Knox	−34	+1	−67	+32	+15	+20	+20	−25
Borden	−17	0	−34	+17	0	+4	+10	−14
Burroughs	−32	+1	−33		+39	+29	+10	
Consumer Power	0				0			
Detroit Edison	+4	+4			+1	+1		
Du Pont	−13		−13		+4		+4	
General Electric	−29	+15	−70	+26	+37	+37	+21	−21
General Motors	−4	+10	−47	+33	−5	+8	+14	−27
Int'l. Harvester	+10	0		+10	+27	+35		−8
Loew's-MGM	0				0			
Montgomery Ward	0				0			
Owens-Illinois	+18	−6		+24	+5	+24		−19
Peoples Gas Light	−9		−29	+20	−7		+9	−16
Pepperell	−3	−10	−20	+27	+14	+30	+6	−22
Phillips	0				0			
Pittsburgh Glass	+9			+9	−7			−7
Procter & Gamble	+4			+4	−4			−4
Republic Steel	0				0			
Reynolds Tobacco	−34		−34		+10		+10	
St. Regis	−89	−2	−136	+49	+43	+42	+40	−39
Sears Roebuck	0				0			
Simmons	−21		−21		+6		+6	
Sinclair	−29	−29			+55	+55		
S. Calif. Edison	+20			+20	−16			−16
Studebaker	−45	+9	−90	+36	+140	+142	+27	−29
Sun Oil	−1	−1			+12	+12		
Swift	0				0			
Texaco	0				0			
Union Carbide	0	0			+16	+16		
Union Pacific	−15	+1	−16		+8	+3	+5	

TABLE 42. Decomposition of Selected Percentage Point Changes (Continued)

	1929–47				1947–60			
	Change in Target Payout	Contributed by:			Change in Target Payout	Contributed by:		
Firms[b]		Depreciation Index (A/P)	Tax Shelter (t_{25})	Interest Rates (i)		Depreciation Index (A/P)	Tax Shelter (t_{25})	Interest Rates (i)
U. S. Rubber	0				0			
U. S. Steel	−1[c]				+2[c]			
White Motors	−63	−63			+12	+12		
Youngstown	+2	+2			+10	+10		

[a] Derived from Table 41. The target changes in this table may disagree with those indicated in Table 41 because of rounding.
[b] For detailed title, see Table 34.
[c] The sales change variable accounted for this change.

ratios are derived by applying the coefficient of each variable in the implied target functions to the data. The sum of the separate contributions completely accounts for the overall change. For example, the model says that the 45 percentage point decline in the theoretical payout ratio for Anaconda between 1929 and 1947 is the net result of (1) a 79 point discouragement of dividends by higher tax rates, and (2) a partial offset of 34 points through a drop in interest rates.

The indicated influence of depreciation liberality and individual tax rates varies so widely from firm to firm that little credence can be placed in the results for any single firm. However, a few fairly clear-cut indications emerge for the group as a whole. According to the models, an over-all relative decline in depreciation between 1929 and 1947 was not a significant brake on payout ratios. The theoretical ratios for only three firms were cut as much as 10 percentage points because of the influence of the depreciation factor, and the ratios for three firms even increased by 10 points or more. These last three—General Electric, General Motors, and Baltimore and Ohio—ran counter to the majority of firms in substantially increasing their depreciation charges relative to their net profits. The increases in depreciation charges relative to net profits were from 20 percent to 31 percent for General Electric, from 14 to 29 for General Motors, and from 20 to 154 for the Baltimore and Ohio. These large increases explain the stimulating effect (according to the models) of depreciation on the dividends paid by these firms in 1947 compared to 1929. The models show a more significant impact by depreciation charges with the postwar liberalization. This development had a positive effect of at least 10 percentage points for fourteen of the corporations, and of 20 or more points for ten of them.

The models show that tax rates had a greater effect on the estimated target ratio between 1929 and 1947 than depreciation had in either interval. The sharp rise in individual tax rates cut the theoretical payout ratio at least 10 points for seventeen firms, at least 20 points for fifteen firms and at least 30 points for twelve firms. The slight fall in tax rates between 1947 and 1960 was less influential, but it raised the theoretical ratio at least 10 points for twelve firms.

The contribution of interest rates to the trends showed less variation from firm to firm. The 1929-47 decline in rates raised the ratio at least 10 points for thirteen firms, at least 20 points for eleven firms. The subsequent rise in interest rates cut the target at least 10 points for twelve firms, at least 20 for eight firms.

A Further Comment on the Problem of Aggregation

The firm models give considerable support to the depreciation, tax rate, and interest hypotheses, but the evidence is far less convincing than that for industries and aggregates. This raises again the possibility that the industry and aggregate results are, in part, aggregation phenomena and that the equations are not actually descriptive of the behavior of the majority of individual firms. It has already been argued that the atypical profit experience of these firms makes this a questionable conjecture; however, more direct evidence on this problem is available.

If the relatively weak support of the hypotheses by the firm models points to an aggregation phenomenon, this would suggest that results for the total of the forty firms should give stronger support to the hypotheses than those for individual firms. To check this point, models were fitted to data for thirty-eight years aggregated over all forty firms in the sample. The equation obtained for the basic Lintner model (with data in millions of dollars) was

$$(7\text{-}1) \qquad D - D_{-1} = 21.6 + .285P - .453D_{-1}$$
$$(16.9) \quad (.025) \quad\;\; (.045)$$

$$\bar{R}^2 = 0.799 \qquad D\text{-}W = 1.93 \qquad r = 0.629$$

This model, with a fixed payout ratio, gives a far better description of the over-all behavior of the sample firms than it did for all corporations or manufacturing corporations. The coefficient of determination is much higher here and the Durbin-Watson statistic is satisfactory.

The success of the simple model in explaining aggregate dividends in the sample was accompanied by a weak showing by the tax and depreciation variables. Inclusion of the Machine and Allied Products Institute depreciation liberality index alone in a variable target function appeared successful. The tax shelter variable was of marginal significance by itself and was useless when the depreciation index was combined with it.

The only significant improvement of the basic model was accomplished by the sales change variable. When included alone, its coefficient was negative, as expected, and differed from zero by more than four standard errors. Combining the sales change and depreciation liberality variables left the former highly significant, but reduced the latter to marginal significance at the 5 percent level. This generalization of the basic model raised the adjusted coefficient of determination $\bar{R}^2$ to 0.875, and the residuals remained satisfactory. The conclusion on the behavior of the total dividends paid by the sample of forty firms is that sales change makes a substantial contribution to the explanation, but depreciation is of marginal importance and the tax shelter fails to explain any variation not explained by the others.

The fact that models for the sample total gave *less* support to the depreciation, tax rate, and interest rate hypotheses than the individual firm equations is evidence against the interpretation that previous success of these hypotheses was manufactured by the process of aggregation. Instead, it reaffirms the atypical nature of the experience and behavior of the firms in the sample.[9]

This argument does not imply that an aggregation problem does not exist. A test of this would require more regressions on firm data and a more representative sample. The point stressed here is that even though the regression equations for these forty firms gave considerable support to the three main hypotheses, the equation for the sample total gave practically none. Far from producing spurious

[9] It may also reflect in part less distortion of the net profits measure by liberalized depreciation in the Moody's data than in the Office of Business Economics data.

association, aggregation of the firm data suppressed the evidence for the hypotheses provided by the individual firms and thus produced the exact opposite of an aggregation phenomenon. This result offers no reason to suspect that the earlier process of aggregation in Chapters III to V exaggerated the influence of these tax factors on the dividend policy of individual firms.[10]

The Determinants of Dividend Payments by Firms

A comparison of Table 42 in this chapter and Table 33 in Chapter VI suggests that, for those firms in which depreciation, individual taxes, and interest rates made an explanatory contribution, the impact of these factors was of the same order as in the industries. For example, where tax rates appeared in the best firm equation, the median impact was —42 points for the 1929-47 interval. For the industries where the variable appeared, its median impact was —34. In the case of the 1947-60 interval, the median impact of the explicit depreciation variables was 20 points for the firms, 26 points for the industries. The main difference between the success of the industry and firm models appears to be that the public policy factors in the firm models yielded explanatory improvement with less frequency and, when such improvement occurred, its estimated impact showed higher variability among firms than it did among industries. This could be because of lesser validity of the models at the firm level, or because of greater estimation difficulties grounded in the relative stickiness of firm dividends.

[10] Probably one of the reasons that the relationships between dividend change and other variables emerged more clearly for each of the firms than would be expected on the basis of the model for all firms was that dividends paid by each firm were not as sticky as might have been expected. The right hand column of Table 40 indicates that almost half of the firms changed their dividends in thirty or more of the thirty-eight years, and only three—including the two railroads which changed least—did so in less than half of the years.

This rather surprising volatility of the dividend series results from the fact that aggregate dividends can change not only because of changed rates per share (including year-end extras) but also because of changes in the number of outstanding shares through new issues (including exercised stock options) and stock dividends. Since dividend changes arising from variations in the number of shares outstanding may be partially inadvertent, it is possible that models explaining dividends *per share* by other per-share variables might refine the present approach.

Although the public policy factors were less successful explanatory variables for firms than for industries, each had an impact on a substantial minority of the firms. The combined effect of the three variables on the 1929-47 and 1947-60 trends in the theoretical ratios is also worth noting. In the case of twenty-six firms, at least one of the variables contributed 10 or more points to these trends. There was a contribution of 20 or more points in the case of twenty-one of the forty firms.

Counting the number of successes of the tested variables is an incomplete evaluation of their importance. There was great variation in the size of the firms in the sample, and the models tended to be more successful in explaining dividend payments by the larger corporations. For example, generalization of the basic model made a substantial contribution to the explanation of dividends paid by American Telephone and Telegraph, General Motors, General Electric, and Du Pont. The models indicate that depreciation, tax rates, and interest rates all made significant contributions to the explanation of General Motors and General Electric dividends, and two of the variables were highly significant in both cases. The models showed tax rates to be a factor in Du Pont dividend payments, and the interest rate variable was highly significant in the American Telephone and Telegraph model. These four companies accounted for more than one-half of the total activity of the forty firms in the sample. In 1960, they charged 54 percent of the depreciation charged by the forty firms, earned 55 percent of the profits, and paid 58 percent of the dividends.[11] The significance of the public policy variables for these four large firms suggests a higher evaluation of their influence than indicated by the fact that the individual variables each failed to contribute a significant explanation of dividends in a majority of cases.

While the firms show less reaction to these factors than do the industries, even this frequency of success of the generalized firm models—especially with large firms—is fairly impressive in light of the failure of the three variables in the time series analysis of the sample total. The models also had to contend with the relative constancy of dividend payments by single firms. In the particular case

[11] This represented a relative gain since the war for the four firms on these three criteria. For example, their shares in 1947 were 47 percent, 38 percent, and 50 percent, respectively.

of depreciation, a lesser impact was to be expected in any case, since company reports showed less postwar liberalization than did the actual charges on which the aggregative analysis was based. Although the results for firms are not consistent enough to permit generalizations about firm behavior, they appear sufficient to account, at least in part, for the aggregate and industry results of Chapters III to VI. The indicated impact of depreciation, individual tax rates, and interest rates on at least one-third of the firms (including some of the largest) in each case could be expected to be reflected in the corporate aggregate. At the same time, there was no indication from this sample that the process of aggregation tends to exaggerate the importance of these factors in dividend policy.

Finally, it should be recognized that this study of forty firms probably has raised more questions than it has answered. The reasons for the lesser success of the explanatory variables at the firm level than in the aggregative analysis remain speculative. The differing relative importance of the variables at the two levels of analysis also remains unexplained; for example, the interest rate variable was at least as important as the shelter variable for firms but not for the aggregate. Furthermore, no attempt has been made here to explain the pronounced differences between firms with respect to the influence of the various factors and the over-all success of the models—particularly the relatively better explanation of the dividend policy of large firms. Resolving these questions would require a detailed analysis of the financial and other characteristics of the individual firms.

CHAPTER VIII

Pooling of Time Series and Cross-Section Data

AN ALTERNATIVE TO the speed-of-adjustment type of dividend model was adopted in this final phase of the study to test whether a basically different technique would substantiate earlier results and thus add to their credibility. Long-run payout ratios were estimated for each year for the sample of firms[1] by a cross-section regression of dividends on profits, using the data for all forty firms. The tax variables and others were then tested for their ability to explain variations in this ratio over time.

Rationale of the Method

The foremost objective of this study has been to isolate the impact of public policy factors on trends in dividend payments. One of the obstacles preventing more reliable estimates of the coefficients for these factors is the correlation among independent variables that makes it difficult to disentangle their separate

---

[1] For characteristics of the sample see the last chapter. It was shown there that these forty firms are by no means representative of all corporations. Thus it should be recognized that these new tests of the earlier hypotheses focus on only one part of the corporate universe.

influences. This difficulty may be illustrated by reference to one of the successful aggregate models. The starting point was the basic Lintner model:

$$(8\text{-}1) \qquad D - D_{-1} = a + c(rP - D_{-1}) + u$$

In place of r (the fixed target payout ratio), may be substituted the target function

$$(8\text{-}2) \qquad r_t = \alpha + \beta \frac{A}{A_2} + \gamma t_{25} + \delta i + \epsilon \frac{S}{S_{-2}}$$

After multiplication of the profit variable P in the basic model by the terms of r_t, the generalized linear model becomes

$$(8\text{-}3) \qquad D - D_{-1} = a + b_1 P + b_2 \frac{A}{A_2} P + b_3 t_{25} P + b_4 i P$$

$$+ b_5 \frac{S}{S_{-2}} P - c D_{-1}$$

This model thus contains six independent variables. The extent of their damaging multicollinearity may be estimated using data for the corporate aggregate. Correlation coefficients for all pairs of these variables are listed in Table 43. These high correlations were to be expected since multiplication of P by the target function made P a component of all the independent variables except D_{-1}. More surprising is the fact that the model was able to produce statistically significant coefficients while hampered by these correlations. Despite the considerable success of the time series models in overcoming the collinearity, it seemed worth while to try to escape its influence through an alternative estimation procedure.

TABLE 43. Simple Coefficients of Correlation Between Pairs of Independent Variables, All Corporations, 1920–60 (Excluding 1936–38)

Independent Variables[a]	Net Profits P	Depreciation $(A/A_2)P$	Tax Rates $t_{25}P$	Interest Rates iP	Sales Change $(S/S_{-2})P$
Depreciation $(A/A_2)P$	.96				
Tax Shelter $t_{25}P$	.97	.91			
Interest Rates iP	.93	.96	.84		
Sales Change $(S/S_{-2})P$	.98	.91	.96	.89	
Lagged Dividends D_{-1}	.83	.88	.82	.83	.77

[a] For definition and measurement of the variables see Appendix A and Appendix B.

The depreciation liberality, tax shelter and interest rate variables—A/A_2, t_{25} and i—are presumed to be macroeconomic influences on firms, affecting them differently, but at least taken as given in any one year. This suggests the possibility of using cross-section data for firms to estimate the simple relationship between dividends and profits for each separate year. This estimation process is aided by the fact that in any given year the three public policy variables are held constant. All corporations are faced by the same over-all tax and interest rate structure. Some may be in more advantageous positions than others, but there are no changes in this external structure to obscure the effect of profits on dividends. This relationship can be estimated without the loss of degrees of freedom that occurs in time series models through the necessity to include these external factors explicitly.

Meyer and Kuh have warned against indiscriminate mingling of cross-section and time series regressions on the ground that it may confound short-run and long-run relationships in a misleading fashion.[2] However, for the problem at hand, the approach is promising. The objective is an explanation of the long-run changes in the relationship between dividends and profits. The long-run relationship may be estimated each year from the cross-section data for firms,[3] and variations in this relationship may then be explained by the time series factors.

Annual Estimates of Long-Run Payout Propensities

The overall long-run marginal propensity of firms to pay dividends out of profits was estimated for each year by a linear regression of dividends on profits using all 40 firms in the sample. The regression coefficient of P (the estimated slope $\Delta D/\Delta P$) was taken as an estimate of this long-run marginal propensity. It was so interpreted on the ground that ΔP, by representing the differences in profits between established firms at a given point in time, was akin

[2] J. R. Meyer and E. Kuh, "How Extraneous Are Extraneous Estimates?," *Review of Economics and Statistics,* Vol. 39, No. 4 (November 1957), pp. 380-393.

[3] For a statement of the argument that cross-section regressions do indeed generally yield long-run relationships see, for example, L. Klein, *Introduction to Econometrics* (Prentice-Hall, 1962), pp. 52-60. The rationale will also be discussed further and qualified below.

to a long-run change in profits for single firms. Assuming that different firms have adapted to the current level of profits almost completely or approximately to the same extent, the corresponding ΔD can be regarded as representing a long-run response by firms to a change in profits. This is in contrast with the short-run marginal propensity which can be estimated from temporal changes for single firms, rather than from interfirm differences.[4]

This interpretation of the cross-section slopes as estimates of the long-run response of dividends to profit changes must be qualified. Although data for a single year are used in estimating each slope, individual firms are affected by their own recent experience, and this may vary substantially among firms. In the first place, it should be recognized that the cross-section explanation of dividends by profits alone is a crude device. Although tax factors are given in a particular year, a more elaborate model might include other differences among firms, such as recent sales change, in an effort to isolate the net relationship between dividends and profits. Secondly, high-profit and low-profit firms may be in their current positions partly because of temporary good fortune or temporary adversity. Their incomplete adjustments would then impart a downward bias to the slope as a long-run measure. Finally it is possible that a bias could arise because in any given year large and small firms differ in their degree of adaptation to current profit levels. However, it is probable that these two possible biases are of relatively minor importance. Given the great variation in size among the firms, it is likely that the major component of the differences in profitability between high-profit and low-profit firms is associated with size and is long-run in nature. Further, although the slope of the regression of D on P is a rather crude measure and could be biased,[5] it may at

[4] Corporations with low profits are presumed to adjust slowly to higher dividend levels when their profits rise. Only after maintaining the higher profit levels will they tend to pay the same dividends as firms already accustomed to the higher levels.

[5] In addition to the possible biases discussed above, the small firms force the regression line very close to the origin, and—assuming the relationship is linear —the slope would tend to be dominated by the large firms. However, this was not necessarily inappropriate for the primarily macroeconomic focus of this study, since large firms pay the bulk of all dividends. For this reason, the data were not normalized by division by a size variable such as assets or sales. The logarithmic transformation could not be used in pursuit of homoscedasticity because of the presence of negative and near-zero profits. This did not seem a great loss, since only the point estimates of the slopes were to be used.

TABLE 44. Annual Estimates of Target Payout Ratios and Their Standard Errors for Sample of Forty Firms[a]

Year	Estimated Target Payout (r_t')	Year	Estimated Target Payout (r_t')	Year	Estimated Target Payout (r_t')	Year	Estimated Target Payout (r_t')
1920	.355 (.048)	1930	.762 (.027)	1940	.780 (.032)	1950	.648 (.016)
1921	.396 (.072)	1931	.942 (.046)	1941	.787 (.038)	1951	.687 (.023)
1922	.594 (.040)	1932	.874 (.086)	1942	.743 (.056)	1952	.669 (.020)
1923	.455 (.045)	1933	1.075 (.099)	1943	.782 (.041)	1953	.642 (.025)
1924	.616 (.035)	1934	1.068 (.078)	1944	.846 (.044)	1954	.610 (.021)
1925	.594 (.026)	1935	.830 (.060)	1945	.836 (.032)	1955	.542 (.020)
1926	.552 (.028)	1936	.837 (.029)	1946	.822 (.042)	1956	.645 (.021)
1927	.602 (.016)	1937	.798 (.045)	1947	.569 (.055)	1957	.645 (.021)
1928	.604 (.016)	1938	.910 (.042)	1948	.517 (.036)	1958	.699 (.024)
1929	.553 (.027)	1939	.849 (.027)	1949	.566 (.026)	1959	.632 (.013)
						1960	.595 (.014)

[a] The r_t' presented are the slopes of the regressions of D on P, which are taken to be estimates of r_t (the unknown aggregate target payout ratio for the sample).

least be biased consistently and thus a good indicator of changes over time in the over-all long-run propensity. If so, a regression of these propensities on the tax factors and interest rates may succeed in isolating the effect of these external factors.

The annual regression slopes are recorded as r_t' in Table 44. These estimated propensities show a far less clear-cut temporal pattern than the observed and target payout ratios for the total of sample

TABLE 45. Simple Correlation Coefficients Between Pairs of Independent Variables Tested in Target Functions, 1920–60 (Excluding 1936–38)

Independent Variables[a]	Depreciation (A/A_2)	Tax Shelter (t_{25})	Interest Rates (i)
Tax Shelter (t_{25})	−.22		
Interest Rates (i)	+.15	−.83	
Sales Change (S/S_{-2})	−.39	+.33	−.40

[a] For definition and measurement of the variables see Appendix A and Appendix B.

firms. On the basis of casual inspection, it appeared unlikely that they could be explained by the tax factors or interest rates, which exhibit clear-cut trends. On the other hand, this might be offset by the stronger estimation potential of this procedure. These variables are designed to explain the target payout ratio r_t itself (as estimated by the regression slopes r_t'). Since they are not to be multiplied by profits, there is now much less collinearity among the independent variables. This is indicated by the correlations shown in Table 45. The correlations are low, and multicollinearity no longer presents a problem except between the tax and interest rate variables.[6]

The plausibility of the estimated long-run target payout ratios in Table 44 may be evaluated by comparing them to the target ratios derived from the basic Lintner model (2-1) which performed well for this sample aggregate. The long-run target ratio was 0.630, and the short-run marginal propensity to distribute was 0.285. The median of the estimated r_t based on cross-section data (excluding 1936-38) was 0.642, which is consistent with the over-all Lintner target ratio. The estimated annual long-run propensities of Table 44 are also well above the single short-run propensity derived from

[6] The high negative association between these two variables is statistically obvious from the trends in the data. Tax rates rose sharply between the late twenties and the war period and dipped somewhat after that. Trends in interest rates were in the opposite direction. The explanation of the association is more difficult. Successful modern countercyclical and growth policies would influence them to move in the same direction. Any such tendency appears to have been swamped by other factors. For example, it is possible that the alternate use of interest rates and tax rates as policy instruments in seeking a given level of aggregate demand may be one factor in the negative association. On the other hand, the negative association may be merely coincidental, or it may be because of a tendency for these two fiscal policy variables to be viewed as substitutes.

the Lintner model, as would be expected according to *a priori* reasoning.

Regression Results: Depreciation, Tax Rates, and Interest Rates

The coefficient representing long-run target ratios is assumed to vary with tax laws and other factors,[7] so the problem is one of explaining the time series of cross-section estimates of r_t by means of these external variables. This means that the time series variables are being asked to explain variations of a dependent variable already subject to estimation error as well as measurement error.[8]

The equation, derived by a regression of the r_t' on the three public policy variables, is reported as relation (8-4), with r_t'' denoting the regression estimate of r_t'.

(8-4)
$$r_t'' = .577 + .688A/A_2 - .324t_{25} - .734i$$
$$(.202) \quad (.119) \qquad (.161) \qquad (.241)$$

$$\bar{R}^2 = .533 \qquad \text{D-W} = 0.91$$

The low Durbin-Watson statistic is strong evidence of positive autocorrelation of the residuals, indicating the standard errors are likely to have a downward bias. Even in this form, however, the relation is fairly convincing. The signs are as expected. The depreciation liberality index appears highly significant despite the low Durbin-Watson statistic. An increase in that variable of 0.5 is associated

[7] For this reason, the dividend hypotheses of this study cannot be tested by simply inserting the cross-section estimate of the income coefficient for dividends as a constant in the original time series model. In one conventional type of pooling of time series and cross-section data (see L. Klein, *op. cit.*, pp. 61-73), one variable, such as quantity demanded, is assumed to depend on others, such as price and income. Suppose the model is $\log q = \alpha + \beta \log p + \gamma \log Y + u$. The income coefficient could be estimated by a simple regression of $\log q$ on $\log y$, utilizing a cross-section of household budget data. Price is ignored at this stage, since it is assumed to be held constant (as are the tax variables in the present problem) by restriction of the data to a single time period. The cross-section estimate of the income coefficient is substituted for γ in the original equation, the income term is transposed to the left, and the price coefficient is then estimated by a simple time series regression.

[8] It should also be noted here that depreciation liberality is crudely measured. The ratio A/A_2 (defined in Appendix A) is based on data for all corporations and could not be computed specially for this sample.

TABLE 46. Decomposition of Percentage Point Changes Into Contributions by Selected Variables Compared for Two Estimates of Target Payout Ratios, 1920–29, 1929–47, and 1947–60

Change in Estimated Payout Ratio	Interval of Change		
	1920–29	1929–47	1947–60
All Corporations[a]			
Contribution by:			
Depreciation index		−5	+20
Interest rates		+10	−8
Tax shelter		−34	+10
Sales change		−6	+5
Change in estimated payout ratio (r_t)		−35	+27
All Sample Firms[b]			
Contribution by:			
Depreciation index	+22	−18	+31
Interest rates	+17	+17	−14
Tax shelter	+3	−15	+4
Change in regression estimates of payout ratios (r_t'')	+42	−16	+21

[a] From Table 33, Chapter VI.
[b] Derived from regression estimates of annual target payout ratios for all sample firms (relation 8-4).

with a 34 percentage point rise in the estimated target payout ratio. A rise of 3 points in interest rates cuts the theoretical payout ratio 22 points, and a 50 point rise in tax rates reduces it by 16 points.

The contribution of the policy variables to trends in the estimated long-run payout ratio is illustrated for selected years in Table 46. The impact of these variables on the theoretical targets for all firms may be compared to those shown for the corporate aggregate in Table 33 (Chapter VI). The present set of estimates shows a greater impact by depreciation liberality and interest rates in both the 1920-47 and 1947-60 intervals, and a smaller role for tax rates. However, the pooling of time series and cross-section information for these firms suggests that these three influences taken together are about as important for the statistical explanation of dividend policy as they appeared to be in the aggregate analysis for all corporations. This is an interesting result in light of the failure of the

CHART 6. Dependent Variable and Regression Estimates, Regression 8-4, 1920–60

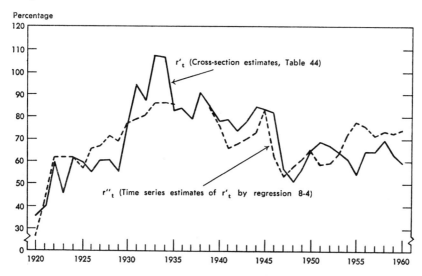

time series analysis of the firm sample total to reveal any convincing relationships. Avoiding the collinearity in the sample series brought out the relationships found earlier for all corporations, especially that for depreciation which had a positive coefficient five times its standard error.

Correction for Autocorrelation*

The low Durbin-Watson statistic of equation (8-4) indicates that the significance of the coefficients is likely to be exaggerated because of autocorrelated errors. The cause of this difficulty is indicated in Chart 6 where it may be seen that during several periods the r_t'' were repeatedly too high or too low. For example, equation (8-4) yields estimates of the long-run ratios (cross-section estimates) that are too high for 1926-29, too low for 1931-34, too low for 1941-44, and too high for 1954-60.

This tendency of equation (8-4) to overestimate or underesti-

* This section derives alternative estimates and corrects for the likely downward bias in the standard errors indicated by the low D-W statistic. It may be omitted by readers not interested in the technical methodology.

TABLE 47. Comparison of Two Alternative Estimates of the Coefficients for Depreciation, Tax Rates, and Interest Rates and Their Standard Errors

Coefficient Estimated	Relation (8–4)		Relation (8–7)	
	Estimate	Standard Error	Estimate	Standard Error
Constant Term (a)	.577	.202	.782	.238
Depreciation (A/A_2)	.688	.119	.486	.183
Interest Rates (i)	−.734	.241	−.877	.354
Tax Shelter (t_{2b})	−.324	.161	−.312	.222
	$\bar{R}^2 = .533$	D-W = 0.91	$\bar{R}^2 = .150$	D-W = 1.60

mate persistently over substantial periods may arise from inadequacies of the public policy variables, poor annual estimates of the long-run payout propensities, or omission of important variables. The first approach to this problem was to recognize autocorrelated errors explicitly in the model. A simple form of the relationship was assumed and estimated from the residuals as

$$(8\text{-}5) \qquad\qquad u = .577u_{-1} + v$$

The error term v is assumed to be random. The original model underlying equation (8-4) may be written as

$$(8\text{-}6) \qquad\qquad r'' = a + bA/A_2 + ct + di + u$$

Substitution of expression (8-5) for the error term in equation (8-6) and algebraic manipulation[9] to eliminate the u leads to the estimating equation

$$(8\text{-}7) \quad r'' - .577r''_{-1} = a(1 - .577) + b(A/A_2 - .577A/A_{2\,-1})$$
$$+ c(t - .577t_{-1}) + d(i - .577i_{-1}) + v$$

Estimates using these transformed variables are compared in Table 47 to the original estimates recorded earlier as relation (8-4). The transformation succeeded in raising the Durbin-Watson statistic from 0.91 to the more acceptable level of 1.60. The standard errors obtained for relation (8-7) are therefore more reliable, and are higher than those in the original estimate which were presumed to have a downward bias. Even though the more reliably-estimated

[9] For a discussion of the type of manipulation required here see, for example, J. Johnston, *Econometric Methods* (McGraw-Hill, 1963), pp. 195-99.

TABLE 48. Decomposition of Selected Percentage Point Changes into Contributions by Selected Variables, Regression Estimates of Target Payout Ratios for All Sample Firms, 1920–29, 1929–47, and 1947–60[a]

Change in Estimated Payout Ratio	Interval of Change		
	1920–29	1929–47	1947–60
Contribution by:			
Depreciation Index	+16	−13	+22
Interest Rates	+21	+21	−16
Tax Shelter	+3	−15	+4
Change in Payout Ratio[b]	+39	−7	+10

[a] These target payout ratios (r_t'') were estimated by Relation (8–6) using the coefficients of Relation (8–7).
[b] The total change may differ from the sum of the contributions because of rounding.

standard errors (except in case of the constant term) are 40-60 percent higher than before, the depreciation and interest rate variables remain significant at the one percent level. However, the tax rate variable is now found to be significant only at the 10 percent level.

The new estimates substantially reduced the contribution of depreciation liberality to the explanation of the estimated long-run target payout ratios; the role of interest rates appears stronger, and that of tax rates is almost unchanged. The new estimates of the coefficients have been used to explain changes in the estimated long-run target ratio for selected years in Table 48. The results are not much different from those based on the original equation, reported in Table 46. Equation (8-4) is mainly revised by the greater importance of interest rates and reduced significance of depreciation indicated by equation (8-7). The 1929-47 decline in the target ratio appears less pronounced because the decline in depreciation liberality is less depressing and the fall in interest rates more stimulating to dividends than indicated by the earlier estimates. Although the new estimate of the tax rate coefficient is less reliable because of its higher standard error, it still shows tax rates depressing the target payout by 15 percentage points over the 1929-47 interval. Despite the downgrading of its importance in the estimates of Table 47, the stimulating effect of increased depreciation liberality was more than enough to offset the rise in interest rates in the 1947-60 interval.

Influence of Investment Demand

This treatment of autocorrelated error, that is, by assuming a particular simplified form of the relationship between the errors, at least provided more reliable estimates of the standard errors. However, it does not provide a fundamental explanation of the tendency of the model to overestimate or underestimate persistently over substantial periods of time. This kind of alternating bias could result from omission of an important variable. On the basis of the aggregative time series analysis in Chapter V, investment demand did not appear to be a factor affecting dividends. This was surprising, although it was in line with earlier findings by Lintner. The hypothesis that high investment demand might depress dividends was reconsidered in the present framework. It seemed plausible that the tendency of the estimated long-run payout ratios (based on cross-section analysis and recorded in Table 44) to fall below those estimated by equation (8-4) in 1926-29 and 1954-60 might be the result of investment booms in those years. Similarly, the tendency of the estimated long-run ratios to lie above those estimated by equation (8-4) in the early thirties and during World War II may have reflected sluggish investment demand in those periods. Therefore, attempts were made to generalize relation (8-4) by including measures of investment demand along with the three public policy variables.

Two basic Office of Business Economics estimates of investment were tested:[10] (1) corporate expenditure on plant and equipment (labeled k), and (2) this same expenditure plus inventory investment. The former measure proved far more successful, so the latter measure was dropped. To obtain relative measures of investment demand, k was divided alternatively by two variables—sales S and income originating in corporations Y. These variables appeared to behave plausibly, showing, for example, low investment demand in the early thirties and during the war. Both were found to improve

[10] The data used are discussed in Appendix A. As in the case of the depreciation liberality index, the investment variable (and the liquidity variable discussed later) are crudely measured since the data used were for all corporations. However, in the ratio form used ultimately, the series behaved plausibly and probably proxy reasonably well for measures of conditions in the sample.

TABLE 49. Regression Results for Models Using Alternative Measures of Investment Demand[a]

(Constant term in billions of dollars)

| Investment Demand Measure[b] | Regression Coefficients[c] | | | | | Coefficient of Multiple Determination ($\bar{R}^2$) | Durbin-Watson Statistic (D-W) |
	Constant Term (a)	Deprecia-tion (A/A_1)	Tax Shelter (t_{25})	Interest Rates (i)	Investment Demand (I)		
Investment-Sales Ratio (k/S)	1.116 (.190)	.302 (.120)	−.302 (.124)	−.640 (.186)	−7.49 (1.52)	.723	1.55
Investment-Income Ratio (k/Y)	1.043 (.196)	.443 (.112)	−.341 (.131)	−.796 (.196)	−2.04 (.47)	.692	1.44
None	.577 (.202)	.688 (.119)	−.324 (.241)	−.734 (.161)		.533	.91

[a] Derived by adding measures of investment to Relation (8–4).
[b] Investment is plant and equipment expenditures; income is income originating in corporations. The last item represents Relation (8–4) without any addition of investment variables.
[c] Figures in parentheses are standard errors of the coefficients.

relation (8-4) significantly, as summarized in Table 49. The investment coefficients have the expected negative sign, supporting for the first time in this study the proposition that a high investment demand will tend to restrain dividend policy in the long run. The coefficients for both investment variables are highly significant, differing from zero in the expected direction by more than four standard errors in both cases. The adjusted coefficient of determination $\bar{R}^2$ is substantially increased over its value for equation (8-4). The Durbin-Watson statistic is also raised to more acceptable levels, even without the manipulation of the error terms as in (8-7). The difficulty with relation (8-4) appears to be primarily that it was incomplete.

The contribution of the indexes of investment expenditure to explanation of the estimated long-run payout ratios is more complex than the role of the other variables, but it is substantial. The two indexes, describing plant and equipment expenditures, declined in the depression of 1921 encouraging dividends. Then, in the 1921-29 period, there was an upward trend that (according to the two models) was sufficient to encourage cuts in the payout ratio of 7 and 11 points, respectively. However, this depressing effect on divi-

dends was far overshadowed by the buoyant effect of rising depreciation allowances and falling interest rates and personal tax rates.

The fall in plant and equipment expenditures in the Great Depression (between 1929 and 1933) was sufficient to explain a 27
point rise in payout according to the first model, 20 points according to the second. The investment ratios returned to average
levels by 1940-41, and then dropped again during the war below
the lowest levels of the thirties. Then, both models indicated that
rising plant and equipment expenditures were sufficient to account
for a 30 point fall in payout between 1943 and 1947. By 1960, investment had slacked off enough to encourage an 8 point rise in
target payout ratios.

The addition of these investment variables did not substantially
revise the coefficients or the significance of the tax rate or interest
rate variables. However, it downgraded considerably the coefficient
for depreciation liberality. Even so, the depreciation variable remained highly significant in both models given in Table 49.

The pooling of cross-section and time series estimates for the
forty firms had already reaffirmed the importance of the three public policy factors, even though the variables did not fare well either
in the analysis of single firms or of the firm sample total. In
resurrecting the investment demand variable, the technique has
shed light on an apparently important factor not recognized in any
of the time series analysis.

The Effects of Changing Liquidity

Despite substantial improvement with the addition of the investment demand factor, the Durbin-Watson statistic was still rather
low. Therefore, additional variables were tested in equation (8-4).
Sales change, which was of some importance in the time series
analysis, failed in this framework. However, corporate liquidity,
which was marginal in the aggregate time series models, was a
much more effective variable in the present analysis. Two measures
of year-end liquidity were tested in this model. The first was cash
plus government securities (L); the second was "working capital,"
defined as L plus inventories plus notes and accounts receivable,
minus notes and accounts payable. The former was the more effective form, and results are reported for it alone. As in the case of in-

vestment, the liquidity variables were normalized in two different ways—by division by sales (S) and by income originating in corporations (Y).

Table 50 reports regression results for the original three public policy variables with liquidity added, and for cases in which both liquidity and investment are included. When liquidity is added by itself, it is about as effective as investment was. The inclusion of both further improved the Durbin-Watson statistic and generally produced better explanations. The regressions reported in the table use various measures of liquidity and investment demand. In all cases, liquidity appears with the expected positive coefficient, reinforcing the earlier, marginal time series evidence of a stimulating effect of liquidity on dividends.

In the first two equations in which a liquidity ratio alone is added, it is significant in both cases at the one-tenth of one percent level, as was the case with investment. The main effect of the inclusion of liquidity on the coefficients of the other three variables was a reduction in the explanatory importance of depreciation liberality. However, the depreciation coefficient was still four to six times its standard error.

Liquidity-sales proved to be the less effective of the two liquidity ratios, especially when the investment ratios were also included. In the latter case, multicollinearity became rather severe, as indicated in the correlation matrix in Table 51. The four coefficients of correlation between pairs of liquidity-investment variables show a high negative association between the two. This apparently reflects a tendency for liquid assets to be accumulated when investment slacks off, as in the early thirties and during World War II, and a reduction of liquid assets during booms.[11] The high correlation be-

---

[11] As with all correlations among ratios, these should be interpreted with caution. For example, L/S and k/S would be positively correlated even if L and k were random variables because of their common denominator. Here, however, the association is negative, suggesting that the denominator is not dominant and that these ratios are effective measures of relative liquidity and investment demand. Sales, for example, were cut in half in the Great Depression while plant and equipment expenditures fell 88 percent and liquid assets dropped only 20 percent. This suggests that the causal sequence was that investment curtailment maintained liquidity. This seems more plausible than the possibility that the negative association of investment and liquidity results from a positive association between investment and sales. If that were the case, a fall in k would be accompanied by a fall in S which would raise L/S for that reason alone.

TABLE 50. Regression Results for Models Using Alternative Measures of Liquidity and Investment Demand[a]

(Constant term in billions of dollars)

Variables Added[b]	Constant Term (a)	Depreciation (A/A₂)	Regression Coefficients[c] Tax Shelter (t_{25})	Interest Rates (i)	Liquidity (L)	Investment Demand (I)	Adjusted Coefficient of Determination ($\bar{R}^2$)	Durbin-Watson Statistic (D-W)
Liquidity-Sales Ratio (L/S)	.336 (.169)	.587 (.098)	−.358 (.126)	−.663 (.181)	3.084 (0.773)		.697	1.64
Liquidity-Income Ratio (L/Y)	.319 (.151)	.418 (.099)	−.265 (.115)	−.504 (.169)	1.144 (0.221)		.752	1.86
Liquidity-Sales (L/S) and Investment-Sales (k/S)	.917 (.300)	.356 (.138)	−.317 (.126)	−.640 (.187)	1.024 (1.189)	−5.830 (2.455)	.721	1.64
Liquidity-Income (L/Y) and Investment-Income (k/Y)	.591 (.223)	.375 (.101)	−.290 (.117)	−.601 (.183)	.901 (.279)	−.905 (.547)	.761	1.90
Liquidity-Sales (L/S) and Investment-Income (k/Y)	.749 (.322)	.492 (.119)	−.349 (.131)	−.742 (.201)	1.533 (1.336)	−1.278 (.818)	.695	1.57
Liquidity-Income (L/Y) and Investment-Sales (k/S)	.681 (.236)	.311 (.110)	−.276 (.114)	−.544 (.174)	.797 (.292)	−3.810 (1.936)	.768	1.92

[a] Derived by adding variables measuring investment and liquidity to Relation (8–4).

[b] Investment is plant and equipment expenditures; liquidity is cash plus government securities; income is income originating in corporations.

[c] Figures in parentheses are standard errors of the coefficients.

TABLE 51. Simple Coefficients of Correlation Between Pairs of Independent Variables[a]

Variable	Deprecia-tion (A/A_2)	Tax Shelter (t_{25})	Interest Rates (i)	Liquidity-Sales (L/S)	Liquidity-Income (L/Y)	Investment Sales (k/S)
Tax Shelter (t_{25})	−.22					
Interest Rates (i)	+.15	−.83				
Liquidity-Sales (L/S)	+.18	+.16	−.18			
Liquidity-Income (L/Y)	+.47	+.03	−.15	+.83		
Investment-Sales (k/S)	−.65	+.08	−.00	−.70	−.78	
Investment-Income (k/Y)	−.52	+.16	−.15	−.75	−.69	+.96

[a] Derived from Table 50 regressions. Variables used are defined there.

tween the different measures of these two variables produced much higher standard errors in equations including both of them, but investment is significant at least at the 5 percent level in three of the four cases, and L/Y is highly significant in both equations in which it is used.

The inclusion of these two competing variables somewhat reduced the importance of depreciation liberality, tax rates, and interest rates indicated by relation (8-4). However, all three remained significant at least at the one percent level in all four of the equations that include both new factors. Depreciation liberality was the only factor among the three original ones that was substantially downgraded by the broadening of the model. Presumably, this was primarily the result of its negative association with the competing investment variables, as shown in Table 51.[12]

Conclusions

The earlier findings of this study concerning the influence of depreciation, tax rates and interest rates (Chapters III-VI) were

[12] This negative relation, though not very strong, is surprising since liberalized depreciation might be expected to stimulate investment because of the tax saving. It is true that liberalization also reduces reported net earnings and may, therefore, discourage investment insofar as corporations fail to allow for the downward bias in earnings. However, it has been the hypothesis of this study that corporations do allow for such a bias in making dividend policy, and presumably they would do the same in arriving at investment decisions. Perhaps the peculiar association rests upon mutual association with other factors or on a tendency for depreciation to be liberalized when investment is low.

CHART 7. Dependent Variable and Regression Estimates by Average of Four Equations, 1920–60

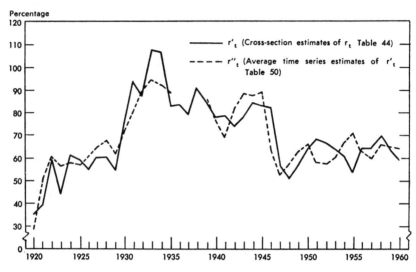

only partially supported by time series analysis of individual firms, and were given no support by the firm sample total (Chapter VII). The alternate approach used in this chapter, based on the same information for the sample of firms, reasserts their importance, as well as indicating other operative factors in the formation of dividend policy. The separate influence of the different factors was brought out more clearly with the reduction of collinearity, but the importance of each varies somewhat from equation to equation. The explanatory contribution of the different variables may be summarized by taking a consensus of the last four equations in Table 50. These equations contain the only two factors that were found to add significantly to the explanation of long-run payout ratios already provided by the original three variables in equation (8-4).[13] In Chart 7, the average of time series estimates by the four equations is compared to the estimated long-run payout ratios based on the cross-section analysis. As was true of the four equations individually, the fit is obviously much better than that in Chart 6 where liquidity and investment were not included. The residuals now appear random, with no persistent bias over long

[13] The sales change variable is not included since it failed in this framework to contribute significantly.

stretches of time. The average adjusted coefficient of determination $\overline{R}^2$ for the four equations was 0.736, and the Durbin-Watson statistic averaged 1.76.

The Impact of Various Factors

The statistical contribution of each of the five independent variables (multiplied by its coefficient) was also averaged over the four equations. These contributions are sketched in Chart 8, measured as percentage point deviations from the mean. They offer a basis for appraising the relative importance of the five factors in dividend policy. When each variable is at its mean level, the model estimates the long-run payout ratio as 68 percent. The effect on the payout ratio of a variable's departure from its mean level may be estimated from the charts. For example, when the depreciation liberality index was low in 1920, the model says this depressed the long-run payout ratio 13 percentage points below what it would have been if depreciation had been at its average level. Similarly, the above-average level of the depreciation variable in 1932 made for a payout ratio 13 points higher than would have been the case if depreciation had been at its average level.

The variability of the contribution of each variable in Chart 8 is an indication of its relative importance according to the model. Two measures of this variability are given in Table 52. According to the range, interest rates were the most influential factor, with depreciation liberality next in importance during the thirty-eight years observed. Interest rates could explain variations in the payout percentage up to 30 points, while depreciation could account for a change up to 26 points. The other three factors carried less weight, but their influence was substantial. As shown in Chart 8, higher tax rates since the early thirties tended to depress the payout ratio by 10 to 17 points. The main effect of liquidity and investment demand was that they worked together to encourage dividends in the early thirties and during World War II, when high liquidity accompanied low investment. A better measure of the importance of the variables is the standard deviation which takes account of all the contributions. Interest rates remained the most important on this criterion, but tax rates slightly surpassed depreciation as the second most important factor.

CHART 8. Contributions of Five Variables to Explanation of Estimated Long-Run Target Payout Ratios, 1920–60

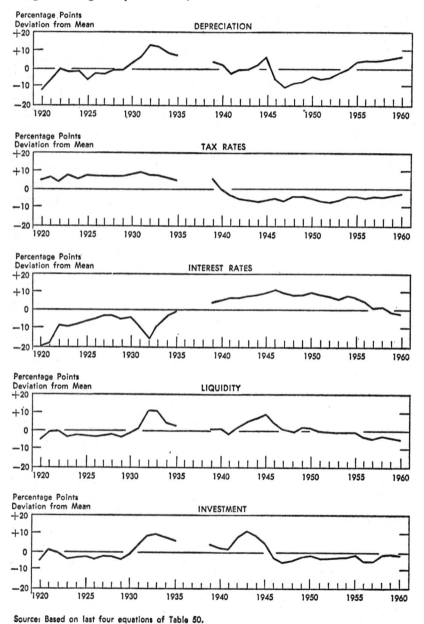

Source: Based on last four equations of Table 50.

TABLE 52. Measures of Variability of the Contribution of Five Factors to the Explanation of the Estimated Long-Run Payout Percentages

Variable	Variation of Contribution	
	Range	Standard Deviation
Depreciation liberality	25.5	5.97
Individual tax rates	17.2	6.17
Interest rates	30.4	8.37
Liquidity	16.3	4.12
Investment demand	16.1	4.84

Influence on Payout Trends

The main trends in the separate contributions shown in Chart 8 may be summed up in turn. Each description of the effect of a change in a variable is made with the "other things remaining equal" proviso. The indicated statistical associations will be described in "causal" language for the sake of brevity, but with the recognition that the hypotheses, though statistically supported, have not been proved.

The consensus of the four equations is that the liberalization of depreciation allowances after 1920 was sufficient to raise the estimated long-run payout ratio 13 percentage points by 1929 and 13 points more by 1932. A reversal after that reduced the theoretical ratio 16 points by 1941. Wartime amortization then increased the ratio 10 points by 1945, but the end of amortization reduced it 17 points by 1947, leaving a net decline of 23 points in the contribution of the variable between 1932 and 1947. Postwar liberalization then contributed 17 points to the rise in the theoretical payout ratio.

Falling individual tax rates after 1920 raised the ratio 3 points by 1929, and 5 points by 1931. Then, high wartime rates cut the ratio 17 points by 1944. There was no net change by the time of the Korean War tax rates of 1952, but lower rates then raised the theoretical ratio 5 points by 1960. A decline in interest rates after 1920 raised the theoretical ratio 17 points by 1928, but high interest rates in the depression cut it 12 points by 1932. A steady downward trend then raised the theoretical payout ratio 26 points by 1946, more than enough to offset the effect of higher tax rates. Higher interest rates then cut the ratio 13 points by 1960.

Relatively high liquidity in 1932 had raised the ratio 14 points after 1929 (16 after 1920). A reversal cut the ratio 12 points by 1941, but higher wartime liquidity put it up again 10 points by 1945. A fairly steady downward trend in liquidity then depressed the ratio 14 points by 1960. The slackening of investment demand in the 1920-21 depression raised the theoretical payout ratio 6 points, but it was down by that amount by 1929. Lack of investment activity in the depression raised the ratio 14 points by 1933. Recovery then depressed the ratio 9 points by 1941, but wartime curtailment of investment raised it 10 points by 1943. The postwar investment boom cut the ratio 17 points by 1947, but a slowdown in the boom raised it 5 points again by 1960.

Trends in the contribution of the five explanatory variables are further described in Table 53 by a decomposition of the most pronounced changes in the estimated long-run payout ratio r_t''. The table shows a tendency for depreciation liberality, liquidity and investment demand to reenforce each other in the determination of the long-run payout ratio. In the first five intervals recorded, which represent the largest moves in the ratio, these three variables worked in the same direction in all cases. It is not surprising, then, to find that inclusion of liquidity and investment reduced the indi-

TABLE 53. Decomposition of Selected Changes in the Estimated Long-Run Target Payout Ratio into Contributions by Selected Variables, Selected Periods[a]

Change in Payout Ratio (r_t'')[b]	Interval of Change						
	1920–29	1929–33	1933–41	1941–45	1945–47	1947–55	1955–57
Contribution by:							
Depreciation index (A/A_2)	+12	+12	−15	+10	−17	+14	+1
Tax shelter (t_{25})	0	0	−11	−3	0	+2	0
Interest rates (i)	+11	−4	+16	+3	0	−2	−6
Liquidity (L)	+5	+14	−12	+10	−9	−2	−3
Investment (I)	+5	+14	−9	+4	−11	+4	−3
Change in payout ratio	+33	+36	−30	+23	−37	+17	−11

[a] Derived from an average for the results of the last four equations in Table 50.
[b] The total change in payout may differ slightly from the sum of the contributions because of rounding.

cated importance of depreciation liberality. However, depreciation still appears to have played a role second only to interest rates.

Evaluation of Results for Firms

This summary should be sufficient to isolate (statistically) the impact of the five different factors on the dividend policy of the sample of forty firms. The results, however, should not necessarily be construed as evidence of causal relationships. The reliability of the findings might be questioned for two main reasons. First, the time series evidence on the effect of depreciation, taxes and interest rates was weak when firms were studied separately and almost non-existent for the sample total. Second, the theoretical long-run pay-out ratios (Table 44), subjected here to time series analysis, are themselves estimates of unknown validity.

The first point may be at least partially countered by the observation that the pooling technique could be expected to be more effective in isolating relationships. The resulting lower correlation among the independent variables permits more precise estimation. It is also true that the direction of association with each of the five independent variables was as hypothesized in all five cases. While the liquidity and investment variables may be marginal, the other three remained highly significant in the face of many combinations of competing variables, and the residuals appear to be random. Finally, the same three variables had already been found effective in the aggregative estimation.

The questionable validity of the measurement of the dependent variable is undoubtedly a drawback. There is no way of testing the accuracy of these theoretical target ratios. On the other hand, they were estimated independently of the independent variables that were ultimately used to explain them. If anything, the error in their estimation by cross-section regression estimates of dividends on net profits should make them more difficult to explain by the time series analysis. The success of the time series thus seems especially convincing.

There is a final point that can be made in favor of these tests of hypotheses by means of the data for firms. Unlike the analysis of the corporate aggregate and manufacturing, the hypotheses were not suggested by the data with which they were tested. The depreciation and individual tax rate hypotheses were conceived in an attempt to explain the observed sharp fall in the aggregate payout ratio during and immediately after World War II and its subsequent recovery. Given the knowledge of the rise in tax rates during the war and the subsequent expansion of depreciation charges, it was almost inevitable that they should improve the statistical explanation of dividends. In contrast, the jumbled nature of the estimated target ratios in Table 44 gave little reason to expect that the tax factors could contribute much to their explanation. That they did so is perhaps more convincing testimony for them than the original aggregative time series analysis. However, this evaluation should be qualified by recognizing that the present findings, since they are based on data for an unrepresentative sample of large firms, may not apply generally.

CHAPTER IX

Summary and Conclusions

THIS STUDY BEGAN within the theoretical framework proposed by John Lintner. His hypothesis that dividends are based primarily on net income levels (after taxes and depreciation) and are adjusted slowly in response to income changes was tested and substantiated. The statistical explanation of dividends was strengthened by generalization of this basic model. First, more relevant income measures were substituted for net profits in defining the dividend-income ratio. Then, other determinants of dividends were isolated by demonstrating their contribution to observed long-run variations in the dividend-income ratio. The original Lintner model made no allowance for these long-run variations in payout policy. However, given the major trends in the actual payout ratio over the years, it appeared essential to allow for and explain these variations by elaboration of the basic model.

Major Factors in Dividend Policy

The first explanatory gain was achieved by recognizing that changes in the liberality of depreciation allowances for tax purposes invalidate officially measured net profits as a measure of the ability to pay dividends. On the basis of data for the corporate aggregate, manufacturing and various industries, it was shown that, for the

195

most part, these distortions of the payout base could be avoided with a resultant improvement in the explanation of dividends under the hypothesis that dividends follow the gross income measure "cash flow" (profits after taxes but including depreciation). The first evidence of the major influence of cash flow on dividends was its successful substitution for net profits in the basic Lintner model for 1942-60, a period of sharp changes in tax provisions concerning depreciation. The use of cash flow as the payout base cut the error variance in half and gave the best explanation of dividend changes during this period.[1]

Direct measurement of the impact of depreciation liberalization in this period is also of importance. For example, the ratio of actual depreciation charges to net profits for all corporations rose from 30 percent in 1947 to 110 percent in 1960. The cash flow model implies that this produces a change from 38 percent to 62 percent in the long-run target payout ratio based on net profits. This more than accounts for the actual change from 36 to 62 in the dividend-profit percentage.

The simple cash flow model, used to explain dividends in the longer period beginning with 1920, continued to show cash flow to be the most influential income factor. However, the statistical explanation for this interval was less satisfactory than for 1942-60, so other possible factors in dividend policy were considered. This led to tests of the second major hypothesis, that rising individual tax rates encourage shareholders to prefer corporate saving as a tax shelter to receiving taxable dividend payments. Allowing the payout ratio to vary with measures of individual tax rates greatly improved the explanation of dividends since 1920. According to all models, rising tax rates were found to depress dividends. The impact of this factor was substantial, and most estimates showed it sufficient to account for the most pronounced downward trend in payout, that which occurred between the late twenties and the early postwar period.

With the introduction of tax rates in the models for 1920-60 (excluding 1936-38), cash flow continued to prove the most influential income factor, as shown in relations (4-3) and (4-5).

---

[1] As an explanatory variable it also performed better than "corrected" net profits and pairs of profit and depreciation variables.

However, its superiority over some rivals was slight. Substitution of net profits for cash flow and explicit inclusion of depreciation liberality along with tax rates in the target relationship produced improved explanations of dividends in a few cases, as shown in Table 15. Even so, the improvement was minor, and use of the cash flow measure as the dividend payout base remained an adequate substitute for explicit recognition of changing tax provisions concerning depreciation.[2] Nevertheless, tests of depreciation liberality in Table 15 were also useful because the explicit depreciation measures were found to influence dividends significantly in 25 of the 28 tests reported there for all corporations and manufacturing.[3]

In Chapter V, rival factors were included along with depreciation liberality and tax rates in the relationships explaining long-run variations in payout ratios. The ratios were found to be negatively related to interest rates and to the change in sales over the previous two years. Although additional variables were tested, no other significant relationships were found in the after-tax models at this stage. Even the interest rate and sales factors were of marginal significance and did not detract from the indicated importance of depreciation and tax rates. In fact, the estimated impact of tax rates was increased by the inclusion of interest rates, and the interpretation of rising individual tax rates as the key factor in the 1929-47 decline in the dividend-profit ratio was considerably strengthened.

With this further generalization of the relationships in Chapter V, the cash flow models continued to hold their own with those containing both net profits and depreciation. Both types performed far better than those that were based on net profits but excluded the depreciation factor. The final conclusion was that depreciation liberality influences the dividend-profit ratio and that this can be adequately treated by assuming dividends to be based on the gross income measure—cash flow.

The last factor considered in the analysis of dividends for all

---

[2] This of course does not necessarily mean that corporations actually base dividends on cash flow. It may simply be proxying statistically for some unobservable net profit measure, or corporations may actually use it as such a proxy in setting dividends.

[3] They were significant at the 5 percent level or better on the standard test, but these results must be qualified as pointed out in the second technical note following Chapter II.

corporations and manufacturing was the corporate tax. It was found that the effect of this tax could be allowed for by using after-tax income to explain dividends.[4] The only impact of the corporate tax on dividends appeared to be through its effect on after-tax income rather than directly on the payout ratio. This effect was found to be of major importance, although the bite out of dividends clearly depends on the extent to which the tax is shifted from profits. That is, the more the tax is shifted the less its effect on after-tax income and therefore the less its impact on dividends.

Alternative Methods Used

To reinforce the findings concerning the behavior of aggregate corporate and manufacturing dividends, the analysis was carried out, in less detail, for seventeen industries approximating, in total, the corporate aggregate. The depreciation liberality and individual tax rate hypotheses were each substantiated by the dividend models for most of the industries, and these industries represent nearly 80 percent of the corporate activity of the country. The interest rate variable was somewhat less influential, and the importance of sales-change was considerably downgraded by the industry estimates. Neither of these factors undermined the indicated impact on dividends of the first two variables, and the importance of tax rates was again enhanced by the inclusion of interest rates. The industry tests gave no indication that the aggregative nature of the analysis of dividends for all corporations might have exaggerated the importance of depreciation and tax rates.

A similar analysis was carried out for forty large firms. These firms were studied for illustrative purposes and were not representative of the corporate aggregate. The results for the firms supported the original hypotheses for a substantial minority of the firms, including some of the largest. However, the evidence was far less impressive than for industries. The reason for the difference in results probably lies in the extent of disaggregation, for the greater the aggregation, the greater the year-to-year variability of dividends, and the more regular the relationship of dividends with other variables.

[4] This is analogous to the fact that depreciation could be allowed for by using gross income including depreciation.

Finally, the speed-of-adjustment models used in the analysis initially were supplemented by an alternative technique using the data for the same forty firms. Annual target payout ratios were estimated by cross-section regressions and explained by time series variables. This stronger technique impressively confirmed the role of depreciation liberality, tax rates, and interest rates in the determination of dividends. It also revealed two additional factors. Dividends were found for the first time to be negatively related to investment demand and positively related to corporate liquidity.

Interpretation of the Best Aggregative Model

The mechanism determining the annual change in aggregate dividends may be described by an interpretation of model (5-1), which was the most successful tested.[5] Corporations in aggregate were assumed to have a target payout ratio based on cash flow and varying over time. According to (5-1), this target ratio varies inversely with individual tax rates and interest rates. For example, the model says that a 10 percentage point increase in the tax rate measure t_{25} reduces the target payout ratio by 5.6 percentage points. Similarly, a one percentage point rise in interest rates cuts the target ratio by 3.4 percentage points. These two factors explained well the actual decline in the payout ratio from nearly 50 percent in the late twenties to a remarkably stable 30 percent since 1941.[6]

In any given year, this payout ratio is applied to cash flow to obtain the target level of dividends. The difference between this and the dividends of the previous year is the amount by which dividends must change in order to reach the target level. However, the model recognizes that firms will modify this adjustment. In the first place, according to (5-1) they will adjust aggregate dividends each year only 38 percent of the way toward the new target level. Secondly, because of the downward rigidity of dividends, the actual change in

---

[5] As pointed out above, the stronger estimation technique made possible by pooling time series and cross-section information for forty firms showed two factors affecting dividends, which are not included in this model. However, model (5-1) is summarized here because of its coverage of the entire corporate sector.

[6] However, see the footnote at the beginning of Chapter I where a 1965 revision of the OBE data is mentioned. Some of the empirical work of this study was redone with the new data, as reported in Appendix G. However, it was found that the revisions did not alter the basic findings presented earlier.

aggregate dividends will tend to stand $210 million above the adjustment indicated by the above behavioral pattern.

This cash flow model gave a far better explanation of 1920-60 dividends than any model based on official net profits without allowance for liberalized depreciation. It even performed slightly better than net profit models that included an explicit measure of depreciation liberalization, as in (5-9).

The economic meaning of the success of the cash flow model should be reviewed briefly. As pointed out in Chapter III, the successful explanation of dividends by a cash flow (gross profit) model without deduction of (or allowance for) depreciation does not imply that corporate officials refuse to recognize depreciation as a cost in the long run. What has presumably happened is that they have rejected depreciation reported for tax purposes as a measure of "true" depreciation. Given this, it is not surprising that dividends tend to follow cash flow. It may be regarded as the best proxy available for changes in "true" profits. While basing dividends on cash flow, firms can still take depreciation roughly into account by paying a smaller fraction out of cash flow than they would pay out of the unknown true net profits. Other firms may base dividends on a net profit measure corrected for liberalized depreciation, but even in those cases, dividends would still follow cash flow if the revised depreciation series grew at about the same rate as cash flow. Under either type of behavior, the superior explanatory performance by cash flow is to be attributed to measurement error in the official profits series, rather than to corporate rejection of the depreciation concept, or to irrationality on the part of corporate officials.

Implications of the Results for Related Problems

The findings on corporate dividend policy contribute to an understanding of various related analytical problems. Several instances of this will be outlined briefly.

Factors Affecting Corporate Saving

The dividend models imply complementary models of the determinants of corporate saving. For example, the target saving percentages (relative to profits after taxes) implied by the four successful models in Chapter V may be obtained from Table 19 by subtracting the payout percentages from 100.[7] The contributions of the three different factors to changes in the desired saving ratio may be obtained by changing the signs in Table 20.

A few quantitative illustrations may be useful. According to the target payout function in model (5-9) for all corporations, the major factor in the increase in the actual saving ratio from 29 percent to 64 percent between 1929 and 1947 was a 40 percentage point depression of the target payout ratio by the rise in individual tax rates.[8] This implies (other things remaining equal) that 1947 corporate saving of $11 billion was about $7 billion higher than it would have been under the individual tax rates of 1929.[9]

The rise in corporate tax rates had the opposite effect. Other things remaining equal, and assuming no shifting of the tax, corporate profits would have been about $24.6 billion in 1947 under 1929 corporate tax rates, as shown in Table 26. Applying the actual corporate saving ratio of 64% for 1947 yields a hypothetical dividend level of $16 billion under 1929 corporate tax rates. However, according to the target function in dividend model (5-9), his hypothetical $16 billion saving is $10 billion higher than the $6 billion level it would have reached under the individual tax rates of 1929.[10] Since the actual corporate saving of 1947 was $11 billion, this reasoning suggests that the stimulating effect of higher individual tax rates on corporate saving in 1947 was $5 billion greater than the depressing effect of higher corporate tax rates.

The effect of liberalization of depreciation on corporate saving is a more complex question. For example, the actual net saving

[7] These are not actually the best fitting models obtained. When the sales change variable was excluded for reasons discussed in Chapter V, the cash flow models (5-1) and (5-2) proved to be the best descriptions of dividend behavior for all corporations and for manufacturing. However, the slightly inferior models (5-9) and (5-10), which are analyzed in Tables 19 and 20, will be used for illustration here because they include the depreciation factor explicitly.

[8] See the contribution by t_{25} in Table 20.

[9] The hypothetical corporate saving in 1947 under 1929 tax rates is about $4 billion—obtained by reducing the actual 1947 saving ratio 40 points to 24 percent.

[10] The hypothetical 1947 corporate saving of $6 billion under the 1929 tax structure allows for both corporate and individual tax rates. The adjustment for corporate tax rates first showed hypothetical 1947 profits of $24.6 billion under 1929 corporate tax rates, according to Table 26. The hypothetical 1947 saving of $6 billion is then obtained by reducing the actual 1947 payout ratio 40 points to 24 percent to allow for individual tax rates and applying this to the hypothetical $24.6 billion 1947 profit figure under 1929 corporate tax rates.

ratio (net of depreciation) declined 26 points—from 64 percent to 38 percent—between 1947 and 1960. According to the first model for all corporations, the major factor in this was a 24 point depressing effect on the theoretical saving ratio exerted by the liberalization of depreciation. However, it should be recognized that this depressing effect of liberalization on the measured saving ratio is not meaningful in an economic sense; it is an accounting phenomenon rather than a behavioral one. Presumably, liberalization is stimulating rather than depressing to "true" corporate saving. Officially measured corporate saving appears to have been depressed because rising allowances reduced measured profits by more than the resulting tax saving increased them. However, from the policy point of view it is important to note that the tax saving increases gross saving and that net saving would also show an increase under consistent depreciation accounting.[11]

Evidence on Postwar Profit Trends

In Table 54, data are gathered comparing profit trends with those of other indicators for selected postwar years. Between 1947 and 1960, officially measured aggregate net profits after taxes fell from nearly 8 percent of GNP to about 4 percent. The profit-sales ratio fell from 5 percent to less than 3 percent. Other comparisons of this type, and for other postwar years, created the impression of a major lag in profits during the postwar period. However, a brief glance at other indicators casts some doubt on this. In the same interval the ratio of cash flow to GNP and sales respectively fell only slightly. Similarly, despite the apparent lag in profits, corporations managed to pay dividends in 1960 at about the same rate (relative to GNP and sales) as in the first postwar years, and the ratio for plant and equipment expenditure was down only about 20 percent. The high investment in 1960 relative to profits and corporate saving is impressive even though it was partly the result of more external financing.

A more complete comparison is available through growth rates

---

[11] The stability of the postwar payout ratio at around 30 percent of cash flow suggests that the tax saving provided by depreciation liberalization raises dividends as well as gross corporate saving. This may detract somewhat from the usefulness of liberalization as a stimulus to investment.

TABLE 54. A Comparison of Postwar Corporate Profits and Other Indicators, 1947 and 1960[a]

(Dollar amounts in billions)

| Item | 1947 | 1960 | Percentage Increase | |
			1947–60	Annual Average[b]
Net Profits (P)	$ 17.55	$ 21.11	20%	2%
Gross National Product (GNP)	234.29	502.60	124	6
Sales (S)	347.80	763.34	119	6
Net Dividends (D)	6.24	13.05	109	6
Plant and Equipment Expenditure (K)	17.50	29.91	71	6
Depreciation Charges (A)	5.28	23.45	344	13
Cash Flow (C)	22.83	44.56	95	6
Corporate Saving	11.27	8.06	−28	−2
P/GNP	7.5%	4.2%		
P/S	5.0	2.8		
C/GNP	9.7	8.9		
C/S	6.6	5.8		
D/GNP	2.7	2.6		
D/S	1.8	1.7		
K/GNP	7.5	6.0		
K/S	5.0	3.9		

[a] Source, see Appendix A.
[b] These growth rates are estimated by least-squares regressions on the logarithms of the data.

of these aggregate indicators from 1946 to 1960. While measured net profits grew at only a 2 percent annual rate, cash flow grew at 6 percent, keeping pace with GNP and sales. This growth of gross income after taxes helps explain the fact that dividends and investment expenditures both grew at nearly a 6 percent annual pace, despite the stagnant behavior of measured profits. The profits series was depressed by the 13 percent rate of increase in depreciation charges. Measured corporate saving was depressed even more by high depreciation, actually showing an average decrease of nearly 2 percent per year.

These figures alone are sufficient to suggest that the lag in profits relative to other indicators is in large part a statistical illusion brought about by liberalization of depreciation allowances.[12] The results of this study give further support to this hypothesis in two ways. Direct evidence of the downward bias in profit trends appears in Table 6 (Chapter III), where growth rates are given for profit series revised by means of independent depreciation estimates. Second, there is some indirect evidence of this bias in the greater success of revised profits measures in explaining dividends in the models presented in this study. The greater the downward revision of the trend in the officially measured depreciation series, the better was the explanation of dividends. If the models are valid, the greater explanatory success of revised profits and cash flow suggests that the official profit series is seriously misleading as a measure of corporate operations that affect management policies.

Effects of Tax Policy on Individual Income Distribution

Postwar studies have shown a reduction of the inequality of (distributed) individual incomes since the twenties. Few of these studies stressed the possibility that the low postwar dividend payout may have led to sufficient accrued capital gains to recoup most of the loss in the share of high income groups in distributed income. Furthermore, most interpreted the leveling of distributed incomes as primarily the outcome of market forces. The ability of taxation to equalize individual incomes over time and within any given year was downgraded. For example, Kuznets found a fall in the relative share ("basic" income variant) of the top one percent of income recipients from 14.6 percent to 8.5 percent between 1929 and 1947.[13] Since this basic income variant was measured prior to the bite of the individual income tax, the impression was given that the indicated equalization took place unaided by the pressure of taxation. In fact, the Office of Business Economics (OBE) refers to income distributions at this level of analysis as "before-tax."[14] How-

---

[12] It should be reiterated that the term "liberalization" refers to changes over time and carries no implication with respect to the adequacy of allowances in absolute terms. Similarly, the discussion of profits refers to the trend over time and makes no judgment as to whether they are overstated or understated in any given year.

[13] Simon Kuznets, *Shares of Upper Income Groups in Income and Saving* (New York: National Bureau of Economic Research, 1953), p. 582.

[14] See, for example, U. S. Department of Commerce, Office of Business Economics, *Income Distribution in the United States* (a supplement to the *Survey of Current Business*, 1953), p. 3.

ever, the dividend models of this study show that these "before-tax" incomes have already been heavily influenced by tax factors. The corporate tax has already shrunk the fund from which dividends are paid, and in 1947, the payout ratio was depressed far more by this tax and by the desire to avoid high individual tax rates than in 1929.

According to model (5-9) as decomposed in Table 20 (Chapter V), the target payout ratio for the corporate aggregate was 40 percentage points lower in 1947 than it would have been at 1929 individual tax rates. If 1929 rates had been in effect in 1947 and the payout ratio 40 points higher, dividends would have been 112 percent higher than they were (other things remaining equal).[15] An indication of the effect on income distribution of this hypothetical increase in dividends is obtainable from Kuznets' data.[16] This higher dividend level would have given the top one percent an income almost 25 percent greater than actually recorded. Its share in the total would have been 10.6 percent rather than the 8.5 percent indicated by Kuznets' series. Thus, higher individual tax rates, through the effect on dividend distributions, account for 27 percent of the 1929-47 decline in the "before-tax" share of this group, as estimated by Kuznets. To evaluate the effect of higher corporate tax rates, actual 1947 profits were increased to the $24.6 billion level that would have prevailed under the 1929 corporate rates (Table 23, assuming no shifting). Then, 40 percentage points were added to the actual 1947 payout ratio to allow for the individual tax rate factor. This yielded a hypothetical dividend level of $18.7 billion in contrast to the actual figure of $6.4 billion. The net result was a total income for the top one percent that was 44 percent greater than recorded, making the relative share of this group 11.3 percent. The two tax factors together thus account for 46 percent of the 1929-47 decline in the share of this top group.[17]

This hypothetical 11.3 percent share of the top one percent under the 1929 tax structure must be qualified in several respects

[15] The actual payout ratio was 35.6 percent in 1947 (Table 1). A 40 point higher ratio implies a 112 percent higher level of aggregate dividends—$13.2 billion compared to the observed value of $6.2 billion.

[16] The estimates are based on Kuznets, *op. cit.,* p. 582 and p. 668, and an estimate of 3.7 percent as the 1947 share of dividends in total individual incomes (basic variant). The latter estimate was based on additional Kuznets data on pp. 585, 671, and 677.

[17] This analysis measures the effect of the corporate tax on distributed income only. Presumably the tax also reduces corporate saving and accrued capital gains.

(in addition to the standard *ceteris paribus*). First, if the corporate tax is partially shifted, a return to the lower taxes of 1929 would have less effect. Second, insofar as higher dividends are associated with lower realized capital gains, the 11.3 percent estimate would also overstate the share of the top one percent.[18] On the other hand, this figure is also biased downward to an unknown extent. The hypothetical increase of 1947 dividends from $6.4 billion to $18.7 billion attributable to reversion to the 1929 tax structure would change the ranks of individual incomes. Those recipients actually in the top one percent in 1947 would receive 11.3 percent of the total income if dividends tripled, but not all of them would continue to be in the top one percent. Therefore, the share of those actually belonging to this rank would be even higher.

Bearing in mind these qualifications, the evidence does suggest that corporate and individual taxes were sufficient to account for nearly one-half of the 1929-47 decline in the share of this top group in what is generally regarded as pretax distributed income. Thus, not only is the leveling of individual incomes exaggerated by exclusion of capital gains, but also the leveling of distributed (pretax) income that did occur was itself in large part the result of taxation. From the viewpoint of this study, about 27 percent of the decline in the share of the top income group resulted from the use of higher corporate saving as a tax shelter. Although this extra corporate saving is not treated as personal income in the national income accounts, it belongs legally to the stockholders, and a case can be made for imputing the common saving to them as a group. If this viewpoint is accepted, the Kuznets and OBE distributions overstate the degree of "before-tax" equalization and obscure the influence of taxation on the process. Even if the imputation of undistributed income and unrealized capital gains to individuals is not regarded as valid, it must at least be recognized that the leveling of distributed incomes by higher corporate saving will very likely have the opposite effect on *wealth* distribution through a stimulation of capital gains.[19]

[18] This would not be true in the more frequently cited OBE estimates, since (unlike *Statistics of Income* and Kuznets' basic variant) they exclude capital gains. In any case, this appears to be a minor factor since the degrees of inequality indicated by OBE and *Statistics of Income* are very close.

[19] There are other reasons for suspecting the indicated degree of income

The leveling effects of lower dividends associated with the rise in individual tax rates should not be allowed to obscure the likely countereffect via increased capital gains. As already indicated, the estimated 40 point 1929-47 reduction in the payout ratio produces a misleading impression of pre-tax leveling. It is important to note also that the greater retention of earnings by corporations sharply curtailed the opportunity for individual rate increases to level incomes. When and if the additional corporate savings were taxed, it was as capital gains at a maximum rate of 25 percent in 1947, compared to rates as high as 20 percent on dividend income in 1929. Since only a small fraction of capital gains is realized, the effective individual rate of taxation on this large slice of income must have fallen between 1929 and 1947.

Relevance of the Findings for Public Policy

This study has demonstrated that federal fiscal policy exercises substantial influence over corporate dividend-saving policy, even without resort to special devices such as an undistributed profits tax. However, the appropriate use of these policies is by no means obvious. In the first place, there are many valid pros and cons with respect to the advisability of encouraging corporate saving, and there is no consensus on how they balance. Increased saving may aggravate some problems while alleviating others, and the appropriate policy at any given time depends on which problems are most acute. Secondly, these policy instruments have an impact on many other variables in addition to corporate saving. Attempts to use them to influence this corporate decision will have many other effects that may complement or offset the original objective. On the other hand, if the basic objective lies elsewhere, the side effect of these policies on corporate saving must also be taken into account. A satisfactory approach to these issues requires that a successful multi-equation system be developed. However, it may be useful to specify and outline some of the questions involved.

---

equalization to be overstated. For example, beginning with World War II, high individual tax rates have bred many tax-avoidance devices in addition to corporate saving. There are other devices besides corporate retention that convert ordinary income to capital gains, and these are also omitted from income distribution data.

The Pros and Cons of Corporate Income Retention

Public policy on this issue has run the gamut from ardent en-
couragement of corporate saving to harsh penalties against it. Between 1947 and 1958, the British tax system provided "nondistribution relief." For example, in 1956, the profits tax rate was 30
percent but the rate of nondistribution relief was 27 percent, leaving a net profits tax rate on undistributed earnings of only 3
percent.[20] The United States policy has not moved in that direction.
In fact, in 1936-37, a controversial surtax was imposed on undistributed profits. This graduated tax ranged from 7 to 27 percent, a
substantial amount in relation to the general rate of 15 percent. The
British and U. S. tax systems in these years appear to have achieved
their respective objectives of suppression and stimulation of dividends.[21]

Advocates of increased corporate saving have stressed three
points. First, it is argued that greater saving leads to greater investment (and growth) than would take place if dividends were paid
and capital raised externally. The prospective external funds are
first trimmed by individual taxes, and they are also more expensive
to the corporation because of flotation costs. Also, small firms are
particularly dependent on internal funds, because they must pay
more than large firms for external funds. It is undoubtedly true
that retained earnings have been a major source of corporate capital, especially since World War II. Nevertheless, the investment argument depends on the assumption that the increased saving would
actually result in new investment rather than moving into government bonds or other liquid assets.

A second claim made for high corporate saving is that it may
serve as an anti-inflationary weapon. It is possible that corporations
are more inclined to accumulate idle savings than stockholders, and
if so, higher retention would oppose inflation by cutting total spend-

[20] In addition to the profits tax, the corporation also paid the "standard" income tax on retained earnings.

[21] For example, see George E. Lent, *The Impact of the Undistributed Profits
Tax, 1936-37* (Columbia University Press, 1948). Incidentally, the large increase
in dividends in response to this tax offers indirect evidence that the corporate tax
could not be completely shifted—at least not in the short run and as of the mid-
thirties.

ing. The more familiar aspect of this anti-inflationary argument is in the context of public policy on incomes and concerns the cost-push type of inflation. This was the argument for "nondistribution relief" made by the 1945-50 Labor government of Great Britain which felt that the line could be better held against wage increases if the dividend policy of corporations were restrained. Of course, neither of these points is a general argument in favor of high retention. They apply only where an anti-inflationary policy is in order.

A third and related point is that an increase in corporate saving promotes income equality by reducing incomes of the wealthy, who receive the bulk of all dividends. However, both the anti-inflation and equality points depend on dubious assumptions. The wage restraint argument depends on the assumption that labor representatives compare the wage share to dividends rather than to earnings. It also assumes that higher corporate saving does not lead to capital gains, or at least that any such gains tend to pass unnoticed by the representatives of labor. The equality argument also depends on the doubtful assumption that corporate saving will not lead to equivalent after-tax capital gains for individual stockholders.

The pro-dividend side of the controversy has many facets. Just as it can be argued that high corporate saving is desirable when inflation threatens, high dividends may serve as a weapon against recession by stimulating aggregate demand through greater spending by stockholders and those wage-earners who obtain parallel wage increases.[22] More familiar are three points made in behalf of the 1936-37 undistributed profits tax. First, this policy-making for high dividends prevents avoidance of the individual income tax and enhances government revenues. Insofar as corporate saving ultimately would lead to capital gains taxed at low rates or not at all, a high-dividend policy leads to greater taxation of high incomes and promotes after-tax equality.

---

[22] Apart from cyclical considerations, increased corporate saving may work a hardship on individuals dependent on dividends for their consuming power. Compensatory capital gains may not be immediately forthcoming. Presumably, even those individuals who live very modestly on the income from stock must be fairly liquid; for example, an income of $3000 per year would require possession of stock valued at $50,000 to $100,000 under the three to six percent range in average dividend yield which has prevailed since the thirties. Still, these individuals might have difficulties in the longer run, and even in the short run a dividend lag could be painful for those averse to dipping into their capital.

The second main objection to high corporate saving is that it promotes the concentration of economic power and tends to stifle competition from new or small firms which may have more difficulty in raising capital. The third and related point made by advocates of the undistributed profits tax is that corporate saving enables entrenched firms to avoid submitting their projects to the test of the capital market which may lead to inefficient allocation of investment.

To sum up, ardent growth advocates are likely to favor high corporate saving as a stimulus to investment. For those opposed to high retention, the strongest point in favor of a high dividend policy is probably that it checks the concentration of economic power. The choice between these alternative policies entails both a value judgment and an assessment of the power of alternative policies aimed at these two objectives.

Corporate Saving and Other Policy Objectives

No general, unqualified evaluation can be made of the desirability of a high or low payout ratio. The appropriate policy will vary with the economic situation. In any case, it is important for policy-makers to bear in mind that depreciation liberality, corporate tax rates, individual tax rates, and interest rates are four public policy instruments found to have an impact on dividends. When these instruments are used to promote such objectives as growth, recovery from a recession, income equality, and satisfactory behavior of prices and the balance of payments, the side effect on dividends and corporate saving should be taken into account. In some cases, this side effect may reenforce the basic policy, but in others it may offset it.

The use of individual income tax cuts and lower interest rates to promote growth will also tend to increase dividends relative to pre-tax profits. Insofar as it can be determined that a high rate of corporate saving is conducive to high investment and growth, this stimulation of dividends counters the basic objective. In such a situation, counter-measures designed to discourage dividends may be in order, such as the postwar "nondistribution relief" granted in the 1947-58 period in the United Kingdom.

The use of any of the same policy instruments to promote recovery from a recession also would stimulate dividends. In this situation, it is entirely possible that this reenforces the basic objective. In a bleak economic environment, corporations may be inclined to accumulate idle savings. Assuming that dividend recipients are less inclined to do so, the stimulation of dividends accompanying these anti-recession policies will augment their effect.

Of the policies affecting dividends, only corporate and individual tax rates would ordinarily be considered to promote income equality. The direct impact of increases and/or greater progression in these taxes on individual incomes would undoubtedly lessen inequality. Such changes in the corporate tax would cut aggregate dividends (and therefore high incomes), and the new individual income tax would level incomes further. In addition, the models of this study show that these changes in individual tax rates would cut the dividend payout ratio. The latter effect appears likely to offset partially the other equalization. The addition to corporate saving escapes taxation as ordinary income and is likely to lead to capital gains, taxed at low rates if they are taxed at all.

The use of higher tax rates and interest rates to combat inflation and/or a balance of payments deficit will at the same time discourage dividends. Insofar as there is a lower marginal propensity to spend retained profits than dividends, aggregate demand is depressed and the intended impact on prices is augmented. A rise in interest rates aimed at improving the balance of payments by reducing capital outflow might be partially offset by the resulting cut in dividends. The additions to corporate saving are likely to lead to higher investment, some of which would go abroad. Furthermore, the lower dividend yield per share might discourage capital inflow in the form of equity investment.

The above examples are intended only to be illustrative, and obviously a much more complete analysis would be needed in each case. They are sufficient, however, to suggest that the influence of these public policy instruments on dividends should be kept in mind even when there is no explicit intent to influence the payout ratio. When policies aimed at other objectives tend to be offset by their inadvertent impact on corporate dividends, it may be in order to consider specific counter-measures, such as the undistributed profits tax or nondistribution relief.

The Dividend Decision As a Built-In Stabilizer

Another implication of the study is that the mechanism of the dividend decision itself makes a contribution to public policy objectives. The indicated sluggish adjustment of dividends to income changes acts as a built-in stabilizer. This can be shown most readily by the simple cash flow model for all corporations in 1942-60 (Table 7, Chapter III). The short-run (annual) marginal propensity to pay dividends out of cash flow was estimated at 15.8 percent. The short-run marginal propensity to save out of cash flow is therefore 84.2 percent.[23]

According to this model, the effect of any billion dollar fall in cash flow in one year tends to be cushioned by an estimated $842 million dollar decline in cash retentions. The net effect on aggregate demand of the income decline depends also on the extent to which corporate investment is tied to saving. According to the model, if investment were autonomous, the billion dollar fall in cash flow would lead to a decline in dividends of only $158 million and an even smaller decline in aggregate demand (since not all dividends are spent). If, however, the fall in saving induces a fall in investment there would be a greater decline in aggregate demand. It seems unlikely, however, that such an investment decline would wipe out the entire stabilizing effect of the fall in corporate saving. Thus, the dividend-saving decision apparently reenforces the stabilizing effect of the corporate tax by cushioning the impact of income changes on aggregate demand.

[23] The corporate saving referred to here is gross, since no depreciation charges have been subtracted. However, it is this magnitude, rather than net undistributed profits, that represents actual cash retentions.

Sources, Processing, and Derivation of Aggregate Time Series

THE MAIN DATA SOURCES were the following.[1] They will be referred to below by the abbreviations following the citation in each case:

(1) U. S. Department of Commerce, Office of Business Economics, *National Income,* 1954 Edition. Washington: Government Printing Office, 1955. (OBE, 1954)

(2) U. S. Department of Commerce, Office of Business Economics, *U. S. Income and Output,* 1958, for data through 1955, and *Survey of Current Business,* 1962 and 1963 for later years. Washington: Government Printing Office. (OBE, 1958ff.)

(3) Simon Kuznets, *National Income and Its Composition, 1919-38,* Volumes I and II. New York: National Bureau of Economic Research, 1941. (Kuznets)

(4) Raymond W. Goldsmith, *A Study of Saving in the United States,* Volume I. Princeton: Princeton University Press, 1955. (Goldsmith)

(5) U. S. Bureau of the Census, *Historical Statistics of the United States.* Washington: Government Printing Office, 1960. (*Historical Statistics*)

[1] However, see the footnote at the beginning of Chapter I where a 1965 revision of the OBE data is mentioned. Some of the empirical work of this study was redone with the new data, as reported in Appendix G. However, it was found that the revisions did not alter the basic findings presented earlier.

(6) U. S. Treasury Department, Internal Revenue Service, *Statistics of Income, Corporation Income Tax Returns.* Washington: Government Printing Office, various years. (*Statistics of Income*)
(7) U. S. Federal Trade Commission and U. S. Securities and Exchange Commission, *Quarterly Financial Report for Manufacturing Corporations.* Washington: Government Printing Office; presented on annual basis in *Economic Almanac,* New York: National Industrial Conference Board, various years. (FTC-SEC)

Several measurement problems arose at the outset. First, a basic choice had to be made between the Office of Business Economics (OBE) and Internal Revenue Service (IRS) time series.[2] The OBE series were chosen as basic data on the ground that most of the adjustments made by OBE in the tax return data appeared appropriate for an analysis of corporate behavior. Only cash dividends were included, since stock dividends represent merely a paper transaction except insofar as they lead to higher cash dividends through failure to compensate by lowering the dividend rate per share. In the OBE profit series, depletion and post-tabulation revisions were added to the IRS data, and profits of financial intermediaries and net capital gains were deducted.

Although these adjustments seem in order, flows between the United States and other countries raise more difficult questions, and the OBE "Rest-of-the-World" component for profits and dividends was not entirely appropriate for this study. For example, the Rest-of-the-World component of the OBE profit and dividend series includes dividends to individuals from abroad and excludes dividends paid to foreign holders of U. S. securities. Dividends from abroad are inappropriate in the measurement of the ability of U. S. corporations to pay dividends and of the amount actually paid by them. On the other hand, omission of the Rest-of-the-World component is not ideal either. This would exclude branch profits and dividends to U. S. corporations from abroad from the profit series and incorrectly include amounts paid to foreign parent companies from the United States.

Despite these defects, the aggregate OBE series excluding the Rest-of-the-World component were selected for the study on several grounds. First, the task of adjusting the data appeared formidable if not impossible. Secondly, the magnitudes at issue appear to be relatively small. Finally, no Rest-of-the-World component was available for the manufacturing sector or for the industry data; its exclusion from the aggregate data was essential if reconciliation of the industry and aggregate results were to be possible.

[2] For the relationship between these see OBE, 1958, p. 230.

The failure of OBE data to extend back before 1929 constituted another problem. Estimates by Kuznets that were closely comparable conceptually to the OBE data were used to develop series for 1919-28. The basic technique used to link the series was a linear regression of OBE data on Kuznets' estimates for the period 1929-38 during which they overlapped.[3] Kuznets' data for 1919-28 were then plugged into each equation to derive estimates of what the OBE estimates would have been for those years. Since the relationship between the two series during the period of overlap was generally remarkably close, the manufactured 1919-28 figures are probably reliable.

Another problem was the failure of the OBE dividend series to exclude dividends paid by investment trusts out of capital gains. Since capital gains are excluded from the OBE income base used to measure ability to pay dividends, it is appropriate to remove them from the dividend payments series also. Dividends paid out of these capital gains have neared 5 percent of all dividends in recent years. Estimates of this component were made as indicated below, and it was subtracted from the dividend series.

The sources and derivation of measures of each variable will be summarized in turn. For each variable, the basis of the series for all corporations (A) and for manufacturing corporations (M) will be discussed in that order:

D = *net cash dividends.* (A) The basic sources were (1) 1946-60: OBE, 1958 ff. Table VI-8; (2) 1929-45: OBE, 1954, pp. 190-91. These were adjusted by subtraction of the Rest-of-the-World component and removal of estimated dividends paid out of capital gains by investment trusts. The latter component was assumed negligible before 1936, and estimates for it for 1936-58 were taken from Daniel Holland, *Dividends Under the Income Tax* (New York: National Bureau of Economic Research, 1962), pp. 100-103. The 1959-60 estimates followed Holland's procedure described on p. 105 of the same study. The series for 1919-28 was obtained by a regression of this adjusted OBE series on the data given in Kuznets, pp. 316-17, for the 1929-34 overlap. (M) The sources and technique were the same as for all corporations except no adjustment was necessary for dividends paid out of capital gains by investment trusts. Adjustment was also not required for the Rest-of-the-World, since it was already excluded from the manufacturing series.

[3] In some cases, shorter periods from 1929 on were used if a discontinuity in the relationship between the two series was apparent. This occurred for some series in 1934, for example, when Kuznets presented two estimates and his later series was not consistent with his earlier one.

$P = $ *net profits (after taxes and depreciation charges).* (A) The basic sources were (1) 1946-60: OBE, 1958 ff., Table VI-7; (2) 1929-45: OBE, 1954, pp. 188-89. The Rest-of-the-World component was excluded. The series for 1919-28 was obtained by a regression of this OBE series on a profit series derived from Kuznets (total net saving minus government saving, on pp. 312-13, plus dividends on pp. 316-17), for the 1929-34 overlap. (M) Sources and methods were the same as for all corporations except that no adjustment was necessary for the Rest-of-the-World component which was already excluded.

$C = $ *cash flow (P plus depreciation charges).* (A) The sources for depreciation charges were (1) 1946-60: OBE, 1958 ff., Table VI-18; (2) 1919-45: Goldsmith, p. 957. (M) This was the same as for all corporations except that data on wartime amortization from *Statistics of Income,* Part II, were added to the manufacturing depreciation series given by Goldsmith, and the 1918-45 series was adjusted upward by 1.7 percent to link with OBE, 1946-47.

$P_1 = C - A_1 = $ *corporate net profits with depreciation estimated according to original cost, straight line and Bulletin F lives.* A_1 for 1929-60 was obtained from unpublished estimates underlying Murray Brown, "Depreciation and Corporate Profits," *Survey of Current Business,* Vol. 43, No. 10 (October 1963), pp. 5-12. (No special computation was necessary for 1919-28, since this special OBE series does not differ from actual charges in that period.)

$P_2 = C - A_2 = $ *corporate net profits based on "realistic depreciation."* Series A_2 was estimated for 1925-60 from unpublished estimates of net stocks and capital expenditures (1960 dollars) of all business underlying *Sixty Years of Business Capital Formation* by George Terborgh (Machinery and Allied Products Institute, 1960).

Net investment was approximated each year by the change in net stocks. The depreciation underlying the MAPI series was then estimated each year as the difference between gross investment and this approximation of net investment. The change in net stocks tends to yield an underestimate of net investment since the former is diminished by retirements as well as depreciation. However, estimates of depreciation in "constant dollars of the year stated" for 1946-60, subsequently made available by MAPI, show this bias to be slight. Furthermore, the annual growth rate of the latter series was 8.7 percent in the 1946-60 interval—very close to the 8.2 percent growth rate of the approximated current dollar depreciation series used in this study. Since the models estimated are responsive primarily to relative changes in the explanatory variables, the approximation was judged to be adequate. The approximation of the MAPI 1960 dollar depreciation series was restored to a current dollar basis by means of the implicit GNP deflator used by MAPI, and the estimated noncorporate component was excluded.

The exclusion of the noncorporate component was accomplished for 1925-49 on the basis of tables in Goldsmith, pp. 346-47, which give business saving on both a business accounting concept and a cash flow concept. The difference between them is an estimate of depreciation, and this is given for both incorporated and unincorporated business. The "all business" estimates were scaled down according to the ratio of corporate depreciation to the total. The 1950-60 data were scaled down to the corporate basis by a cruder method. The ratio used was based on data on plant and equipment expenditures by all business and by unincorporated business given by Raymond W. Goldsmith, *The National Wealth of the United States in the Postwar Period* (Princeton: Princeton University Press, 1962), p. 267. The series for 1920-24 was an extremely crude estimate derived from a regression of the revised MAPI data on an estimate of double declining balance, current cost depreciation, for the 1925-34 overlap. The latter estimate was derived from a regression of the double declining balance, current cost depreciation underlying the corresponding profit series of Murray Brown (*op. cit.*) on actual charges. Crude as this procedure was, at least this association was close. This attempt to push MAPI data back before 1925 is certainly unreliable, but the weakness of these few observations probably does not seriously undermine the series as a whole.

$P_3 = C - A_3 = $ *manufacturing net profits with depreciation estimated according to original cost, straight line and Bulletin F lives.* A_3 was based on an estimate of *establishment* depreciation.[4] The source for the latter in the 1929-60 period was OBE, 1958 ff., Table V-13. No reliable estimate of establishment depreciation could be made for 1919-28, but it was taken as $0.80A_1$, which was the relation prevailing in 1929-30. This was then reduced to exclude noncorporate depreciation. For 1919-38, the noncorporate share of depreciation was taken to be 5 percent, based on its share of capital expenditures (Goldsmith, p. 889). For 1939-45, the ratio was interpolated linearly to reach the 9 percent ratio given for 1946 by OBE, 1958 (Tables VI-18, VI-19). For 1946-60, the ratios applied were those of OBE 1958 ff., Tables VI-18 and VI-19.

[4] The use of depreciation estimates on an establishment basis to adjust corporate depreciation charges is open to question. However, in 1934-39, before amortization was introduced, Murray Brown (*op. cit.*) took actual charges as an adequate approximation of straight line, historical cost depreciation. In this period, corporate charges and OBE estimates of establishment depreciation were very close.

$P_4 = C - A_4 =$ *manufacturing net profits with depreciation estimated according to current cost, straight line and Bulletin F lives.* A_4 was based on an estimate of *establishment* depreciation. The source for the latter in the 1929-60 period was OBE, 1958 ff., Table V-13. The figures for A_4 in the 1919-28 period were obtained by adjusting A_3 according to the ratio of original cost depreciation to current cost given (for all corporations) by Goldsmith, p. 955, col. 3. The series was then put on a corporate basis by the same method as that used for A_3.

$P_5 = C - A_5 =$ *manufacturing net profits based on adjusted FTC-SEC estimates of depreciation.* The FTC-SEC estimates of depreciation and depletion for 1951-60 were taken directly from the *Economic Almanac.* There was a discontinuity between old and new series in 1951, and the figures for 1948 were therefore adjusted according to the ratio of the two estimates in 1951—the only year of overlap.[5] To obtain an estimate for 1942-47, an alternative series was derived by multiplying FTC-SEC estimates of depreciation and depletion as a percentage of sales (*Economic Almanac,* 1956) by OBE sales data. The 1942-47 figures were adjusted according to the ratio of this series to the later one in the 1948-50 overlap.

$T =$ *corporate tax liabilities.* (A) The source for 1929-60 was OBE, 1958 ff., Table I-17. The 1919-28 figures were obtained from a regression of the OBE series for 1929-39 on IRS, *Historical Statistics,* p. 714, columns 288-89. (M) Data for 1919-28 were taken from an unpublished manuscript by Challis A. Hall, Jr., *Direct Shifting and the Taxation of Corporate Profits in Manufacturing, 1919-59,* Appendix B, Table C, p. 84. For 1929-45, the source was OBE, 1954, pp. 186-87, and for 1946-60, OBE, 1958 ff., Table VI-6.

$V =$ *inventory valuation adjustment.* (A) The source for 1919-28 was Goldsmith, p. 903; for 1929-45, OBE, 1954, pp. 194-95; for 1946-60, OBE, 1958 ff., Table VI-11. (M) The 1929-45 and 1946-60 data were taken from the same OBE sources as for all corporations. The 1919-28 series was derived from a regression of 1929-38 OBE data on Kuznets, p. 904 (with sign changed).

$L =$ *cash plus government obligations.* (A) The series estimated was the difference between all corporations and financial, insurance, and real estate corporations. (The two series were constructed, and L was defined as the difference.) For 1926-55, the data are taken from *Historical Statistics,* pp. 580-81, with two manipulations required: (1) Government obligations were separated from total "investments" by means of annual *Statistics of Income;* (2) Figures for 1934-41 (when

---

[5] The three-quarter figure for 1948 was first increased by one-third.

consolidated returns were not permitted) were adjusted by the method outlined by Goldsmith, p. 394, note 2, and in *Historical Statistics,* p. 576. For 1919-25, cash was derived from a regression of the 1926-33 *Statistics of Income* data in Goldsmith, p. 393, col. (1) minus col. (3). To this was added government obligations as derived from a regression of 1926-33 *Statistics of Income* data on Goldsmith, p. 575, col. (1). The data for 1956-60 were taken directly from *Statistics of Income.* (M) For 1926-55, data were taken from *Historical Statistics,* p. 582, with the same two adjustments as discussed above for all corporations. For 1919-25, cash was estimated by Goldsmith's index, p. 395, col. (5). To this was added a crude estimate of government obligations derived from a regression of 1926-33 *Statistics of Income* data on Goldsmith's data for all corporations, p. 575. The data for 1956-60 were taken from *Statistics of Income.*

$W = $ *year-end "working capital" (L plus inventories plus notes and accounts receivable minus notes and accounts payable).* (A) Finance, insurance, and real estate were again excluded throughout. For 1926-60, all three additional series were obtained in the same way as variable L above. A 1919-25 series for inventories was derived from a regression of *Statistics of Income* data for 1926-33 on Kuznets, pp. 903-10, col. 1, excluding finance, p. 908. Then W was derived from a regression of W data for 1926-33 on L plus inventories. (M) Data for 1926-60 were obtained in same way as variable L. For 1919-25, inventories were derived from a regression of *Statistics of Income* data for 1926-33 on Kuznets, p. 904, col. 1. Then W was derived from a regression of W data for 1926-33 on L plus inventories.

$K = $ *expenditure on plant and equipment.* (A) Data for 1946-60 (all business) were taken from OBE, 1958 ff., Table V-7. Figures for 1919-45 were derived from a regression of this OBE series on MAPI, *op. cit.,* 1946-60. This series was reduced to a corporate basis by the same method as MAPI depreciation A_2. (M) The 1946-60 data are based on OBE, 1958 ff., Table V-7. Figures for 1919-45 based on *Historical Statistics,* p. 410, col. 24. The latter series was multiplied by 1.275; this conversion factor was obtained by a regression through the origin of OBE, 1958 ff., Table V-7 or Table V-12, 1946-60. Then the series was reduced to the corporate basis by methods discussed above under variables P_1 and P_2.

$I = $ *net change in corporate inventories, nonfarm, book value.* (A) The source for 1946-60 was OBE, 1958 ff., Table V-8; for 1929-45, it was OBE, 1954, pp. 210-11; 1919-28 data were derived from a regression of 1929-38 OBE data on Kuznets, sum col. (2), pp. 903-10. (M) First a series including the noncorporate sector was estimated from the same sources as those used for all corporations. Then the series was reduced to the corporate basis by methods discussed under variables P_1 and P_2.

$S = corporate\ sales$. (A) The source for 1946-60 was OBE, 1958 ff., Table VI-17; for 1929-45, it was OBE, 1954, pp. 204-5; 1919-28 data were derived from a regression of OBE data for 1929-34 on *Historical Statistics,* p. 714, col. 282. (M) OBE sources for 1929-60 were the same as for all corporations. For 1918-28 two regressions were used: (1) a regression of the sales series in *Economic Almanac,* 1964, p. 250, on "gross income" given in *Statistics of Income,* 1929, p. 298 (1926-31 overlap), and (2) a regression of OBE on *Economic Almanac,* 1964, p. 250, 1929-34. The *Economic Almanac* was extended back to 1919 by means of the first regression, and these data were used in the second equation to extend the OBE series back to 1919.

$E = wholesale\ price\ index,\ 1947-49 = 100\ (erosion-via-inflation\ variable)$. (A) For 1919-57, the source was *Historical Statistics,* p. 117 (all commodities other than farm products and foods); for 1958-60, *Statistical Abstract of the United States,* 1963, p. 351. (M) For 1947-57, the source was *Historical Statistics,* p. 118; for 1958-60, *Statistical Abstract of the United States,* 1961, p. 332. Data for 1919-46 were derived from a 1947-51 regression of the latter series on an older series for manufactured products (Bureau of Labor Statistics. *Handbook of Labor Statistics,* 1950, p. 118).

$H = ratio\ of\ all\ stock\ prices\ to\ the\ consumer\ price\ index,\ 1947-49 = 100\ (hedging\ or\ speculative\ confidence\ variable)$. (A) The measure of all stock prices was Standard and Poor's index of all common stock prices, *Historical Statistics,* p. 657, col. 351 and *Statistical Abstract of the United States,* 1963, p. 472. The consumer price index was taken from *Statistical Abstract of the United States,* 1961, p. 334. The ratio of the two series was adjusted so that 1947-49 = 100. (M) The stock price index used was Standard and Poor's index of industrial prices, same source as for all corporations. The same consumer price index for "all items" was used in the ratio for manufacturing as in that for all corporations.

$Y = national\ income\ originating\ in\ corporations$. (A) The source for 1929-60 was OBE, 1958 ff., Table I-12; for 1922-28, *Survey of Current Business,* Vol. 36, No. 1, January 1956, p. 20. The 1919-21 estimates were derived from a regression of the latter series for 1922-28 on Kuznets, p. 310, Table 44 (excluding agriculture, services, government and miscellaneous). (M) For 1929-60, the source was OBE, 1958 ff., Table I-10; for 1919-28, Challis Hall, *op. cit.,* Table C, Appendix B, p. 84. (Noncorporate manufacturing is inappropriately included.)

$N = $ *total assets, net of depreciation charges.* (A) The series for all corporations and for financial, insurance, and real estate corporations were estimated separately and the difference between them was used. Data for 1926-55 were taken from *Historical Statistics,* p. 580 and p. 584, with the two adjustments discussed under variable L. Later data came from *Statistics of Income.* For 1918-25, net investment implied by *Historical Statistics,* p. 580 and p. 584, was derived for 1927-33. A regression was then run relating this series to net investment implied by variables derived earlier in this study (net investment = K + I − A). The net investment series derived from this equation was then used to extend the net asset series back to 1919. (M) The sources and estimation technique for manufacturing were identical to those for all corporations.

Eight of the series used most extensively in this study are tabulated in Tables A-1 and A-2 for all corporations and manufacturing, respectively. Although no depreciation series are given, actual depreciation charges may be derived as the difference between C and P. The alternative depreciation series used to revise the profit figures are also excluded from the tabulation, but they are implied by Charts 1 and 2 in Chapter III.

TABLE A-1. Basic Time Series Used in Analysis for All Corporations, 1919–60[a]

(In billions of dollars)

Year	Net Cash Dividends (D)	Net Profits (P)	Cash Flow (C)	Cash and Government Obligations (L)	Expenditure on Plant and Equipment (K)	Corporate Sales (S)	National Income (Corporate) (Y)	Total Assets (N)
1919	2.69	6.29	8.28	8.16	4.67	86.2	42.7	93.4
1920	2.98	4.65	6.84	8.39	5.52	102.0	44.8	109.9
1921	2.72	.85	3.19	8.24	2.95	78.7	32.0	104.3
1922	2.79	4.67	7.33	8.60	3.33	87.1	30.4	113.4
1923	3.53	5.86	8.57	8.75	4.97	102.7	37.7	130.0
1924	3.46	5.11	7.93	9.10	4.67	103.3	36.1	138.6
1925	4.02	6.67	9.57	9.59	5.07	116.3	38.3	151.7
1926	4.35	6.66	9.93	9.89	5.78	123.1	42.3	162.8
1927	4.63	5.99	9.34	10.26	5.26	125.1	40.7	174.6
1928	5.03	7.48	11.08	11.10	5.55	132.4	41.8	181.5
1929	5.72	8.03	11.90	10.86	6.56	138.6	45.2	195.1
1930	5.46	2.34	6.33	10.42	4.76	118.3	38.9	194.0
1931	4.12	−1.27	2.73	9.11	2.48	92.4	28.3	175.5
1932	2.61	−3.37	.32	9.13	.90	69.2	18.4	169.3
1933	2.08	−.37	3.15	8.83	.80	73.0	17.3	162.7
1934	2.58	.91	4.27	9.27	1.38	89.6	23.4	189.2
1935	2.80	2.03	5.38	9.66	2.01	102.0	27.0	188.0
1936	4.54	4.23	7.52	10.21	3.07	119.5	32.3	188.5
1937	4.66	4.61	7.95	9.40	4.16	128.9	37.6	191.6
1938	2.96	2.02	5.37	10.41	2.71	108.6	32.3	179.9
1939	3.64	4.78	8.22	11.48	3.23	120.8	36.2	182.7
1940	3.89	6.25	9.78	13.46	4.46	135.2	42.4	186.5
1941	4.34	9.14	13.02	16.03	5.92	176.2	56.4	201.7
1942	4.18	9.24	13.57	23.26	3.26	202.8	72.9	184.5
1943	4.34	10.24	14.85	31.97	2.50	233.4	88.1	195.0
1944	4.55	10.08	15.01	35.55	3.83	246.7	90.1	197.2
1945	4.57	8.06	13.99	35.71	5.99	239.5	82.4	192.3
1946	5.58	13.02	17.29	32.41	12.30	270.9	86.3	208.3
1947	6.24	17.55	22.83	32.53	17.50	347.8	104.7	236.8
1948	6.95	19.68	26.02	35.84	18.81	388.7	120.4	260.0
1949	7.14	15.16	22.38	37.92	16.03	370.1	115.5	261.6
1950	8.74	21.76	29.66	42.96	17.21	431.9	132.3	299.8
1951	8.52	18.49	27.62	44.78	21.44	488.4	153.3	330.5
1952	8.55	16.11	26.53	44.91	22.13	499.5	158.5	347.0
1953	8.83	16.96	28.99	46.72	23.67	523.3	169.0	359.9
1954	9.22	15.43	29.12	46.80	22.42	516.5	163.3	372.8
1955	10.46	21.48	37.41	52.02	23.98	599.4	184.2	413.8
1956	11.21	21.70	39.19	47.40	29.32	632.4	195.2	444.4
1957	11.63	20.36	39.69	47.05	30.88	671.8	202.9	467.9
1958	11.43	16.97	37.52	49.73	25.22	658.2	195.8	492.0
1959	12.39	22.68	44.59	53.32	27.20	739.4	220.8	529.9
1960	13.05	21.11	44.56	51.10	29.91	763.3	226.2	556.1

[a] Source, see text of Appendix A.

TABLE A-2. Basic Time Series Used in Analysis of Manufacturing Corporations, 1919-60[a]

(In billions of dollars)

Year	Net Cash Dividends (D)	Net Profits (P)	Cash Flow (C)	Cash and Govern- ment Obli- gations (L)	Expendi- ture on Plant and Equipment (K)	Corporate Sales (S)	National Income (Corporate) (Y)	Total Assets (N)
1919	1.24	3.77	4.65	4.24	2.67	51.6	19.10	52.6
1920	1.46	2.65	3.60	4.34	3.88	55.8	22.50	57.5
1921	1.30	−.10	.94	4.01	1.70	37.9	14.28	54.1
1922	1.28	2.57	3.78	4.27	1.81	44.1	14.82	56.6
1923	1.72	3.39	4.60	4.68	2.55	55.4	18.85	60.5
1924	1.61	2.66	3.89	4.84	2.06	53.2	17.54	60.7
1925	1.86	3.46	4.84	5.10	2.42	59.8	18.93	62.8
1926	2.06	3.43	4.96	5.35	2.91	61.9	20.43	64.7
1927	2.16	2.91	4.52	5.56	2.55	63.0	19.37	65.6
1928	2.44	3.67	5.36	6.08	3.27	66.1	20.20	67.1
1929	2.65	4.23	6.01	5.82	3.51	70.3	21.89	70.3
1930	2.54	1.26	3.11	5.76	2.19	58.5	18.23	69.2
1931	1.86	−.51	1.24	5.21	1.22	42.8	12.42	63.8
1932	1.10	−1.43	.17	5.22	.61	31.0	7.21	59.0
1933	.99	.56	2.11	5.07	.85	34.3	7.56	57.8
1934	1.19	1.02	2.36	5.16	1.09	40.1	10.90	66.6
1935	1.52	1.64	2.95	5.32	1.22	46.8	13.26	66.8
1936	2.33	2.83	4.16	5.42	1.81	56.0	16.18	68.8
1937	2.36	2.88	4.28	4.96	2.55	61 5	19.30	70.7
1938	1.21	1.11	2.53	5.75	1.58	50.0	15.01	69.5
1939	1.74	2.90	4.37	6.42	1.82	57.2	17.92	72.0
1940	1.93	3.78	5.34	7.69	2.66	65.8	22.34	76.8
1941	2.27	5.58	7.30	9.73	3.70	92.0	33.03	88.9
1942	2.14	5.11	7.17	14.78	2.39	116.3	45.34	85.1
1943	2.27	5.56	7.92	20.90	2.02	141.9	58.15	94.8
1944	2.40	5.46	8.03	23.24	2.61	151.0	60.12	96.0
1945	2.42	4.03	7.14	22.29	4.23	138.7	52.01	91.0
1946	2.86	6.66	8.61	18.21	6.21	136.9	48.48	96.3
1947	3.41	10.06	12.44	18.95	7.99	177.8	58.72	111.4
1948	3.74	11.18	14.00	19.33	8.42	197.1	66.78	121.7
1949	3.95	8.49	11.66	22.05	6.56	184.5	62.70	123.8
1950	4.85	12.67	16.11	25.57	6.88	216.8	74.37	141.6
1951	4.53	10.64	14.64	27.30	10.01	251.2	88.50	160.9
1952	4.50	8.85	13.56	26.63	10.82	257.3	90.17	170.3
1953	4.72	9.72	15.35	27.82	11.20	276.8	97.95	176.8
1954	4.79	9.07	15.58	27.68	10.48	266.1	91.06	181.9
1955	5.65	13.20	20.70	31.18	10.88	303.6	104.49	201.4
1956	6.05	12.97	21.08	26.63	14.27	316.5	109.27	216.4
1957	6.33	12.22	21.09	26.32	15.26	331.0	112.48	224.9
1958	5.95	9.32	18.76	28.00	10.97	323.2	103.82	235.8
1959	6.37	13.18	23.01	30.63	11.59	339.2	119.93	252.1
1960	6.67	11.46	21.72	28.25	13.68	366.2	121.02	262.3

[a] Source, see text of Appendix A.

223

APPENDIX B

Derivation of Individual Tax
Rate Variables

THE RATIONALE FOR each measure of the individual tax rate structure used in the study was discussed in Chapter IV. The data processing procedure will be outlined here.

Derivation of Standardized Income Levels

Chart 4 in Chapter IV displayed the four tax rate series used. Although the t_s series measures statutory rates, the three series relied on most frequently were the t_{10}, t_{25}, and t_{50} series measuring marginal tax rates on dividends at income levels that vary over time. The objective was to abstract from growth and inflation and to standardize the income base by measuring marginal tax rates on dividends at given ranks in the dividend distribution. Three income series were developed that cut off the top 10 percent, 25 percent, and 50 percent of all dividends received. Each income series was assumed to trace the experience of dividend recipients in a given relative position over time.

Data presented by Holland on dividends reported by income class were used to develop the series.[1] The figures include dividends reported

---

[1] Daniel Holland, *Dividends Under the Income Tax* (New York: National Bureau of Economic Research, 1962), pp. 40-41. His data for 1952 and 1953 were corrected for an apparent reversal of the figures for the $10,000-$25,000 and $25,000-$50,000 classes. Holland's data for 1919-57 were supplemented by 1958-60 figures taken directly from U. S. Internal Revenue Service, *Statistics of Income.*

on taxable returns of individuals and estates and trusts. For 1936-53, Holland had to make a special estimate of the dividend component of total individuals' income from estates and trusts. The dividend estimate for each class was expressed as a percentage of aggregate dividends (variable D as defined in Appendix A, but before exclusion of dividends paid out of capital gains by investment trusts). For each year, the cumulative percentage of total dividends accruing to incomes above the lower limit of each class was plotted against these lower income limits on double logarithmic graph paper. Estimates of the income levels cutting off the top 10 percent, 25 percent, and 50 percent of all dividends were obtained by graphical interpolation. This yielded series of statutory net incomes through 1943. After that the income data do not exclude personal deductions, so the income levels were adjusted downward to estimate statutory net income. This was done by means of interpolation of data provided by Kahn on personal deductions as a percentage of adjusted gross income.[2]

Estimation of Marginal Personal Tax Rates

For each year, the marginal tax rates on dividends and on capital gains were derived for a couple with two dependents for the three statutory net income levels. The rates were derived each year on the basis of the rate structure provided in *Statistics of Income*. There were many special provisions which had to be taken into account in the computations. The maximum earned income credit was assumed. From 1920 through 1935, dividends were exempt from normal tax and subject to surtax only. On the other hand, in the 1919-33 interval, all net income was subject to surtax and no exemptions were allowed. In 1923, a 25 percent reduction was allowed.[3] In 1940, there was a defense tax that added 10 percent to the regular rate. The 1943 Victory Tax was computed according to a method suggested by Seltzer.[4] For 1954-60, the dividend credit required subtraction of 4 percentage points from the regular rate.

The main methodological difficulty was created by the introduction of income splitting in 1948 that produced a substantial cut in the tax rates for married couples. Use of the series for married couples here would exaggerate the tax cut, however, since only about 75 percent of all dividend income is reported on joint returns. Unmarried taxpayers

[2] C. Harry Kahn, *Personal Deductions in the Federal Income Tax* (New York: National Bureau of Economic Research, 1960), p. 44.

[3] See *Statistics of Income, op. cit.,* 1950, p. 322.

[4] Lawrence Seltzer, *The Nature and Tax Treatment of Capital Gains & Losses* (New York: National Bureau of Economic Research, 1951), p. 524.

TABLE B-1. Measures of Marginal Tax Rates on Individual Incomes, Various Income Levels, 1919–60[a]

(In percentages)

Year	Rates on Dividends				Rates on Capital Gains		
	t_{10}	t_{25}	t_{50}	t_s	g_{10}	g_{25}	g_{50}
1919	60.0	36.0	10.0	24.0	60.0	36.0	10.0
1920	56.0	28.0	9.0	24.0	56.0	28.0	9.0
1921	52.0	21.0	6.0	24.0	52.0	21.0	6.0
1922	49.0	28.0	6.0	23.0	12.5	12.5	6.0
1923	36.8	18.0	3.8	15.3	12.5	12.5	3.8
1924	38.0	26 0	6.0	18.0	12.5	12.5	6.0
1925	20.0	18.0	7.0	13.0	12.5	12.5	7.0
1926	20.0	19.0	8.0	13.0	12.5	12.5	8.0
1927	20.0	20.0	8.0	13.0	12.5	12.5	8.0
1928	20.0	20.0	8.0	13.0	12.5	12.5	8.0
1929	20.0	19.0	6.0	13.0	12.5	12.5	6.0
1930	20.0	16.0	2.0	13.0	12.5	12.5	2.0
1931	20.0	12.0	1.0	13.0	12.5	12.5	1.0
1932	48.0	18.0	1.0	23.0	12.5	12.5	1.0
1933	48.0	18.0	1.0	23.0	12.5	12.5	1.0
1934	52.0	21.0	5.0	27.0	31.2	12.6	3.0
1935	53.0	27.0	6.0	27.0	31.8	16.2	3.6
1936	64.0	31.0	10.0	31.0	38.4	18.6	6.0
1937	64.0	31.0	11.0	31.0	38.4	18.6	6.6
1938	62.0	23.0	8.0	31.0	15.0	11.5	4.0
1939	62.0	25.0	9.0	31.0	15.0	12.5	4.5
1940	68.2	44.0	13.2	48.4	16.5	16.5	6.6
1941	69.0	54.0	21.0	59.0	15.0	15.0	10.5
1942	85.0	61.0	26.0	69.0	25.0	25.0	13.0
1943	85.8	63.8	28.8	71.8	25.0	25.0	13.0
1944	92.0	68.0	33.0	75.0	25.0	25.0	16.5
1945	92.0	65.0	33.0	75.0	25.0	25.0	16.5
1946	84.6	61.8	32.3	68.4	25.0	25.0	16.2
1947	84.6	65.6	36.1	68.4	25.0	25.0	18.0
1948	75.7	57.2	30.2	54.0	25.0	25.0	15.1
1949	75.7	57.2	30.2	54.0	25.0	25.0	15.1
1950	79.8	59.8	32.1	57.1	25.0	25.0	16.0
1951	85.4	65.8	35.8	63.4	25.0	25.0	17.9
1952	84.6	68.2	38.5	68.4	25.0	25.0	19.2
1953	82.3	64.4	33.4	68.4	25.0	25.0	16.7
1954	78.8	58.1	26.0	60.4	25.0	25.0	13.0
1955	79.2	58.0	26.0	58.4	25.0	25.0	13.0
1956	79.2	61.0	30.2	58.4	25.0	25.0	15.1
1957	78.9	58.0	30.3	58.4	25.0	25.0	15.1
1958	76.5	58.1	26.0	58.4	25.0	25.0	13.0
1959	76.5	55.1	26.0	58.4	25.0	25.0	13.0
1960	74.2	51.9	24.7	58.4	25.0	24.5	12.4

[a] See text of Appendix B for explanation of symbols and sources.

did not benefit from income splitting, so separate series were derived for single returns with four exemptions. Then, a weighted average of the marginal rates for married and single returns was taken as a measure of the overall rate for each given income level. The weights used were estimated fractions of dividends on joint returns and on single returns in the various income brackets. The weights for each income cut-off level were approximated by the weights for the bracket in which that income level fell.

The rate series obtained by this averaging process pertains to neither joint nor single returns. However, it probably provides a better measure of the overall level of individual income taxation than would a series picturing either one or the other type of return.

In addition to these tax rate series, a rate series t_s was also derived for a couple with two dependents and a $50,000 statutory net income. This series was also adjusted to allow for income splitting as above.[5] The statutory rate series is included in Table B-1 along with the six series that take account of changing incomes.

The "t" series are illustrated in Chart 4, Chapter IV where they may be compared with selected estimates of the weighted average marginal rates for individuals.[6]

[5] The series differs from a similar series constructed by Seltzer, *Ibid.,* p. 524, because of that adjustment and because Seltzer did not exclude the normal tax for 1919-35, when dividends were exempted from it.

[6] The latter estimates for 1929-52 are from Daniel Holland, *op. cit.,* p. 120 and the estimate for 1956 is from C. Harry Kahn, *op. cit.,* p. 155.

APPENDIX C

Sources of Industry Data

FIVE TIME SERIES were developed for corporations in each of seventeen industries. The variables were D (net cash dividends), P (net profits after taxes), A (depreciation allowances), T (federal and state taxes), and S (sales).

The Industry Classification and Sources for 1929-60

In order that the industry analysis would be consistent with the aggregate, the Office of Business Economics (OBE) reports discussed in Appendix A were chosen again as the basic sources for 1929-60. Data on the five variables are given for about seventy industries (or combinations of industries) in OBE, 1954 and OBE, 1958 ff. (as identified in Appendix A). However, for many of these relatively narrow industrial groups there was no reliable basis for extension of the data back to 1919. It became necessary to settle for broader groups. Although the Kuznets estimates for 1919-28 are conceptually closer to those of OBE than the Internal Revenue Service (IRS) data are, it was found that the latter provided a more detailed breakdown. Accordingly, the OBE industry series were grouped in such a way that they could be linked to the broader IRS groups for 1919-28.

The 1929-60 sources for the resulting seventeen industries are: Variable D was taken from the same tables as the aggregate series, as described in Appendix A. (The estimate of dividends paid out of capital gains by investment trusts was subtracted from the data for the finance,

228

insurance, and real estate industry.) Variable P was taken from the same tables as the aggregate series. For the years 1946-60, variable A was taken from OBE, 1958 ff., Table VI-18. Since no industry depreciation figures for 1929-45 are given by OBE, 1954, it was necessary to extract these from annual issues of IRS *Statistics of Income*.[1] Variables T and S were taken from the same tables as the corporate aggregates.

Sources and Derivation of 1919-28 Industry Series

The basic technique for extending the D, P, and S series back to 1919 was a linear regression of OBE data on IRS data for 1929 through 1933 or 1934.[2] In each case, the equation obtained for this period was used to estimate what earlier OBE data might have been. This was done by substituting IRS data for 1919-28 into the right hand side of the equation.

This procedure is subject to the criticism that there are many inconsistencies between the OBE and IRS data.[3] The two series were far from identical. However, despite these definitional differences, the linear relationships between them were surprisingly close during the period of overlap.

No adjustments were made in the IRS data for taxes and depreciation in the 1919-28 period.[4] The OBE series for those two variables were practically the same during the period of overlap.

To sum up, the 1919-28 data for the five industry variables are undoubtedly less reliable than the aggregate series discussed in Appendix A. The Kuznets data used there were more consistent with the OBE estimates. Even so, the closeness of the linear relationships between the 1929-34 OBE and IRS measurements suggests that the industry extrapolations for the twenties are reasonably reliable.

[1] These *Statistics of Income* figures are consistent with OBE data since the latter depreciation figures embody no adjustment of the IRS data. The series adopted for each industry excluded depletion but included amortization.

[2] Later data were not used since, beginning with 1934, the filing of consolidated returns was not permitted for a number of years. This produced a discontinuity in the IRS series. However, the 1934 data were used in most cases since the relationship between OBE and IRS data in that year appeared consistent with the earlier data.

[3] For a reconciliation see, for example, OBE, 1958, p. 230.

[4] It was, of course, necessary to remove depletion, and in some early years this was not reported separately. In such cases, a crude estimate had to be made on the basis of later relationships between depreciation and depletion. However, this problem was minor except in mining and petroleum and even there it arose in only the very early years.

APPENDIX D

Sources of Firm Data

FORTY FIRMS WERE SELECTED for study on the basis of the criteria outlined in Chapter VI. The sources of the data and definitional issues are discussed briefly here.

Sources

As in the case of the industry analysis the five variables selected for study were D (net cash dividends), P (net profits after taxes), A (depreciation allowances), T (federal and state taxes), and S (sales). Practically all of the data were taken directly from annual reports published by Moody's Investors Service. However, it was necessary to "manufacture" some data for the very early years to fill some gaps, especially in the case of the sales and tax variables. Since these variables proved to have only a minor role in dividend determination, and since this study has not stressed the results of the firm analysis, the lengthy details of these manipulations will not be recounted here. However, the following examples will illustrate the types of manipulations that were required.

Where sales figures were missing (as for Anaconda 1929-31), they were estimated from profits on the basis of a graphical correlation of sales and profits in adjacent years (1926-28 and 1932-34 in the case of Anaconda). Where tax data were missing (as for Anaconda in 1919-29), they were filled in by application to the firm's profits of tax-profits ratios available annually for industries in the Internal Revenue Service *Statistics of Income*. These two techniques were used generally for the

230

sales and tax variables, although the gaps in the sales and tax data were of minor significance. There were also a few gaps in the depreciation data. For example, depreciation data were missing for St. Regis Paper in 1926-29. In this case, and in others where it was necessary, the gap was filled on the basis of a graphical correlation of depreciation and sales based on data for adjacent years. The profit and dividend variables were missing only in a trivial number of cases. Profits were filled in according to relationships with sales in nearby periods. Missing dividends were "derived" on the basis of the dividend-profit ratio in nearby periods.

While little can be said in defense of these data-manufacturing techniques, the assertion here is that the extent of their use was minimal, particularly in the case of the depreciation, profit and dividend variables. The results of the manipulations are presumed to have had little effect on the regressions based on thirty-eight observations. Probably more important are the conceptual problems outlined below.

Differences Between Moody's and OBE Definitions

The analysis in Chapters VII and VIII of the dividend policy of firms is not directly comparable to that in Chapters III-VI, which is based on Office of Business Economics (OBE) data. The main discrepancies are in the profit and depreciation variables.[1] The data from Moody's are based primarily on reports to stockholders in which the usual accounting definition of profits differs from that of the OBE. The OBE data is based on tax data as adjusted by adding back depletion charges and eliminating capital gains and losses and dividend receipts. Company reports do not make these adjustments. Another possible discrepancy is that the OBE data are based on only partially consolidated accounts. The Moody's data is probably on a more completely consolidated basis. The discrepancy between the OBE and Moody's concept of profits is substantial but probably of minor importance in the problem of explaining changes in dividends over time. Inclusion of net capital gains in the Moody's profit series makes for a more erratic series, but there should be no systematic discrepancy in the measured changes in profits over time.

Undoubtedly the primary contrast between the Moody's and the OBE data is in the depreciation series. Since Moody's reflects stock-

[1] Insofar as firms count stock dividends among their dividend payments this would be a further source of discrepancy, but this appears to be rare. Only the one case of Southern California Edison (discussed in Chapter VII) was actually discovered.

holder reports, its depreciation data is less susceptible to changes in depreciation regulations than the OBE series which is wedded to tax returns. The importance of this is that the dividend policy of firms is likely to be better explained by the Moody's net profit series than OBE dividends can be explained by OBE profits. It is to be expected then that the explanation of firm dividends should require less allowance for depreciation liberalization and show less success for the cash flow variable than was found in the analysis based on OBE data.

APPENDIX E

Regression Results Underlying Significance Tests for Industry and Firm Models

TABLE E-1. Ratios of Regression Coefficients to Their Standard Errors, Best Industry and Aggregate Models, 1920–60 (Excluding 1936–38)

Industry[a]	Constant Term (a)	Income (Y) Net Profits (P)	Income (Y) Cash Flow (C)	Depreciation (A)	Tax Shelter (tY)	Interest Rates (iY)	Sales Change $(S/S_{-2}Y)$	Lagged Dividends (D_{-1})
Mining	−1.28	3.27		3.38	−2.43	−2.31		−4.21
Construction	3.25	4.20		5.31	−4.45	−2.94		−5.65
Food	3.23		5.24					−4.57
Textiles	3.53	5.01			−1.73			−7.37
Lumber	3.51		6.51		−4.13			−6.95
Paper	1.85		10.72					−9.81
Printing	2.52	4.06		1.50	−3.62	−1.81		−6.25
Petroleum	2.44		3.74		− .94		−1.05	−5.56
Rubber	.89	2.48		2.40				−3.04
Leather	1.68	1.98		1.70	−1.72	−1.66		−3.53
Stone, glass	1.72		5.01		−2.15	−2.41	−1.75	−6.07
Metals and products	3.29	7.40		3.60	−4.28	−2.96	−4.22	−8.93
Wholesale trade	3.31	3.30		.40	−2.57	−1.69		−5.73
Retail trade	4.44		4.47		−3.03	−2.24	− .08	−7.78
Finance	.13	6.96			−4.55			−1.97
Public utilities	.95		4.93		−2.80			−4.71
Services	2.24	3.18		4.97	−2.37	−2.51		−5.63
All corporations	2.25		8.64		−6.04	−3.69	−1.51	−9.57
Manufacturing corporations	2.73	6.08		2.54	−2.87	−1.32	−3.03	−7.09

[a] Abbreviated title. See Table 27 for detail.

233

TABLE E-2. Ratios of Regression Coefficients to Their Standard Errors, Best Firm Models, 1920–60 (Excluding 1936–38)

Firms[a]	Constant Term (a)	Income (Y) Net Profits (P)	Income (Y) Cash Flow (C)	Depreciation (A)	Tax Shelter (tY)	Interest Rates (iY)	Sales Change (S/S_{-2} Y)	Lagged Dividends (D_{-1})
Allis-Chalmers	.27	2.98					−1.24	−3.06
A. T. & T.	2.18	5.33				−3.50		−3.20
Anaconda	.11	4.25			−3.94	−1.93		−8.11
Babcock & Wilcox	1.13	4.04		.37	−2.39			−4.99
Baltimore & Ohio	−3.97		8.10		−8.03		−2.41	−7.64
Bethlehem Steel	−3.29	5.40		1.23	−3.81			−4.20
Blaw-Knox	− .09	2.25		1.08	−2.10	−1.36		−4.15
Borden	− .18	5.26		1.01	−3.38	−2.06		−5.05
Burroughs	1.77	4.25		1.84	−2.66			−5.18
Consumer Power	−1.72	6.79						−7.05
Detroit Edison	−1.05	5.09		1.61				−5.26
Du Pont	−2.76	12.79			−2.45			−21.70
General Electric	−1.33	3.41		3.50	−3.03	−2.07		−4.95
General Motors	.14	4.82		3.20	−2.88	−2.97		−9.02
Int'l. Harvester	1.06	3.49		2.50		−1.46		−3.78
Loew's-MGM	− .19	3.43						−3.48
Montgomery Ward	.01	3.41						−2.78
Owens-Illinois	3.32	5.17		2.63		−3.52		−4.82
Peoples Gas Light	−1.40	3.86			−2.05	2.04		−5.93
Pepperell	1.58	2.49		2.66	−1.02	−2.67		−6.54
Phillips	− .13	6.98						−5.56
Pittsburgh Glass	3.74	6.27				−1.84		−8.26
Procter & Gamble	3.34	5.78				−1.09		−7.17
Republic Steel	−1.99		3.21		−1.00		−1.30	−4.76
Reynolds Tobacco	.15	4.97			−2.65			−4.20
St. Regis	−2.08	4.70		2.02	−4.25	−2.98		−3.62
Sears Roebuck	− .79	6.88						−5.07
Simmons	.54	5.65			−2.03			−5.55
Sinclair	−1.70		3.54				−1.86	−5.29
S. Calif. Edison	−1.19	3.16				−1.68		−1.58
Studebaker	.57	3.47		.70	−4.91	−1.92		−6.77
Sun Oil	1.77	3.17		3.18				−3.48
Swift	.97	2.93						−2.61
Texaco	2.74	6.52						−5.37
Union Carbide	1.64	6.57		2.79				−5.57
Union Pacific	.22		3.91		−2.01		−2.34	−4.52
U. S. Rubber	−1.46	6.02						−5.78
U. S. Steel	− .10	5.41					−1.57	−7.63
White Motors	−1.47	1.00		2.76				−4.32
Youngstown	− .13	4.46		1.55				−3.59
All 40 firms	2.68	10.32					−4.34	−13.01

[a] For more detailed title, see Table 34.

Tests of the Forecasting Ability of the Industry and Firm Models

THE "BEST" INDUSTRY AND FIRM models of Chapters VI and VII were checked for their ability to explain dividends beyond the period of observation. These tests of the validity of the models are reported as a supplement to the significance tests.

Forecasting Ability of the Industry Dividend Models

The validity of the regression equations in Table 30 as descriptions of industry dividend policy may be tested further by applying them beyond the 1920-60 range of observation. For most of the industries, the latest information available for use in such "forecasts" was that for 1961. While the success of any one equation in predicting behavior in a single year is of little interest, an overall check on the seventeen industry and two aggregate equations may give an indication of the models' stability over time. As in the case of the aggregate forecasts discussed in Chapters III and V, the objective here is not a test of forecasting ability *per se,* but rather of the stability of the relationships. If the equations represent any kind of fundamental association, they should be able to give reasonably good estimates beyond the 38 years' data to which they were fitted.

Table F-1 gives actual 1960-61 changes in dividends as reported in the July 1964 *Survey of Current Business*[1] and three alternative fore-

---

[1] The data exclude agriculture, the "Rest-of-the-World" and an estimate of

TABLE F-1. Forecasts of 1960–61 Dividend Changes by Various Industry and Aggregate Models[a]

(In millions of dollars)

Industry[b]	Actual Change	Forecasts			Errors			Standard Error of Estimate
		Naive	Basic	General[c]	Naive	Basic	General[c]	
Mining	62	106	1	21	44	− 61	− 41	47.4
Construction	19	16	− 10	3	− 3	− 29	− 16	6.9
Food	32	71	40	24	39	8	− 8	33.9
Textiles	5	11	7	8	6	2	3	17.4
Lumber	− 10	5	− 13	1	15	− 3	11	11.5
Paper	7	22	− 11	6	15	− 18	− 1	8.8
Printing	− 2	17	− 6	0	19	− 4	2	8.6
Petroleum	−151	78	− 10	10	229	141	161	59.8
Rubber	− 16	− 1	− 2	0	15	14	16	8.1
Leather	− 9	9	− 3	− 1	18	6	8	4.9
Stone, glass	− 30	29	− 23	− 7	59	7	23	9.9
Metals and products	198	53	−180	− 23	−145	−378	−221	72.7
Wholesale trade	− 7	39	− 7	− 10	46	0	− 3	22.7
Retail trade	44	35	− 22	34	− 9	− 66	− 10	23.3
Finance	89	109	− 20	100	20	−109	11	70.1
Public utilities	243	138	180	254	−105	− 63	11	92.6
Services	− 71	58	− 25	− 4	129	46	67	11.8
All corporations	403	795	− 86	455	392	−489	52	223.9
Manufacturing corporations	24	294	−199	22	270	−223	− 2	136.3

[a] Source, U. S. Department of Commerce, *Survey of Current Business* (July 1964).
[b] For detailed title see Table 27.
[c] The "general" models are the "best" ones given in Table 30.

casts of that change. The "naive" forecast is a duplication of the 1959-60 change. The other two forecasts are derived from the basic Lintner model and from the best generalized model (Table 30) for each industry. While less successful at forecasting than the aggregate equations, the best regression models were more successful than the naive model in several respects. In a year of erratic behavior by industry dividends (half up, half down), the general models correctly forecast the direction of change in fourteen of the seventeen cases compared to ten correct naive forecasts. The absolute error by the general models was smaller for thirteen of the seventeen industries, and the sum of these errors was 613 com-

---

dividends paid out of capital gains by investment trusts for reasons discussed in Appendix A.

TABLE F-2. Forecasts of Aggregate 1960–61 Dividend Changes by Consensus of Industry Forecasts

(In millions of dollars)

Sector	Actual Change[a]	Forecasts			Errors		
		Naive	Basic	General	Naive	Basic	General
Manufacturing corporations	24	294	−201	18	270	−225	− 6
Nonmanufacturing corporations	379	501	97	397	122	−282	19
All corporations	403	795	−104	416	392	−507	13

[a] Source, see Table F-1.

pared to a sum of 916 for the naive forecasts. A consensus of the general model forecasts also gave a much better forecast of aggregates, as is indicated in Table F-2. These consensus forecasts by the general industry models were remarkably accurate for both manufacturing and nonmanufacturing, and about equal in quality to those made by the aggregate equations themselves (as indicated at the bottom of Table F-1).[2] This comparison should be qualified by recognition of the large compensating errors in forecasts by the general models for petroleum and metals. Still, it is apparent that they performed much better than the naive and basic models. An alternative naive forecast of *no* 1960-61 dividend change fares even worse. Such naive models are automatically defeated at turning points. In the 1960-61 case, the "same change" hypothesis missed the slowdown in dividend growth in the 1960-61 recession, and the "no change" model was undermined by the tendency for dividends to rise even in the face of falling profits.

The basic model performed no better than the "same change" naive model. Its absolute error was smaller in eleven of the seventeen cases, but its sum of absolute errors was higher at 955, and its consensus forecasts, shown in Table F-2, were slightly inferior. The basic model had smaller errors than the more general equation in eight industries, but its total of absolute errors was 59 percent higher and its consensus forecasts were very low. This was to be expected in view of its reliance on net profits as an income base despite the depressing effect of rising depreciation allowances on reported profits.

Although it has been shown that the general models allowing for

---

[2] While only a fragment of evidence, this parallels the failure (discussed in Chapter VI) of the consensus of industry estimates to explain any more of the variation of dividends than the aggregate model.

tax factors and other influences did the best job of forecasting 1960-61 dividend change, there is another criterion to be considered. How do these forecasts compare with regression estimates within the period of observation? For this comparison, the adjusted standard error of estimate is also given in Table F-1. The errors made by the general models fall within one standard error of estimate for ten of the seventeen industries, close to the 11.5 figure that would be expected on the assumptions of normality and equal accuracy outside of the range of observations.

Apparently, the worst black mark is that along with some very good forecasts, there were five that were off by two or more standard errors of estimate. By far the worst forecast was in the case of services. It was off by almost six standard errors, suggesting the possibility of an altered relationship in that case. The data support this conjecture: with a 1960-61 decline in net profits from $208 million to $93 million, dividends were cut drastically from $213 million to $142 million. The general model predicted only a slight fall in dividends, since the equation fitted to 1920-60 data had shown depreciation to have a strong influence. Depreciation allowances—over $1,100 million in 1960 and still rising—dominated the forecast, but apparently net profits were a controlling factor in 1961.

The side-by-side existence of very good and very bad forecasts (as measured by the standard error of estimates) invited some kind of an over-all comparison. The square of each standard error gives the mean squared error for each industry. The sum of these can be compared to the sum of squared 1960-61 forecast errors. The latter sum is three times as large. However, if petroleum and metals are excluded, the sum of squared forecast errors becomes 41 percent of the sum of mean squared errors and 18 percent if services are also excluded. This is not to say that the bad forecasts in these three industries may be ignored, but it suggests that if structural changes are indicated, they seem to be concentrated in a few industries. For example, in nonmanufacturing alone (about one-half the total), the forecasting error is only one-half the error in the fitted period according to the above criterion. It is not surprising, then, to find that the 1960-61 forecasting error in the model for all corporations is much less than one standard error of estimate. This comparison of forecast errors in a single year to the errors in the fitted period is not entirely satisfactory. Although there were seventeen industry forecasts, the 1960-61 dividend changes may have been either more or less difficult to forecast by models of this type than the typical annual changes; there may have been more or less than the usual exogenous factors involved. Still, these forecasting tests probably reenforce somewhat the plausibility of the behavioral models. More convincing, however, is the performance by the more general tax-oriented model relative to the others. In those comparisons, each model faced the same forecasting problem, and the tax variables and others produced a general improvement.

Forecasting Ability of the Firm Models

Models of the dividend policy of the 40 firms were tested for their ability to "forecast" the 1960-61 change. Table F-3 gives the actual changes (as reported in Standard and Poor's *Standard Corporation Records*) and three alternative forecasts of that change. The forecasting performance of the three models may be compared according to a number of criteria.

The naive model (repeat of 1959-60 change) forecast the direction of change correctly for thirty out of the thirty-five firms in which a change actually occurred. The general model was right on the direction for twenty-eight of the thirty-five firms, and the basic model was right for twenty-two. The general model made a smaller absolute error than the naive for sixteen of thirty-nine firms (with one tie). The basic model made a smaller error than the naive for only fifteen of the forty firms. On the other hand, the sum of absolute errors made by the basic model was lowest at $255 million, compared to a total of $270 million for the general model and $296 million for the naive. The sum of squared errors showed the basic model slightly better than the general and both considerably better than the naive.

The forecasts of 1960-61 dividend change for the sample aggregate by a consensus of firm forecasts showed the general model with the smallest error at $202 million, as shown in Table F-4. However, the basic model was best for nonmanufacturing corporations, and the naive model showed the smallest error in manufacturing.

Summing up these various comparisons, it is apparent that none of the three models stands out as significantly better than the other in the 1960-61 forecasts. This is in contrast to the industry analysis in which the general models containing various public policy variables performed better on most criteria. The present finding is also rather surprising in view of the fact that the general models added variables that, in many cases, significantly improved the explanation provided by the basic Lintner model. The failure of the generalization of the model to improve the forecasts for firms, even though only one year has been analyzed, suggests the possibility that the added variables may no longer be in-

TABLE F-3. Forecasts of 1960–61 Dividend Changes by Various Firm Models[a]

(In millions of dollars)

Firms[b]	Actual Change[c]	Forecasts			Errors			Standard Error of Estimate
		Naive	Basic	General	Naive	Basic	General	
Allis-Chalmers	− 2.27	2.55	− 1.92	− 2.22	4.82	.35	.05	1.28
A. T. & T.	97.21	35.14	75.64	63.79	−62.07	−21.57	−33.42	10.07
Anaconda	.00	.00	.14	− 1.65	.00	.14	− 1.65	4.26
Babcock & Wilcox	1.22	1.19	.29	.71	− .03	− .93	− .51	.56
Baltimore & Ohio	− 1.53	− 2.29	− 4.98	− 4.74	− .76	− 3.45	− 3.21	1.39
Bethlehem Steel	.05	.32	.02	4.06	.27	− .03	4.01	4.05
Blaw-Knox	.08	.08	− .14	− .02	.00	− .22	− .10	.41
Borden	1.08	1.16	1.42	1.10	.08	.34	.02	.63
Burroughs	.00	.02	− .08	1.00	.02	− .08	1.00	1.13
Consumer Power	.65	2.15	1.24	1.24	1.50	.59	.59	3.07
Detroit Edison	2.25	1.01	2.22	2.06	− 1.24	− .03	− .19	.82
Du Pont	35.09	−10.95	11.17	18.38	−46.04	−23.92	−16.71	7.55
General Electric	.96	1.15	1.39	4.99	.19	.43	4.03	10.74
General Motors	143.00	2.00	4.29	3.95	−141.00	−138.71	−139.05	25.81
Int'l. Harvester	.01	4.76	− .88	.38	4.75	− .89	.37	1.64
Loew's-MGM	.95	3.07	1.33	1.33	2.12	.38	.38	1.30
Montgomery Ward	− 6.39	.00	− 3.08	− 3.08	6.39	3.31	3.31	2.69
Owens-Illinois	.03	.31	.73	.46	.28	.70	.43	.73
Peoples Gas Light	2.06	2.58	1.53	1.39	.52	− .53	− .67	.56
Pepperell	.00	.24	− .06	.08	.24	− .06	.08	.26
Phillips	.00	.00	3.54	3.54	.00	3.54	3.54	1.98
Pittsburgh Glass	.44	.45	− 1.92	− 2.68	.01	− 2.36	− 3.12	1.45
Procter & Gamble	5.47	6.39	5.93	5.02	.92	.46	− .45	2.12
Republic Steel	.09	.09	− .89	.40	.00	− .98	.31	2.02
Reynolds Tobacco	8.00	6.00	6.51	7.42	− 2.00	− 1.49	− .58	2.03
St. Regis	1.67	2.25	− .23	1.09	.58	− 1.90	− .58	.67
Sears Roebuck	.16	15.16	3.10	3.10	15.00	2.94	2.94	3.25
Simmons	.02	− .71	− .34	− .31	− .73	− .36	− .33	.37
Sinclair Oil	− 8.16	− 7.68	− 4.06	− 1.12	.48	4.10	7.04	3.42
S. Calif. Edison	1.17[d]	.16	2.76	2.30	− 1.01	+ 1.59	+ 1.13	.84
Studebaker	.22	.00	0.70	1.10	− .22	.48	.88	1.77
Sun Oil	.73	.58	.54	.76	− .15	− .19	.03	.38
Swift	.02	1.55	− 1.79	− 1.79	1.53	− 1.81	− 1.81	1.96
Texaco	18.96	19.36	12.74	12.74	.40	− 6.22	− 6.22	5.67
Union Carbide	.01	.02	− .74	2.05	.01	− .75	2.04	4.15
Union Pacific	.00	.00	− .51	1.60	.00	− .51	1.60	1.93
U. S. Rubber	.04	.88	− 1.70	− 1.70	.84	− 1.74	− 1.74	1.90
U. S. Steel	.28	.18	−23.97	−24.11	− .10	−24.25	−24.39	7.34
White Motors	1.02	.80	− .64	1.27	− .22	− 1.66	.25	.73
Youngstown	.02	.06	− .88	− .92	.04	− .90	− .94	1.01
Total	304.61	90.03	88.42	102.97	−214.58	−216.19	−201.64	—

[a] The general models are the "best" ones given in Table 38.
[b] For more detailed names see Table 34.
[c] Source, Standard and Poor's, *Standard Corporation Records.*
[d] Dividend payments for 1961 listed in company report corrected to exclude stock dividend.

TABLE F-4. Forecasts of 1960–61 Dividend Changes for the Sample Aggregate by a Consensus of Firm "Forecasts"

(In millions of dollars)

Sector	Actual Change[a]	Forecasts			Errors		
		Naive	Basic	General	Naive	Basic	General
Manufacturing (28 corporations)	216	41	13	37	−175	−203	−179
Nonmanufacturing (12 corporations)	88	49	75	66	− 39	− 13	− 22
All 40 corporations	305	90	88	103	−215	−216	−202

[a] Source, see Table F-3.

fluential, or that their influence was weaker than suggested by the goodness of fit. On the other hand, it may be an indication that these additional variables are needed only to explain substantial long-run changes in payout policy.

While no model stands out, the forecasts seem generally about as good as the estimates within the period of fit, suggesting no widespread changes in relationships. The forecasting errors made by the general models were within one adjusted standard error of estimate (Table F-3, as estimated for the period of fit) for twenty-eight of the forty firms. This was somewhat more often than would be expected under the assumption of normality. The forecast error by the basic model lay within the same standard error of estimate twenty-six times, and the naive error was within for twenty-nine firms.

Because of a few large errors, the sum of squared forecast errors by the general models was nearly twenty times the sum of all forty mean squared errors in the period of fit. However, if General Motors, U. S. Steel, and A. T. & T. are excluded from the comparison, the forecasting error is only slightly larger than that of the fitted period, on this criterion. Finally, the models for the firms taken together showed no consistent bias in the 1960-61 forecasts. In fact, twenty-one positive and nineteen negative errors were made by the general models.

To sum up, the forecasts were no worse than the estimates in the period of fit, attesting to the stability of the relationships. However, generalization of the basic model to include the public policy variables produced no gain in forecasting accuracy for firms.

Statistical Results Based on 1965 Revisions of OBE Data

AFTER THIS STUDY WAS COMPLETED, the Department of Commerce issued substantially revised estimates of some of the basic time series used here.[1] The revisions were both statistical and definitional, and the series most affected among those used in this study was that for corporate profits. The main definitional change credited stock life insurance companies and all mutual institutions with profits of their own, rather than attributing them to policyholders or depositors. This substantially increased profits for the corporate aggregate but had no effect on data for the manufacturing sector. Profits also were generally increased by statistical revisions such as increased allowances for unreported profits indicated by audits, and a changed treatment of bad debts. "Nevertheless, short-term fluctuations and long-term trends (in the profit series) are substantially unchanged."[2]

The revisions of dividends and depreciation were less important. The main revision of dividends was the exclusion of dividends paid out of capital gains by investment trusts—an adjustment already made in the series used in this study. Although there were substantial changes in noncorporate depreciation, the revisions of the corporate depreciation series were very small. In particular nothing was done to allow

[1] U. S. Department of Commerce, Office of Business Economics, *Survey of Current Business*, Vol. 45, No. 8 (August 1965), and Vol. 45, No. 9 (September 1965).

[2] OBE, *op. cit.* (August 1965), p. 6.

TABLE G-1. Revised Data on Dividends and Profits After Taxes and Payout Percentages, Selected Years, All Corporations[a]

(Dollar amounts in billions)

Year	Dividends	Net Profits	Payout Percentage
1920	$ 2.96	$ 5.09	58.2
1929	5.71	8.39	68.1
1947	6.12	19.51	31.4
1960	12.60	24.80	50.8

[a] As in Table 1, the data exclude the "Rest of the World" component.

for the liberalization of depreciation allowances since the beginning of World War II.

Since even the important revisions of the profit series had little effect on short-term fluctuations or long-term trends, it was to be expected that substitution of the new data would make little difference in the statistical results. Nevertheless, since the estimated corporate income base was significantly broadened, it seemed advisable to repeat some of the basic statistical analysis using revised dividends (D'), revised profits (P'), and revised depreciation allowances (A').

The new data were first checked to compare trends in the payout ratio with those indicated earlier in Table 1. According to Table G-1 there was a fall in the payout ratio between 1929 and 1947 which was even more pronounced than indicated by the original data in Table 1. The subsequent relative increase in the payout ratio by 1960 was about the same in the two sets of data. The main difference between the two sets of figures is the lower level of the payout ratio. Because of the upward revision of profits this ratio was considerably lower in the new data—especially in the two postwar years.

Relations (G-1) and (G-2) for all corporations show the new 1942-60 regression results for the basic Lintner model and the simple cash flow model, respectively. These may be compared to the results for the original data given in the first and fourth equations in Table 7. The new

(G-1)
$$D' - D'_{-1} = -\underset{(.248)}{.435} + \underset{(.022)}{.118P'} - \underset{(.048)}{.183D'_{-1}}$$

$$\overline{R}^2 = .612 \qquad \text{D-W} = 1.83 \qquad r = .647$$

(G-2)
$$D' - D'_{-1} = \underset{(.157)}{.472} + \underset{(.016)}{.138C'} - \underset{(.070)}{.547D'_{-1}}$$

$$\overline{R}^2 = .805 \qquad \text{D-W} = 1.83 \qquad r = .252$$

data yield somewhat higher values of $\overline{R}^2$, and the cash flow model improves upon the $\overline{R}^2$ of the net profits model to about the same extent as before. The Lintner model continues to yield the implausible negative constant term and a relatively high target payout ratio, although the latter is well below the 90 percent estimate yielded by the original data. The cash flow model explains dividends in much the same way with the new data as with the old, except that the target payout ratio applied to the higher income base is 25 percent, rather than 29 percent.

Depreciation is included explicitly in equation (G-3) which may be compared to relation (3-3) using the original data. Although the degree

$$(\text{G-3}) \qquad D' - D'_{-1} = \underset{(.246)}{.273} + \underset{(.017)}{.142P'} + \underset{(.028)}{.114A'} - \underset{(.084)}{.498D'_{-1}}$$

$$\overline{R}^2 = .806 \qquad \text{D-W} - 2.08 \qquad r_t = .286 + .230A'/P'$$

of explanation is again somewhat improved in the new data, the positive depreciation coefficient continues to differ from zero by about four standard errors. In sum, the new data for 1942-60 confirm the conclusions of Chapter III.

In Chapter IV, it was shown that the introduction of an income tax shelter variable such as t_{25} greatly improved the explanation of dividends for the entire 1920-60 period. The new data confirm this, as shown, for example, in relation (G-4).

$$(\text{G-4}) \quad D' - D'_{-1} = \underset{(.138)}{.253} + \underset{(.022)}{.219P'} + \underset{(.020)}{.042A'} - \underset{(.032)}{.190t_{25}P'} - \underset{(.050)}{.297D'_{-1}}$$

$$\overline{R}^2 = .832 \qquad \text{D-W} = 1.93 \qquad r_t = .738 + .142A'/P' - .640t_{25}$$

The shelter variable is again negative and highly significant, with a t-ratio of about six, while the t-ratio for depreciation remains over two. These results may be compared to those for the fourth model in Table 15. The latter results for the old data again show a lower $\overline{R}^2$ than for the new data; they also show somewhat less significance for the shelter variable and somewhat more significance for the depreciation variable than do the new data.

Tests of the interest rate and sales change variables discussed in Chapter V were also repeated with the new data for the corporate aggregate. The best equation basing dividends on net profits was (5-3); the result for the same equation fitted to the new data is given in (G-5).

$$(\text{G-5}) \qquad D' - D'_{-1} = .302 + \underset{(.051)}{.299} + \underset{(.026)}{.046A'/P'} - \underset{(.054)}{.203t_{25}}$$

$$- \underset{(.075)}{.053i} - \underset{(.024)}{.044S/S_{-2}} \; P' - \underset{(.049)}{.313D'_{-1}}$$

$$\overline{R}^2 = .846 \qquad \text{D-W} = 2.00$$

$$r_t = .956 + .148A'/P' - .650t_{25} - .169i - .142S/S_{-2}$$

The shelter and depreciation variables continue to be significant, although in this equation the depreciation variable barely demonstrates significance at the 5 percent level on the one-tail test. The interest rate variable is even weaker in this equation than it was in relation (5-3). Sales change also shows somewhat less importance in the new data, but it remains significant at the 5 percent level.

Finally, the new data confirm the old in showing interest rates to be a significant factor in the cash flow models where the sales change variable fails. This mixed evidence from the profit and cash flow models reaffirms the suggestion that interest rates and sales change are of marginal importance. However, in Chapter V it was concluded on the basis of forecasting tests in addition to $\overline{R}^2$ that equation (5-1) offered the best explanation of aggregate dividend behavior obtained in the study. Fitted to the new data this model yields equation (G-6).

$$(\text{G-6}) \quad D' - D'_{-1} = .279 + \underset{(.032)}{(.260} - \underset{(.033)}{.194 t_{25}} - \underset{(.034)}{.116 i)} C' - .381 D'_{-1}$$

$$\overline{R}^2 = .826 \quad \text{D-W} - 1.80 \quad r_t - .683 - .511 t_{25} - .303 i$$

Although the $\overline{R}^2$ is appreciably lower for the new data, the coefficients and t-ratios are very close to those obtained in the original data. The shelter variable and interest rates remain highly significant in the cash flow models fitted to the new data, and the success of the cash flow model itself continues to reenforce the profit-plus-depreciation models in indicating the importance of depreciation liberality.

To sum up, no evidence was found that the 1965 revisions of the national income statistics require any important amendments to the conclusions of the aggregative analysis of Chapters III to V.

INDEX

Index